SYDNEY

FODOR'S TRAVEL PUBLICATIONS

are compiled, researched, and edited by an international team of travel writers, field correspondents, and editors. The series, which now almost covers the globe, was founded by Eugene Fodor in 1936.

OFFICES
New York & London

Fodor's Sydney:

Editors: Debra Bernardi, Staci Capobianco
Area Editors: Emery Barcs, Pauline Murphy, Patricia Rolfe, Bruce Stannard
Drawings: Alida Beck
Maps and Plans: Jon Bauch Design, Pictograph

SPECIAL SALES

Fodor's Travel Publications are available at special discounts for bulk purchases (100 copies or more) for sales promotions or premiums. Special editions, including personalized covers, excerpts of existing guides, and corporate imprints, can be created in large quantities for special needs. For more information, write to Special Marketing, Fodor's Travel Publications, 201 East 50th Street, New York, NY 10022.

FODOR'S
SYDNEY
1988

FODOR'S TRAVEL PUBLICATIONS, INC.
New York & London

Copyright © 1988 by Fodor's Travel Publications, Inc.

All rights reserved under International and Pan-American Copyright Conventions. Published in the United States by Fodor's Travel Publications, Inc., a subsidiary of Random House, Inc., New York, and simultaneously in Canada by Random House of Canada Limited, Toronto. Distributed by Random House, Inc., New York.

No maps, illustrations, or other portions of this book may be reproduced in any form without written permission from the publisher.

ISBN 0-679-01570-1
ISBN 0-340-41968-7 (Hodder & Stoughton)

MANUFACTURED IN THE UNITED STATES OF AMERICA
10 9 8 7 6 5 4 3 2 1

CONTENTS

FOREWORD vii

Map of Australia, viii–ix

Australia's Bicentennial xi

FACTS AT YOUR FINGERTIPS 1

Facts and Figures, 1; Tourist Information, 1; Passports, Visas, and Customs, 2; When to Go, 2; What to Pack, 3; Currency, Credit Cards, and Banking Matters, 3; What It Will Cost, 4; Cruises, 5; Hints to Motorists, 5; Accommodations, 6; Dining Out, 6; Tipping, 7; Drinking Laws, 7; Business Hours, Holidays, and Local Time, 8; Seasonal Events, 8; Sports, 9; Gambling, 9; For Women Visitors, 9; Disabled Visitors, 10; Postage, 10; Electricity, 10; Metric Conversion, 10; Telephones, 11; Security 11; Departure Tax, 12

"I TAKE BUT I SURRENDER": An Introduction to Sydney, by Emery Barcs 13

EXPLORING SYDNEY, by David Swindell 27
Orientation Map of Sydney, 30–31
Map of Sydney Harbour and Beaches, 32
Map of The Domain–Macquarie St.–Hyde Park, 36
Map of The Rocks, 39
Map of Kings Cross, 44
Map of Paddington, 47

PRACTICAL INFORMATION FOR SYDNEY 51
How to Get There, 51
Hotels and Motels, 52
How to Get Around, 57
Tourist Information, 60
Tours, 61

CONTENTS

Special-Interest Sightseeing, 63
Parks and Gardens, 63
Theme Parks, 66
Zoos, 66
Beaches, 67
Sports, 71
Sites of Architectural and Historic Interest, 73
Museums, 80
Film, 86
Music, 87
Dance, 90
Theater, 91
Art Galleries, 92
Shopping, 94
Dining Out, 97
Coffee Shops, Tea Shops, Brasseries, 118
Nightlife, 119

OUTSIDE SYDNEY, by David Swindell — 128
Map of the Outside Sydney Area, 129
Exploring the Blue Mountains, 130
Practical Information for the Blue Mountains, 131
Exploring the Hunter Valley, 134
Practical Information for the Hunter Valley, 135
Exploring Opal Country and the Outback, 139
Practical Information for Opal Country and the Outback, 140

INDEX — 142

FOREWORD

During intermission at an Opera House performance one evening, you may step out onto a terrace and marvel at Sydney Harbour below: the lights of the Harbour Bridge, Luna Park, and the ferries all glowing in the water. On another evening, you could find yourself drinking schooners of Foster's amid a group of Aussies who are reminiscing about the night Australia won the America's Cup: the country stayed up until dawn, and few made it to work the next day. Or possibly you're at an Italian restaurant, eating gnocchi gorgonzola that is rivaling any you've had in San Francisco or New York.

Daylight and you could be on a ferry—to the beach at Manly, or to the zoo to see your first Tasmanian devil. At the museums you can learn as much as you want about Sydney's culture and history: about Governor Macquarie and his progressive attitude toward the convicts that built the young city; about the fables the aboriginal peoples told to explain the natural phenomena of their land. Wandering through the Royal Botanic Gardens, watching surfers at Bondi Beach, sampling local wines and rock oysters at an outdoor café—this is all only part of a visit to Sydney.

Fodor's Sydney is designed to help you plan your own trip to Sydney, based on your time, your budget, your energy, your interests—your idea of what this trip should be. Perhaps having read this guide you'll have some new ideas. We have, therefore, tried to put together the widest possible *range* of activities and within that range to offer you *selections* that will be safe, worthwhile, and of good value to you. The descriptions we provide are designed to help you make your own intelligent choices from among our selections.

While every care has been taken to ensure the accuracy of the information contained in this guide, the publishers cannot accept responsibility for any errors that may appear.

All prices quoted in this guide are based on those available to us at the time of writing. In a world of rapid change, however, the possibility of inaccurate or out-of-date information can never be totally eliminated. We trust, therefore, that you will take prices quoted as indicators only, and will double-check to be sure of the latest figures.

Similarly, be sure to check all opening times of museums and galleries. We have found that such times are liable to change without notice, and you could easily make a trip only to find a locked door.

When a hotel closes or a restaurant produces a disappointing meal, let us know, and we will investigate the establishment and the complaint. We are always ready to revise our entries for the following year's edition should the facts warrant it.

Send your letters to the editors at Fodor's Travel Publications, 201 East 50th Street, New York, NY 10022. European readers may prefer to write to Fodor's Travel Publications, 9-10 Market Place, London W1N 7AG, England.

AUSTRALIA

→→→ PRINCIPAL RAILWAYS
✈ AIRPORT
⚓ PORT

0 200 400
Scale of Miles

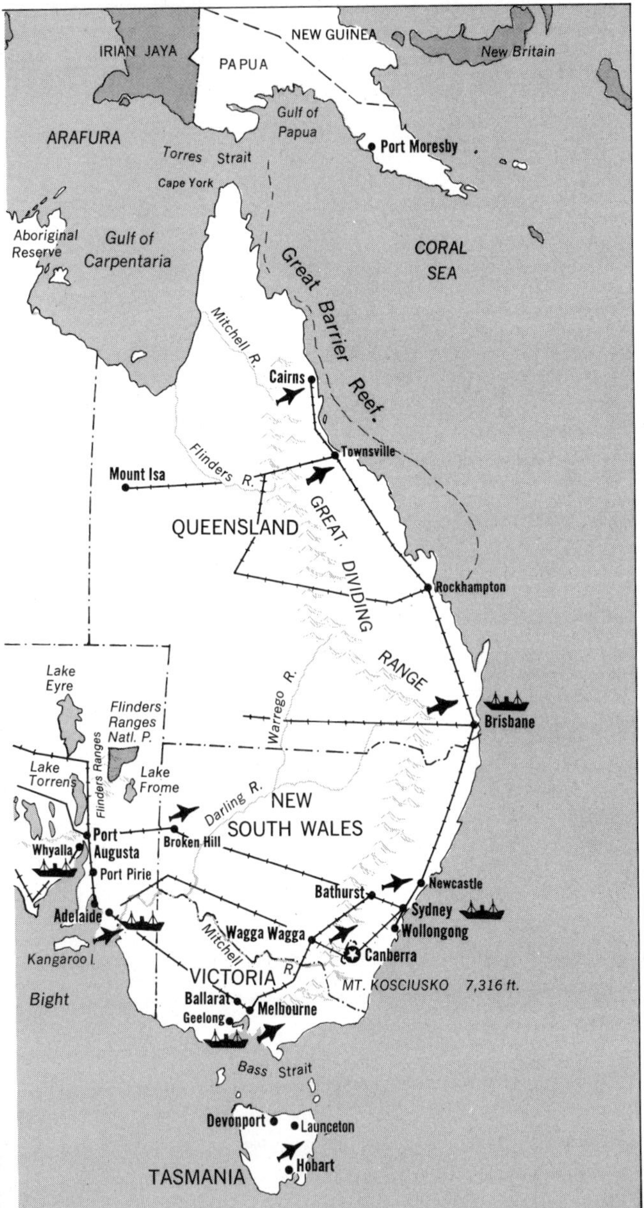

IRIAN JAYA
PAPUA
NEW GUINEA
New Britain
Gulf of Papua
Port Moresby
ARAFURA
Torres Strait
Cape York
Aboriginal Reserve
Gulf of Carpentaria
CORAL SEA
Great Barrier Reef
Mitchell R.
Cairns
Townsville
Flinders R.
Mount Isa
QUEENSLAND
GREAT DIVIDING RANGE
Rockhampton
Lake Eyre
Flinders Ranges Natl. P.
Flinders Ranges
Warrego R.
Brisbane
Lake Torrens
Lake Frome
Darling R.
NEW SOUTH WALES
Port Augusta
Whyalla
Broken Hill
Port Pirie
Newcastle
Bathurst
Sydney
Wollongong
Adelaide
Wagga Wagga
Mitchell R.
Canberra
Kangaroo I.
VICTORIA
MT. KOSCIUSKO 7,316 ft.
Bight
Ballarat
Melbourne
Geelong
Bass Strait
Devonport
Launceton
Hobart
TASMANIA

Australia's Bicentennial

On January 26, 1788, the First Fleet expedition from England landed in soon-to-be-named Sydney Cove. The 1,017 persons aboard (including officers, crew, and the infamous convicts banished to exile) became the founders of modern Australia. To commemorate its 200 years of growth, Australia is celebrating 1988 with numerous special events. The theme of the Bicentennial is "Living Together," a reference to the various backgrounds of the Australian population (including the Aboriginal people who inhabited the continent for over 40,000 years before the landing of the First Fleet).

Sydney promises to be in the thick of things as it marks its 200th birthday along with the national Bicentennial. The following is a list of special Bicentennial events scheduled to take place in Sydney. Please check with the Australian Tourist Commission (see *Facts at Your Fingertips*) or the New South Wales Bicentennial Council in Sydney, (02) 221–1988, for additional details, information contacts, and events that were not scheduled at our press time.

January 9–17, **Australian Bicentenary Baptist Celebration.**

January 19–26, **Tall Ships** in Sydney Harbour. Tall ships and pleasure craft from around the world will arrive in Sydney, commemorating the importance of sailing and water transport—particularly in preaviation times—to the development of the city and the country.

January 26, **Australia Day/First Fleet reenactment** in Sydney Harbour. To mark the nation's 200th anniversary, a fleet of 11 ships will reenact the historic 1788 trip of the First Fleet from England to Sydney Cove (now called Circular Quay). The modern fleet left London on April 24, 1987, and, following the path of the original First Fleet, will arrive in Sydney on January 26 in time to join the tall ships to open the celebration of Australia Day.

January 31, **Bicentennial International Wool Cloth and Design Display.**

March 5–6, **Vaucluse Bicentennial Regatta,** Double Bay to Manly.

May 8–20, **FIVA** (Federation Internationale Vehicules Anciens) **Australian Bicentennial International Relay.** May 8 marks the start of a road rally featuring vintage cars from around the world that will travel from various state capitals in Australia (including Sydney) to Canberra, the Australian federal capital.

May 11, **Around Australia Relay** reaches Sydney. On May 9 in Canberra a runner will begin the first leg of a relay run following Australia's Highway 1. The relay will include 16,000 runners covering 17,500 km and will end up back in Canberra in December. On May 11, the arrival of the relay in Sydney is sure to draw cheering crowds and spur on local festivities.

October 8–16, **Bicentennial Air Show,** Richmond RAAF Base, near Sydney. The air show will feature vintage airplanes, aerobatic displays, sky diving, and hot-air ballooning.

December 12–18, **Australian Bicentennial Exhibition.** The exhibition, having traveled throughout Australia since January, will end its 25,000-km journey in Sydney. The exhibition uses video, audio, and still displays and models to highlight Australia's achievements and culture of the past, present, and for the future. A fitting way to end the celebration of where it all began.

Facts at Your Fingertips

FACTS AND FIGURES. Australia is one of the world's oldest land masses, and archaeologists estimate that the first wave of human migration to the continent swept down from Asia 40,000 years ago. However, it wasn't until 200 years ago that the first European settlers made it to Australia. There had only been a few recorded sightings of the Australian continent before 1768, when Captain James Cook, an English explorer, sailed into Botany Bay, near what is now Sydney's Kingsford Smith International Airport, and claimed Australia for the British crown. Twenty years later, the first English colonists, in the form of transported convicts and sailors from the First Fleet, landed in Sydney at the area now called The Rocks, and Sydney thus became the first European colony in Australia.

Today, with a population of 3.43 million, Sydney is Australia's largest city and the commercial, entertainment, and financial hub not only of Australia, but of the entire South Pacific. Sydney is an ethnically diverse metropolis with large Greek, Lebanese, Italian, Chinese, and Maori communities. One look at the names of Sydney's restaurants and you know you're in a very cosmopolitan city.

TOURIST INFORMATION. Before you leave home, write the *Australian Tourist Commission*, Suite 1200, 12th Floor, 2121 Avenue of the Stars, Los Angeles, CA 90067, (213) 552–1988, or 489 Fifth Ave., New York, NY 10017, (212) 687–6300, for free information about Sydney. In Canada: 120 Eglington Avenue East, Suite 220, Toronto, Ontario M4P 1E2; (416) 487–2126. In the city, the *Travel Centre of New South Wales,* 16 Spring St., (corner of Pitt and Spring sts.), Sydney, NSW 2000, (02) 231–4444, can provide information and help in deciding what to see and do. Stop in when you get there. The *Sydney Morning Herald,* the only local newspaper that does not lean toward the sensational, lists daily entertainment and sporting events. In hotel lobbies, pick up a free copy of *This Week in Sydney, Sydney's Tourist Attractions, Where,* or *Sydney's Top Ten* for pages and pages full of goings-on in the city.

Some helpful phone numbers are:
Emergency Police, fire, ambulance, 000
Emergency medical, 230–0111
Weather, 1196
Time, 1194
Tourist information services, 669–5111
Sports results, 1187
Foreign exchange rates, 1–1500
News, 1199
Bus timetables, 2–0543 or 29–2622
Train schedules, 2–0942 or 29–2622
Ferry schedules, 29–2622

FACTS AT YOUR FINGERTIPS

PASSPORTS, VISAS, AND CUSTOMS. You'll need a passport and visa to enter Australia. (No visa is required if you're entering from New Zealand.) Visas are free and obtainable by mail or in person from any Australian Consulate. A visa application form is also contained in *Destination Australia,* a free travel guidebook available from the Australian Tourist Commission (see "Tourist Information," above). Consulates are located in New York, Chicago, Washington, D.C., Houston, San Francisco, Los Angeles, Honolulu, Toronto, Ottawa, and Vancouver. You must also have a ticket out of Australia and enough funds for your stay.

Most personal items are allowed into Australia duty-free. Each visitor eighteen years or older is allowed to bring into the country duty-free 250 cigarettes, or 250 grams of cigars or tobacco, one liter of an alcoholic beverage, and gifts or souvenirs valued at no more than $A400. Additional items are subject to customs duty and sales tax. There are strict controls on importing food, animals, plants, and plant and animal products. (They'll actually spray your plane on arrival, before passengers are allowed to disembark.) There's little use in bringing your pets along, because the quarantine period would no doubt be longer than your vacation. Firearms and motor vehicle imports are also strictly controlled, and there are severe fines and jail penalties for bringing into Australia marijuana or narcotics.

No inoculations are needed to enter Australia if you're coming directly from North America.

WHEN TO GO. Sydney's mild, semitropical climate is quite similar to that of Southern California; therefore, any time of the year is a good time to visit. Because Sydney lies in the Southern Hemisphere, seasons are the reverse of those in North America—Christmas is the big summer holiday. Beaches are crowded from November to March, and even on winter days the sun is often strong enough to allow for a few hours at one of the protected harbor beaches.

Opera and ballet seasons normally last through the fall and winter months, but there is a brief summer opera season in January and February and a short ballet season during the few weeks leading up to Christmas. During most weekends of the year, it is not unusual to find outdoor concerts taking place in front of the Sydney Opera House or in the city's parks. In fact, during January (and February in 1988), when the Festival of Sydney occurs, the Australian Opera stages a performance outdoors on the parklike area called the Domain.

Sydney's mean annual temperature is 17 degrees Celsius, or about 65 degrees Fahrenheit. (Temperatures in Australia are measured in Celsius; for a quick conversion to Fahrenheit, double the Celsius number and add 30.) Summer (December, January, February) temperatures are naturally the hottest of the year, with a mean of 22 degrees Celsius, but cool breezes off the harbor and the South Pacific Ocean temper them a good bit. Autumn (March, April, May) mean temperature is 18 degrees Celsius; winter (June, July, August) mean temperature is 13 degrees Celsius; spring (September, October, November) mean temperature is 17 degrees Celsius. Rain falls an average 149 days of the year in Sydney, with June having the most rain and September the least.

WHAT TO PACK. You won't need a heavy winter coat, scarf, or gloves in Sydney even if you do visit in the middle of winter; a lightweight jacket or raincoat will do fine. In late fall and early spring, a sweater will keep you plenty warm, but at any other time of the year, especially summer, pack your coolest clothes. The Australian national costume is shorts, T-shirt, and thongs, so don't feel you have to dress up for summer in Sydney. Don't forget a swimsuit, and sensible shoes if you plan to do a lot of sightseeing on foot. A raincoat and umbrella will come in handy any time of year. Sydneysiders rarely dress up to go out to restaurants, though the "national costume" would be unwelcome in most establishments, and when attending an opera, ballet, or concert, they wear all sorts of things—from black tie to high fashion to the clothes worn to work that day. Australians are not exactly a fashion-conscious people and will rarely look askance at anything you might choose to wear.

Don't forget to pack a camera; Sydney is a photo-opportunity city. You can buy Kodak, Agfa, and all other brands of film in Sydney for about what it would cost at home. If mosquitoes (called "mossies" in Australia) bug you, carry repellent in summer, when they seem to be everywhere.

It's also a good idea to bring a converter and an adapter plug; see "Electricity," below.

CURRENCY, CREDIT CARDS, AND BANKING MATTERS. The Australian dollar, abbreviated internationally $A, but simply $ in Australia, is the national unit of currency. It is printed in $A2, $A5, $A10, $A20, $A50, and $A100 notes, and coins are issued in 1-, 2-, 5-, 10-, 20-, and 50-cent pieces; there is also a $A1 coin. You may bring into Australia as much money as you wish, but you can leave with only $A250 in notes and $A5 in coins.

All prices given in this book are in Australian dollars unless otherwise noted. At presstime the exchange rate was: $1 American=approximately $1.40 Australian.

American Express, Diner's Club, Visa, and MasterCard are widely accepted in Sydney at restaurants and in shops and department stores. You can also buy tickets to the theater, opera, ballet, or concerts with these cards. All major hotels in Sydney accept these cards for payment.

Traveler's checks are also universally accepted in Sydney for the payment of goods and services. It's best to convert your traveler's checks to Australian dollars at banks in Sydney; they give the best exchange rates. Hotels, shops, and restaurants will change traveler's checks with a purchase, but do not usually offer the best exchange rate available.

Banking hours in Sydney are Mon.–Thurs., 9:30 A.M.–4:00 P.M.; Fri., 9:30 A.M.–5:00 P.M. Banks are closed on weekends and public holidays.

4 FACTS AT YOUR FINGERTIPS

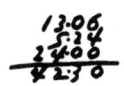

WHAT IT WILL COST. Basically, Sydney is no more or less expensive than major cities in North America, except for the cost of getting there, a week in Sydney will cost you about the same as a week in New York, Los Angeles, or San Francisco. And, as in those cities, you'll find you can vacation on a budget, spend a fortune, or strike the happy medium. It's really up to you. There are deluxe hotels and restaurants where you can pay $2 for a cup of coffee, or you can turn the corner and pay 90 cents for coffee at a milk bar (Sydney's version of a delicatessen), take-out food shop, or coffee shop. You can use public transportation to travel around the city and hardly feel a pinch, or you can take a cab everywhere or rent a car and watch transportation costs consume your vacation budget. You can stay in the best hotel in town and pay $A215–$300 a night for a room, house yourself in a moderately priced hotel for half that or less, or spend your nights in a budget hotel for about a third of the price.

Anyway you slice it, however, getting to Sydney is not going to be cheap, although APEX (advance purchase excursion) air fares are about as low now as they have ever been. At press time, the cheapest airfare between Sydney and the U.S. West Coast was an APEX fare priced $1,096 (U.S.) round trip for an economy-class ticket (subject to change). That fare was available only during the Australian winter (our summer), known in travel industry lingo by the unfortunate title of "off season"—pure nonsense in Sydney, as no season is really "off." Full economy fares, business-class, and first-class fares to Sydney are also sold, and once in a while an airline will offer a promotional fare even cheaper than an APEX ticket. Your travel agent is often the best source of information about air fares to Sydney, or you can call the airlines themselves, which may or may not give you a straight answer. That totally depends on how well informed the agent is and how willing to find you the best fare.

Here's an idea about what you might expect to pay for some typical tourist items in Sydney:

Bus sightseeing tour, $A18 half day, $A35 full day
Cruise on Sydney Harbour, $A10–$A16
Theater ticket, $A15–$A27, depending on seat
Concert, opera, or ballet ticket, $A16–$A60, depending on seat
Movie ticket, $A8
Entrance to museum or art gallery, free–$A5
Ticket to a sports event, $A7–$A20
Hotel room per day for one person, deluxe $A215 and up, moderate $A100, inexpensive $A70 and up
Breakfast in a coffee shop, $A6 per person
Lunch at a café or bistro, $A10 per person
Dinner at a fine Sydney restaurant, $A50 per person without wine
Bottle of Australian wine, $A6 and up
Glass of beer at a pub, $A1.10
Cocktail, $A6
Commuter rail ticket, 60 cents–$A10.60, depending on distance traveled

FACTS AT YOUR FINGERTIPS

City bus fare, 60 cents–$A2.40, depending on distance traveled
Ferry ride at Sydney Harbour, $A1.10–$A2.40, depending on destination

CRUISES. Several shipping lines offer air/sea cruises; you first fly to the South Pacific (Sydney, Tahiti, Singapore, Hong Kong) and join a cruise there. It's possible to buy an air/sea package, or just purchase the cruise alone. There are also some cruise ships that call at North American ports, cruise to the South Pacific, and include Australia on their itinerary. If there's a disadvantage to cruising to Sydney, it's that your time in the city will be limited.

For detailed information contact: *Cunard Line,* 555 Fifth Ave., New York, NY 10017, (800) 221–4770 in the U.S. *P & O Princess Cruises,* 2029 Century Park East, Los Angeles, CA 90067, (213) 553–7000 (U.S.), or 2 Castlereagh St., Sydney, NSW 2001, Australia. *Royal Viking Line,* 450 Battery, San Francisco, CA 94111, (415) 398–8000 (U.S.). *Sitmar Cruises,* 10100 Santa Monica Blvd., Suite 1800, Los Angeles, CA 90067, (213) 553–1666 (U.S.). Or see your travel agent.

HINTS TO MOTORISTS. The best advice to visitors who might want to drive in Sydney is: Forget it. Traffic during normal business hours on weekdays and Saturdays is heavy, and parking on the street in the city center is virtually impossible. The last thing Sydney needs is another driver in the fray. Sydney's public transportation system—buses, trains, and ferries—is excellent and inexpensive, although it does not operate 24 hours a day. By midnight many of the buses, trains, and ferries are asleep for the night. Cabs, however, are still quite plentiful in the wee hours. As an added incentive to leave the car behind, the Urban Transit Authority operates a free shopping bus (no. 777) around the inner city between 9:00 A.M. and 3:30 P.M. weekdays, at ten-minute intervals. Another free bus (no. 666) operates from Wynyard rail station downtown to the Art Gallery of New South Wales, across town.

If you insist on driving, the major adjustment will be driving on the left-hand side of the road with the steering wheel on the right-hand side of the car. Seat belts are mandatory for all passengers throughout Australia, and this law is strictly enforced. The police can pull you over in Sydney anytime anywhere to administer a breath test to determine whether you are driving while intoxicated. If you are—and by Sydney law you probably are if you've had a couple of drinks and/or wine with dinner—expect to go to jail. There are no exceptions for foreign passport holders. Of course, you'll need a valid driver's license to rent and operate a car in Sydney, but a license from any U.S. state or Canadian province is honored.

The maximum speed limit in the city is generally 60 km/h (kilometers per hour), or about 35 mph. Speed limits on expressways are higher. Gas stations are all over the city, but not all accept credit cards as payment.

FACTS AT YOUR FINGERTIPS

Road conditions can be quickly determined in Sydney by a call to 1–1571. If you need road assistance, NRMA (National Roads and Motorists Association) will come to your aid; call 632–0500.

Avis, Budget, Hertz, and Thrifty, in addition to a slew of local companies, are Sydney's major car rental agencies. You'll find their offices at Kingsford Smith International Airport and at many locations in the city. Average unlimited-mileage rates are $49 a day for a small car, $59 for a medium-size car, and $69 for a large car. You'll need a valid driver's license and a major credit card to rent a car in Sydney. Your travel agent or international airline can reserve the car for you.

ACCOMMODATIONS. Hotels, motels, and self-catering apartments are readily available in Sydney to serve as your home away from home, and you'll find that whatever your vacation budget can afford, there's accommodation to match. Many of the names you know from home—Sheraton, Hilton, Hyatt, Inter-Continental—operate deluxe hotels in Sydney, but there is a wide range of moderate-price and budget accommodations located all over town. The Australian Tourist Commission in Los Angeles and New York (see "Tourist Information," above) has information about accommodations, so you can decide before you go just where you want to stay, and your travel agent can reserve a room for you in the city. It's a good idea in a big and busy city like Sydney to reserve your hotel room well in advance. In the unlikely event that you arrive with no place to stay, your first stop after clearing customs should be the Travel Centre of New South Wales, corner of Pitt and Spring sts., which may be able to direct you to an empty room. Their publications *Budget-Priced Accommodation in Sydney and Near Suburbs, Serviced Apartments and Hotels with Cooking Facilities in Sydney,* and *Camping and Caravan Parks in Sydney* may be helpful. (Again, see "Tourist Information" for mailing address.)

Another accommodation option is a stay in a **private home** or on a **farm** or **ranch** in the Sydney area. For information contact *Bed & Breakfast Australia,* part of Bed & Breakfast International, 396 Kent St. or Box Q 184, Sydney, NSW, Australia 2000; (02) 264–3155, or (02) 498–1539 after hours.

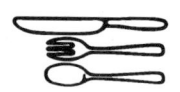

DINING OUT. You'll find every cuisine under the sun at Sydney restaurants, and meals priced from a couple of dollars to more than $50. Because Sydney is a cosmopolitan city, ethnic restaurants abound—Chinese, Greek, Japanese, French, Thai, Indian, Italian, Yugoslav, Mexican, Spanish, to name a few. American-style fast food shops reached Sydney long ago, so that today there are McDonald's and Kentucky Fried Chicken outlets in almost every neighborhood.

Australian cuisine is hearty and not unfamiliar. Quality beef and lamb are Down Under specialties, as is fresh seafood. Try a dozen Sydney rock oysters for a taste of a local shellfish that is superb. Australian red and white wines and Australian beer are also exceptional. Many restaurants are licensed to sell

FACTS AT YOUR FINGERTIPS

alcohol, but those that are not display signs advising patrons to "BYO"—bring your own bottle. The restaurant will serve the wine or beer you bring along. Liquor stores, called bottle shops, are certainly plentiful, and odds are there will be one near the unlicensed restaurant where you may be eating.

You needn't worry about the water in Australia. It is as pure as any you'll ever drink anywhere in North America. Because Australian health and food regulations are strictly enforced, vegetables and fruits present no problem to eat. Australian fruits are among the juiciest in the world.

Bookstores in Sydney are stocked with restaurant guides to the city, so you might want to pick one up as a reference. (The *Sydney Morning Herald's Good Food Guide* is an interesting one.) If you're on a tight vacation budget, get a copy of *Cheap Eats in Sydney,* which lists hundreds of restaurants in the city where you can get a meal for $15 or less.

Bed & Breakfast International (Australia) can arrange dinners in private Australian homes. See their address and phone under "Accommodations," above.

TIPPING. Tipping is not as widespread a practice in Australia as in the U.S., but it is generally expected in the service industry if service has been worth it. Sydneysiders would, however, be the first to withhold tips for unsatisfactory service. As always, tipping is a matter of personal preference, but you'll find none of the pressure to tip in Australia that is so common in North America. If you wish to recognize a special service at a hotel or restaurant, for example, 10 percent of the bill is sufficient. Taxi drivers and porters have set price scales and do not expect to be tipped, but many people will round off a taxi fare in favor of the driver. Bartenders may well remind you to pick up your change if you leave some on the bar as a tip. Service charges are not added to hotel or restaurant bills in Australia.

DRINKING LAWS. The minimum age to purchase or consume alcoholic beverages, including beer, is 18 in Sydney and throughout Australia. Strict drunk-driving laws are enforced in Sydney, so don't be surprised if the police pull you over to administer a breath test. Those who drive while intoxicated will find themselves in a judicial mess, or worse.

Australian laws have stipulated that establishments had to have rooms for guests if they served liquor. Though now there are some pubs that are permitted to only serve drinks, many "hotels" are hotels in name only: they are actually pubs, and may have a room or two somewhere, but keep them permanently empty. Many pubs close by 11 P.M.

Australian wines and beers are of high quality; but be aware that the beer is stronger here than that legally allowed in the U.S. (The Foster's you have back home has to be watered down.)

8 FACTS AT YOUR FINGERTIPS

BUSINESS HOURS, HOLIDAYS, AND LOCAL TIME. Normally business hours in Sydney are 9:00 A.M.–5:00 P.M. Banks are open Mon.–Thurs., 9:30 A.M.–4:00 P.M.; Fri. until 5:00 P.M. Australia Post, the national post office, is open weekdays, 9:00 A.M.–to 5:00 P.M. Most department stores open at 9:00 or 9:30 A.M. and remain open until 5:30 P.M. Usually stores are open late Thursday nights. Some stores close at noon on Sat., but more and more are beginning to stay open a full day.

Public holidays in Sydney during 1988 are *New Year's Day; Australia Day,* Jan. 26; *Good Friday,* Apr. 1; *Easter Monday,* Apr. 4; *Anzac Day,* Apr. 25; *Queen's Birthday,* June 13; *Bank Holiday,* Aug. 1; *Labour Day,* Oct. 3; *Christmas,* Dec. 26; and *Boxing Day,* Dec. 27. In addition, there are school holidays several times a year, when you might notice an abundance of children roaming the streets and especially the beaches.

Sydney is located in Australia's *eastern time zone.* It is ten hours ahead of Greenwich mean time most of the year. Daylight savings time is usually in effect from the last Sun. in Oct. until the first Sun. in Mar. If you live in the Eastern time zone in North America, the time in Sydney will be ahead by 16 hours from Nov. to early Mar., ahead by 15 hours from early Mar. to Apr., and ahead by 14 hours from May to Oct. If you live in the Pacific time zone in North America, the time in Sydney will be ahead by 19 hours from Nov. to early Mar., ahead by 18 hours from early Mar. to Apr., and ahead by 17 hours from May to Oct.

SEASONAL EVENTS. Special events of one kind or another are always being staged in Sydney. If you want to know about them in advance of your arrival, write to the Australian Tourist Commission in Los Angeles or New York for details (see "Tourist Information," above). Otherwise, the Travel Centre of New South Wales can tell you all about them when you arrive in town. Major events are listed in newspapers and in free publications found in hotel lobbies, such as *This Week in Sydney.*

The major regular events are the *Royal Easter Show,* Sydney's biggest annual event, which begins the Fri. before Easter weekend and runs for ten days; the *Sydney–Hobart Yacht Race,* starting the day after Christmas from Rushcutter's Bay is one of the yachting world's major events, after the America's Cup Race (you can watch from ferries, Watson's Bay, North Head, Dobroyd Point, Nielson Park); the *Festival of Sydney,* which starts New Year's Eve and runs for the entire month of Jan., and Feb. in 1988, featuring all sorts of cultural and sporting events; *Chinese New Year,* which features the traditional lion dance through the streets of Chinatown; and the *Sydney City to Surf* mini-marathon, which takes place in late winter, when runners travel from Sydney to Bondi Beach.

In 1988 Australia celebrates its *Bicentenary,* the 200th birthday since European settlement. Special events, planned throughout the year, include a spectacular celebration on Sydney Harbour on *Australia Day,* Jan. 26: sailings of a fleet of tall ships and many local pleasure craft; and in the evening there will

FACTS AT YOUR FINGERTIPS

be fireworks displays. In Oct. a major international air show will be held. (See pages xi–xii for more information.)

SPORTS. Sydney, like the rest of Australia, is sports mad. You'll find a complete range of participant and spectator sports available to you in the city—including **golf, tennis, squash, horse racing, dog racing,** Australia-rules **football, rugby, cricket,** and all the **water sports** imaginable. If you want to spend a day at the races, *Randwick Racecourse, Canterbury, Rosehill,* and *Warwick Farm* are the major tracks. If you're interested in seeing a cricket match, cricket season is during summer, and there are matches staged all over town.

Most sporting clubs in Sydney will allow visitors to use their facilities. All are listed in the yellow pages. Details of sporting events are always listed in the sports pages of Sydney newspapers and in *Coming Events in Sydney,* published by the Tourism Commission of New South Wales and distributed free. The Travel Centre of New South Wales can tell you the best places to play golf or tennis, and usually your hotel concierge has information on where you might play.

If you like **fishing,** you'll love the ocean beaches and coastal cliffs. Fishing is also fine in nearby Georges and Hawkesbury rivers. Information and licenses, available at the New South Wales State Fisheries, McKell Building, Rawson Place, (02) 217–6110 or (02) 217–5093. The Travel Centre of New South Wales can tell you about fishing charters and equipment rental.

GAMBLING. There are plenty of ways to lose your money gambling in Sydney. You can bet on **horses, dogs,** and **sports events,** and there is a **state lottery** that promises to make you an instant millionaire. **Poker machines,** or one-armed bandits, are found only at clubs that have a license to operate them. You can place your bets on horses, dogs, and sports matches at TAB (Totalizator Agency Board) offices in most shopping areas, and lotto tickets are sold at newsstands all over the city.

FOR WOMEN VISITORS. Women traveling alone in Sydney will be comfortable doing all the things they feel comfortable doing alone at home. If an elegant restaurant is your kind of place, then you'll feel just fine dining alone at one here. If you like rowdy pubs, drink up with the Sydneysiders; no one will look at you askance. The people are friendly, so be prepared to talk with strangers if you're out for a drink by yourself. If you don't like that idea, a table in a hotel lounge would probably be your best choice.

All the establishments listed in this guide are fine for women on their own unless otherwise noted. If you're out for the evening, however, take taxis rather than stroll too far by yourself. Sydney is a safe city, but still a large one, and there's no sense in risking trouble in areas such as Kings Cross (see "Security," below).

FACTS AT YOUR FINGERTIPS

DISABLED VISITORS. Facilities for disabled visitors are located in Sydney at most public places. A free booklet, *Guide to Sydney for the Disabled,* is available in the city; phone (02) 80–4488. A specialist in travel for the disabled is Meryl Bolin. She can provide information, plan and book tours, and be an escort as well if required. Contact: *Meryl Bolin Enterprises,* Box 339, Avalon, 2017; telephone (02) 918–9770.

POSTAGE. Airmail postcards cost 60 cents; an aerogram 53 cents; an airmail letter 90 cents.

ELECTRICITY. The current is different than in North America: in Australia it is 240/250 volts. And the wall outlet is different from North American and European outlets (so the set of adapter plugs you have at home may not work here). The Australian outlet takes a 3-prong plug: the 2 prongs at the top are set at an angle. If you're staying in a large hotel, they will probably be able to supply you with an electrical converter and adapter plug for your small appliances. Otherwise, get them before you leave home—they are hard to find in Sydney.

METRIC CONVERSION

CONVERTING METRIC TO U.S. MEASUREMENTS

Multiply:	by:	to find:
Length		
millimeters (mm)	.039	inches (in)
meters (m)	3.28	feet (ft)
meters	1.09	yards (yd)
kilometers (km)	.62	miles (mi)
Area		
hectare (ha)	2.47	acres
Capacity		
liters (L)	1.06	quarts (qt)
liters	.26	gallons (gal)
liters	2.11	pints (pt)
Weight		
gram (g)	.04	ounce (oz)
kilogram (kg)	2.20	pounds (lb)
metric ton (MT)	.98	tons (t)
Power		
kilowatt (kw)	1.34	horsepower (hp)
Temperature		
degrees Celsius	9/5 (then add 32)	degrees Fahrenheit

FACTS AT YOUR FINGERTIPS

CONVERTING U.S. TO METRIC MEASUREMENTS

Multiply:	by:	to find:
Length		
inches (in)	25.40	millimeters (mm)
feet (ft)	.30	meters (m)
yards (yd)	.91	meters
miles (mi)	1.61	kilometers (km)
Area		
acres	.40	hectares (ha)
Capacity		
pints (pt)	.47	liters (L)
quarts (qt)	.95	liters
gallons (gal)	3.79	liters
Weight		
ounces (oz)	28.35	grams (g)
pounds (lb)	.45	kilograms (kg)
tons (t)	1.02	metric tons (MT)
Power		
horsepower (hp)	.75	kilowatts
Temperature		
degrees Fahrenheit	5/9 (after subtracting 32)	degrees Celsius

TELEPHONES. Australian telephones may ring a bit funny to the ear of a North American, and phone numbers may not have as many digits, but the system works as well as the phones back home. Local calls from a public pay telephone cost 30 cents. Dial the operator if you have difficulty on the line, or to place long-distance calls. You can dial direct to North America from many hotel room phones.

Sydney's area code is 02; the area codes for the areas outside of the city vary. When calling Sydney from overseas, you'll need the country code, 61, and city code, 2 (the area code without the 0), then the phone number.

SECURITY. Sydney is a safe city and none of the areas tourists frequent are particularly risky. Perhaps the roughest area of town is Kings Cross, but even that part of the city favored by prostitutes, drunks, and rowdy youths is more colorful than dangerous (though women alone at night may want to use taxis if traveling through The Cross). In any city, Sydney included, it's a good idea to check valuables in a safe deposit box at your hotel.

DEPARTURE TAX. Hang on to your last $A20, because that's what it will cost you to leave Australia. Australia has the highest departure tax of any nation on earth. You can pay this tax at any Post Office during your stay (be sure not to lose your receipt), or after you have checked in for your international flight out of Australia, at a specially marked window at Sydney's Kingsford Smith International Airport.

"I Take but I Surrender"

An Introduction to Sydney

by
EMERY BARCS

Hungarian-born Emery Barcs, a Sydney resident since 1939, writes for Australia's weekly news magazine The Bulletin. *His most recent book, the critically acclaimed* Backyard of Mars, *is an account of Australia's refugee period, 1939–44. This Introduction is a summary of the feelings he has developed about his city, from the perspectives of both insider and outsider.*

I disagree with the opinion of many tourism experts that the most rewarding introduction to Sydney comes from sailing into Port Jackson, the majestic harbor of the oldest and largest city of Australia and the South Pacific.

Port Jackson, with its 5,504-hectare (13,595-mi) water surface, certainly is one of the largest and loveliest natural harbors of the world, and a magical surprise does await those who arrive here by sea. At one moment the voyager sees only yellowish sandstone shoreline, but suddenly, after the ship has negotiated a narrow opening between two steep cliffs—North Head and South Head—an inspiring panorama unfolds.

When the weather is good—and in Sydney the sun shines on an average of 342 days a year—a visitor is greeted by the sight of countless pleasure craft with billowing sails gliding over the dark blue expanse. Ferryboats, which, for maneuverability, are powered with propellers on both ends, ply between suburbs where homes in luxuriant gardens border the shore. Above all looms the single-span, silver-gray bulk of the Harbour Bridge—affectionately nicknamed "the coat hanger." To the left of it the "sails" of one of the most controversial masterpieces of modern architecture, the Sydney Opera House, seem ready to lift the building from its anchorage at any moment.

Farther on emerges the city proper: tall, angular glass-walled buildings, which give the impression of a Manhattan in the Southern Hemisphere. And around the Port stretches a 224-km (139-mi) winding shore with bays and coves, many with berths, which dock some 3,000 ships a year, handling more than 10 million tons of cargo. By the time the newcomer reaches the overseas terminal at Circular Quay, he or she has probably fallen in love with that city, which may appear like a dream come true.

Yet, just because of this chance of falling in love at first sight, it is advisable to arrive in Sydney by plane. Port Jackson is an overstatement, a promise that Sydney may not be able to keep. On the other hand, Sydney's and Australia's main airport is an understatement—and probably a welcome one.

Named after the nation's foremost air pioneer, Sir Charles Kingsford Smith (1897–1935)—but referred to popularly by its location, "Mascot"—the terminal has badly outgrown its facilities, despite constant additions. (The trouble is the universal one: Nobody wants the noisy monster of an airport in the vicinity, and the quarrel over whether to build a new one or extend the old has been going on for years between the federal government in Canberra, the government of the state of New South Wales, local government authorities, and various resident action groups.) Sydney urgently needs a new international air terminal. A site for it has now been chosen at Badgery Creek, 42 km (about 26 mi) from the city center. But when it will be finished is anybody's guess.

After an arrival at Port Jackson, the pleasant surprises that Sydney has to offer may not be immediately apparent. For despite a veneer of

INTRODUCTION

carefree serenity and bonhomie, Sydney is not one of those rare spots where one slides with ease into the rhythm of life, feeling comfortably at home. The city's coat of arms, depicting an 18th-century sailor and an aborigine holding a shield with a three-masted ship, carries the motto: "I take but I surrender." As nobody seems to know what this enigmatic inscription is supposed to mean, anybody may interpret it. My solution: It is a warning to all newcomers that Sydney will squeeze a lot out of them before it begins to give something back.

Some Statistics

Officially, the name Sydney belongs only to a relatively small area of some 23,093 square km (about 15 square mi), with an estimated resident population in 1986 of over 80,000. But the entire metropolitan area—a conglomerate of five separately administered cities (Sydney, Parramatta, Liverpool, Penrith, and Campbelltown), four shires (Sutherland, Baulkham Hills, Hornsby, and Warringah), and 31 municipalities (each with its own elected local council)—extends over 5,203 square km (3,226 square mi), with a population of about 3.5 million. It stretches some 90 km (55 mi) along the Pacific coast and 55 km (34 mi) inland. These cities, shires, and municipalities together form the fourth-largest urban settlement in what was the British Commonwealth, exceeded in population only by London, Calcutta, and Bombay.

As Sydney is the capital of New South Wales (one of the six states that, with the Australian Capital Territory and the self-governing Northern Territory, form the Commonwealth of Australia), the city is the seat of the NSW state government. Here, in walking distance of one another, are the buildings of the State Parliament, the Ministries, the Supreme Court, the Public Library, the Art Gallery, etc. Separately they may not be much to rave about; together they serve as a dignified backdrop to what is arguably the most distinguished square mile in Sydney.

Normally the city is governed by an elected council of 27 aldermen headed by a Lord Mayor. But in March 1987 the New South Wales State government sacked the council after charging it with inefficient management and appointed three commissioners to run the city's business, which is financed by a $100-million annual budget.

Except for a few streets and squares, the city they govern is neither elegant nor impressive. Most of it looks somewhat ordinary, is noisy and during working hours is hopelessly overcrowded. On the other hand, "after hours" (5:30 P.M. and later) the city empties out.

Yet, like so many things here, this "mainly for business" attitude of Sydneysiders toward the heart of their metropolis is changing. It is mellowing into an appreciation of their city, in which they begin to take some civic pride and which they are beginning to enjoy. For instance, Martin Place, one of Sydney's more distinguished-looking thoroughfares, in recent years has been closed to vehicular traffic and become pedestrians-only Martin Plaza. As a convenient rendezvous spot, it has been a great success. The free concerts and other performances held at noon on most weekdays in the plaza's sunken open-air auditorium attract considerable crowds—mainly lunching office workers.

Sydney is not only a big trade and finance center but also Australia's largest industrial city, with the busiest port in the Southern Hemisphere. Its approximately 14,000 factories include 5,300 machine and motor works, 2,900 textile and clothing factories, and 1,500 food, drink, and tobacco manufacturing establishments. A quarter of Australia's wool production is auctioned in and shipped from Sydney. Altogether, its industries employ about half a million workers—20,000 in the port alone.

But how did this big city develop in the short span of less than two centuries?

The History

The aboriginal people were, of course, living in Australia well before the Europeans came ashore. The two causes of the British founding of Sydney are quite well known: the chronic overcrowding of British jails in the 18th century and the American War of Independence, which prevented the British from disposing of their malefactors in the New World. After long deliberation about what to do with the flotsam and jetsam of society, and a misfired attempt to establish a penal colony in West Africa, the British government of the day decided to transport criminals to the faraway land of Australia, which Captain James Cook had discovered in 1770. Those "criminals" included men and women sentenced for petty misdeeds such as the theft of goods worth only a few cents, or for membership in certain (mainly Irish) political movements.

The First Fleet—consisting of 11 ships under the command of Arthur Phillip—sailed from Spithead in May 1787. On board were the involuntary founders of Sydney (and of Australia)—about 300 officers, seamen, and jail wardens, and 520 male and 197 female convicts.

Eight months later, on January 18, 1788, they reached their destination: Botany Bay. But the bay looked unsuitable for a settlement, and Phillip decided to land his wards a few kilometers north, at what became Port Jackson. On January 26, the expedition landed in a sheltered dent of the port, which Phillip named Sydney Cove, after Home Secretary Viscount Sydney; today it is called Circular Quay. Oddly,

INTRODUCTION

however, the name Sydney has never been officially conferred on the spot which in 200 years has grown from a miserable camp at the edge of the continent.

Here is a short chronological run-down of that spectacular development:

1788 Settlement at Farm Cove.
1789 James Ruse granted land at Rose Hill (now Parramatta) and becomes the first settler there.
1792 First foreign trading vessel, *Philadelphia,* arrives.
1793 First church built (on Hunter Street).
1802 First book (*General Standing Orders*) printed in Sydney.
1803 First newspaper, *Sydney Gazette and N.S.W. Advertiser,* published.
1809 First post office opened.
1810 First racetrack opened in Hyde Park, now on the fringe of the commercial center.
1823 Legislative council appointed to assist the governor in colonial affairs.
1831 First immigrant ship arrives, and the first steamer, *Sophia Jane,* reaches Sydney.
1838 David Jones opens the first shop.
1841 Gas used for street lighting.
1842 First omnibus licensed.
1844 Exports exceed imports for the first time.
1849 The last convict ship arrives.
1850 University of Sydney founded.
1856 Comprehensive registration of births, deaths, and marriages inaugurated.
1858 First electric telegraph line.
1871 National Art Gallery founded.
1883 Sydney–Melbourne railroad established.
1898 Sydney and Newcastle connected by phone.
1910 Saturday half-holiday established.
1932 Harbour Bridge opened.
1973 Sydney Opera House opened.
1988 Celebration of Sydney's (and Australia's) Bicentennial.

The Growth of the City

Historical developments, adverse circumstances, and, frequently, disregard for the common good shaped the Sydney of today. To begin with, Sydney has the congenital defect of having developed in the direction of least resistance.

18 INTRODUCTION

The first governor of the settlement, Captain Arthur Phillip, was a man of vision. His plan, drawn up in 1788, provided Sydney with wide streets, roomy squares, and substantial public buildings. Alas, subsequent governors did nothing to implement this plan. They watched with indifference as the early residents erected their houses and hovels wherever it was easiest to build. As historian C. H. Bertie has pointed out, Sydney's main thoroughfares were constructed by the feet of transported convicts, who followed the least tiring routes from one point to another. By the time the authorities became concerned about what was happening, it was too late. Sydney was bedeviled by traffic arteries that were too narrow even for the coach epoch and are totally unsuited to the motorized age.

Another slice of historical bad luck for the city's development was that its adolescence coincided with the Victorian era, when architecture experienced what some consider was one of its poorest periods. Hence, many of Sydney's public buildings—including the Town Hall, the General Post Office, and most state government buildings—are monuments to mid-19th-century kitsch. They are worth preserving only as architectural witnesses of the youth of a nation and because they are still usable. To replace them just for aesthetic reasons would be too expensive.

Finally, it was also bad luck that for long periods builders, land speculators, so-called developers, and similar "unselfish" people had been able to persuade city fathers that what was good for business was also in the public interest. This period may not have vanished.

Whether because of the distance (about 20,000 km) from the mainstreams of modern Western architectural trends or for reasons of ingrained artistic conservatism (probably a combination of both), Australian architecture limped half a century behind the times until well past the end of World War II. It was only in the 1950s that modern constructions began to pierce a flattish skyline. Since then, the change has been dramatic.

However, not all Sydneysiders have been happy about their city's entry into the 20th century. Many men and women still argue that the switch to modernism has produced a blanket to the city's ventilation by stopping sea breezes from blowing through the streets, which the tall buildings have transformed into dark canyons. These people assert that, while the skyscrapers have rejuvenated the city's appearance, they have not improved it. Be that as it may, that "airlessness" cannot be *so* bad: Sydney has experienced a movement from the suburbs back to the city in the past few years. Huge and very expensive apartment houses have been and are being built for those who can afford to settle nearer the facilities of a modern metropolis. This means not only giving up better air and noiseless suburban nights for air-conditioned comfort,

INTRODUCTION

but also good riddance to congested roads, overcrowded trains and buses, and other commuter problems.

A Suburban Life

Still, for most people living in Sydney means residence in one of the sprawling suburbs. It can be life in one of the pretty upper-crust harborside quarters such as Vaucluse or Mosman, with their villas and boat sheds; in plutocratic Bellevue Hill overlooking them; in leafy North Shore "villages" such as Killara, Pymble, or Wahroonga, where the homes are spacious and the gardens large and well tended, and where the two- or three-car garage is the rule rather than the exception. Or it can be life in one of the dozens of suburbs that look as if they were turned out on a production line. In these—rather unfairly dubbed—"dormitory suburbs,"—centered around shopping centers that all seem to look alike, the statistically average Sydneysiders lead their lives.

The opinion most Sydneysiders share with many other Australians is that one "suffocates" in a flat (apartment) and "only mugs pay rent for years and end up without their own roof over their head." Although buying an apartment (called a "home unit") has become fashionable in recent years, most Australians consider it their birthright to own a separate house on a separate plot of land. As a result, the suburban sprawl of Sydney continues relentlessly.

Town planners and administrators argue and complain in vain that this practice is costly, wasteful, idiotic. Objectively, they may be right. Astronomical amounts are being spent to provide the steadily extending suburbs with essential infrastructure such as roads, gas, electricity, public transportation, sewers, and telephones.

Take, for instance, water. Sydney's supply comes from rain caught in huge dams and reservoirs. But the prevailing climate brings periods when reserves sink to alarmingly low levels and water becomes scarce. Sydney's longest drought on record lasted eight years—from October 1934 to October 1942. The situation had become so desperate by the end of 1941 that water had to be rationed severely. According to Sydney Water Board calculations, the city and suburbs would need only half of the water consumed now for personal use, industry, and keeping the innumerable gardens green if people lived in apartments instead of in separate houses.

Sydney's transportation system between the city center and suburbia is quite efficient, but transportation between the suburbs is poorly developed, and a car is a necessity unless you are prepared to accept near exile. Consequently, Sydney has become one of the most motorized metropolises of the world, averaging one car for fewer than every three people.

Unfortunately, road building and maintenance lag badly behind what is needed, and traffic snarls at certain "strategic" points, such as the Harbour Bridge, are frequent.

The Sydneysiders

What do that "average" male and female Sydneysider look like? A few leisurely walks in the crowded city streets will go a long way to answering that question.

One is surrounded by a well-fed, well-clothed, and healthy-looking crowd—people who generally enjoy a high standard of living and a lot of leisure. (The five-day week of 36 to 40 work hours leaves plenty of time for outdoor activities.) The newcomer is at first impressed by the masses of healthy physiques, suggesting a city with secret sources of rejuvenation.

However, if a visitor is looking for ultra-elegance and supreme sophistication, this city is not Paris or New York. Rather, rugged good looks seem to prevail here, a style that is down-to-earth. The people look approachable, and for the most part they *are* approachable—friendly, open, with a fondness for visitors. (Until the 1986 "wheat-sales crisis," Americans—as World War II comrades-in-arms—could expect an especially warm welcome).

While Sydney may not be graceful, sensitive, and elegant, neither is it uncouth or monotonously gray. It has one suburban shopping center that is quite different from the others and could be in any—well, almost any—of the world's smartest cities; the shop windows here are restrained, not overstuffed with goods. That center is about 5 km (3 mi) from the city, in the eastern suburb of Double Bay. Strategically situated in the midst of the affluent quarters of Darling Point, Edgecliff, Bellevue Hill, Rose Bay, and Vaucluse, it is nicknamed "Sydney's Faubourg St. Honoré." Many shop owners here travel several times a year to Europe or the United States to buy the latest fashions in London, Paris, or New York. Still, bargains are not rare in Double Bay—if you don't mind buying things of a season almost past.

Though Double Bay now ranks as the finest shopping area, the city proper also has some elegant shops and good department stores. There the main retail business area has evolved in an oblong bordered on the north by Circular Quay, on the east by Hyde Park and Macquarie Street, on the west by George Street, and on the south by Bathurst Street. From one of the tall buildings during the lunchtime break, the sight of thousands of workers swarming out of offices into the narrow streets resembles streams full of sardines. In the summer heat (between November and March), walking in this crush can be exhausting. As a subtropical city, Sydney ought to indulge in a siesta at least during summer, but such a midday rest is out of the question. What would city workers who live long distances away from their workplace do with a couple of hours' break? Traveling home and returning to the office would take too much time and cost too much money. Hence, Sydney offices and shops work mostly from 9:00 A.M. to 5:30 P.M. in winter and summer, when one just sweats it out and hopes that a "southerly buster"—the wind that roars in from the South Pole—will reach the city to lower the temperature by several degrees in a few minutes.

On January 18, 1988, Sydney will celebrate its 200th birthday (which, of course, is also the birthday of Australia). But how much will the celebrants have in common with those first arrivals? Very little, if only for the simple reason that the convicts produced very few progeny. Yet the question is still being argued as to whether the first convicts and those who followed them until 1849 have left any lasting impact on the character of successive generations. Some historians assert that the Sydneysiders' alleged passions for gambling and alcohol and prejudice against authority, in favor of the "underdog," have their origins in the mental and emotional makeup of the First Fleeters and their descendants. But, more likely than not, such assertions are romantic and scientifically untenable fables. Many Australians *are* passionate gamblers—but this is true even in, say, Melbourne and Adelaide, which never had penal colonies. Per capita alcohol comsumption in Sydney is less than it is in London, New York, and Paris. And, in fact, the per capita consumption beer, called by some, "Australia's national pastime," has fallen by 10 percent between 1982 and 1985. The contemporary vice of drug taking—rife as it is in Sydney—is not worse here than in other large Australian cities. And although it is difficult to compare crime statistics (because the methods of collating them are so different), crime is no more widespread in Sydney than in other Western metropolises. Mugging and bag snatching do occur in Sydney, but relatively rarely; the city has no official red-light district, but prostitution thrives in the Kings Cross area and off William Street. Tourists can avoid this easily.

The Social Structure

If Sydneysiders once upon a time felt hurt when one reminded them of their city's convict past, times have changed; these days descent from a First Fleeter is claimed with a certain pride. It suggests that the claimant is a "dinkum Aussie"—a genuine Australian, not the offspring of some Johnny-come-late immigrant.

It is true that Australian society tends toward egalitarianism, but this does not mean that it is classless—and, until recently, descent has had an important bearing on the class to which one belonged.

Most of the relatively well-to-do free settlers were English, Welsh, and Scottish Protestants; the majority of poor settlers and convicts were Irish and Catholics. To this day, the "upper crust" of what passes for Sydney society is basically Anglo-Saxon Protestant. So are the conservative Liberal and National (agrarian) political parties, which most of them support. On the other hand, the social democratic Labor Party is backed largely by Catholics—including the mainly Irish Roman Catholic Church. These are not hard and fast rules. Frontiers are being crossed, and moving upward on the social ladder is probably easier in Australia, including Sydney, than in more traditional and more settled societies.

The proud working-class saying that "Johnny is as good as his master" is no empty slogan here, though the proverbial "Johnny" can be tiresome because he frequently behaves as if he were not "as good" but much better. Many Australians want to demonstrate their conviction that rank, money, and higher education do not entitle a person to greater respect than that accorded their more modest fellow human beings.

Naturally, snobbery exists (as it does everywhere), though its roots are not easily ascertainable. Money does matter a great deal, but while Sydney has a fair number of millionaires, its idle rich are few. There is no aristocracy, and the publisher of a social register based on birth would be laughed out of town. Papa's social standing carries weight, but probably most with the membership committees of the city's elite clubs—the Australian and the Union for males, Queen's for females—than elsewhere. Sheep and cattle breeders on a sizable scale (Australians call them "station owners" or, currently, "cockies") are definitely "in" people, though for some mysterious reason sheep seem to be classier than cattle. Banking, high finance, and mining and other industries are also "in." But until quite recently retail trade was "out"—even if it meant the owner of a billion-dollar chain of department stores. Law and medicine are, as almost everywhere, favorably regarded professions. The old school tie remains very important socially and career-wise, and thousands of ambitious parents make considerable financial sacrifices to send their offspring to "public" (which, following British tradition, means private) schools instead of to free state schools.

A Shift from the British Ways

But new values have emerged. Since the great post–World War II immigration flood, Sydney's markedly British way of life has changed enormously. One in every three Sydneysiders was born in or is the child of someone born in another country. It is the impact of these "ethnics" that has altered the city's character since 1945.

INTRODUCTION

The tea shops have mostly gone, replaced by espresso bars run by some "ethnic"—most likely a Central European. Almost vanished, too, is the prewar restaurant with its "roast and three vegs" staple menu, which had managed to prove that excellent raw material (Australia produces some of the world's best-quality foodstuffs) can be transformed into tasteless feed. Now Sydneysiders can pick and choose from hundreds of good eateries representing the cuisines of dozens of nations.

Prewar indifference to fine cooking has changed into an almost hedonistic adoration of eating. Expertise in food and wine (Australia produces some excellent wines) is expected from anyone wanting to progress socially. Restaurants for all pockets appear and disappear quickly. Those that survive mostly can be relied upon to supply the right stuff and the right service in the right ambience. Burgeoning delicatessens (also usually run by "ethnics") are other signs of a still-increasing taste for the culinary arts. The variety of the international range of foodstuffs on their shelves must be seen to be believed.

Until well after World War II, eyebrows were raised and lips were dropped if one dared speak in a foreign tongue in a public place. On occasion the speaker was sternly rebuked for the insolence of not speaking English. But no one gives a hoot today if you talk in French, German, Swahili, or Eskimo, for Sydney has become one of the world's most polyglot cities. Fortunately, so far this has not led to any great formation of foreign-national ghettos. While there are areas favored by certain ethnic groups—Liverpool by Italians, Bankstown by Vietnamese, Parramatta by Slavs—none of them has become the exclusive habitat of this or that single immigrant group. They are peopled by a healthy mixture of sometimes as many as 30 or 40 nationalities around an English-speaking Australian nucleus.

The role of immigrants in this officially encouraged evolution toward multiculturalism has been that of a leavener. But the new era of attitudes came mainly as a reaction to the experience of young Australians from Sydney and elsewhere who returned home from overseas trips and wanted the things they had seen and enjoyed abroad. By and large, their demands have been or are being satisfied, and by no means solely in matters connected with creature comfort.

The level of culture and cultural aspirations is rising steadily. During the past 20 or 30 years, Sydney has become a respectable center of the arts and of learning of international standards. It has three universities, with an aggregate enrollment of more than 47,000 undergraduates. Music, theater, and film are thriving; fine-arts exhibitions (many imported from overseas) draw large crowds.

There are a couple of dozen commercial art galleries in Sydney and most of them carefully choose the artists whose works they exhibit. A volume would be necessary to introduce all the Sydney-based artists whose works are displayed and sold in the city. The doyen of contemporary Australian art is Lloyd Rees, age 92, one of the finest landscape artists by any standard. (His colleague, Desiderius Orban, produced advanced, mainly semi-abstract work up to his death in September 1986, two months before his 102d birthday.) Others who have made a name for themselves far beyond Australia include Brett Whitley—considered by many art critics as Australia's most outstanding younger painter (he also exhibits in New York, London, and other world capitals), the water colorists John Caldwell and Eva Kubos, the vigorous expressionist Stanislaus Rapotec, the portraitist Judy Cassab, and Kevin Connor, highly esteemed for his expressionist views of Sydney. Space prevents me from mentioning many more.

Sydney's professional live theater, deeply rooted in the traditions of the English stage, is very good. Of course one may not like all the plays performed but one can rarely find fault with the polished standards of performance. The leading permanent groups are the Sydney Theatre Company, Ensemble, Nimrod, and Northside.

Dance in Australia has reached world class with companies such as the classical Australian Ballet and the more modern, highly innovative Sydney Dance Company. The Sydney Orchestra can reach the same category if it really tries to. The chamber music concerts of the Musica Viva society regularly fill the 2,700-seat Opera House concert hall as well as the smaller Seymour Centra.

There are five television networks (two public, three private), a dozen radio broadcasting stations, three morning and two afternoon general daily newspapers, and a large number of weeklies and monthlies that compare favorably with similar products internationally.

The Good and the Not-so-Good

Private and public organizations make considerable efforts to attract tourists to Sydney, and their exertions are not in vain, for the number of foreign visitors is increasing steadily. Most leave satisfied with what Sydney has offered to them. If they complain at all, one of the most frequently heard cause for dissatisfaction is that (as in many other tourist countries) service in Sydney is not as good as it ought to be. Whatever the reasons for this may be elsewhere, here the main cause of beds made late in the day, slow room service, and similar annoyances is the high cost of labor—especially on holidays and weekends, when hotel and motel employees get "penalty rates"—so management gets by with as few staff as possible.

Another complaint concerns the relative paucity of Sydney's nightlife, which consists largely of some restaurants, a few discos, and joints offering "adult entertainment" at Kings Cross. Those desperately wanting company can find it—at a price—by calling on one of the escort agencies that advertise in free weekly tourist guides.

Sydney is no longer a wowsers' citadel where (as recently as 20 years ago) one can't legally obtain a drink after 6:00 P.M. or on Sundays and religious holidays. But the suburban way of life and the high cost of quality nightclub entertainment restrict the city's nightlife mainly (though of course not entirely) to overseas patrons, who are not numerous enough to sustain it. Besides, wowserism in not quite dead either. The linguist Sydney J. Baker defined the word as "a puritanical enthusiast, a blue stocking, a drab-souled philistine haunted by the mockery of others' happiness." As the *Daily Telegraph* of Sydney put it on July 31, 1937: "If Australia had given nothing more to civilisation than that magnificent label for one of its melancholy products—the word 'wowser'—it would not have been discovered in vain." Though considerably diminished in number and influence, wowsers are still around.

But while, admittedly, Sydney's nightlife cannot produce anything quite as attractive as in other cities, it has developed something else in which it is able to match practically any offering. That "something" is in the sporting arena.

Sydney's more than 30 major beaches, with golden sands and great surf, are unparalleled by those of any other big city. Compared with Bondi, Cronulla, and Palm Beach in Sydney on a fine surfing day, Waikiki is a tame pond.

Few rivals can compete with sailing in Port Jackson, Broken Bay, and on other large protected water surfaces. Deep-sea fishing is excellent. A golfer can play on a different course every day for two months, leaving a few more for the third month. Tennis fans can chose from hundreds of courts and meet some of the world's best amateurs for a friendly game. The diversity of sporting facilities has practically no limits. Athletically inclined visitors can easily find horses to ride, boats for sailing and rowing, and a great variety of other activities, because one or another is the favorite leisure occupation of the sports-crazy Sydneysider.

Summing Up

Sydney today is a fast-growing metropolis whose lifestyle, character, and even soul are changing rapidly. Whether one considers it to be the *most* attractive, *most* entertaining, *most* cosmopolitan city of Australia or the *least* plain, boring, and narrow-minded city of the Fifth Continent depends on one's personal approach not only to this city but to the whole of Australia. But if one takes the small effort to learn something about the enormously difficult circumstances in which this megalopolis has developed, one can hardly fail to admire what has happened here in less than two centuries.

Sydney was founded in the epoch of the international sailing ship, when it took the better part of six months to receive an answer to a letter sent to London. It took even longer to get goods ordered from "home"—that is, England.

The first steamer reached Sydney in 1831; the first cable service between Europe and Australia was established in 1872. Regular plane service between Sydney and London opened shortly before World War II.

One remembers all this, looks around, and thinks: "What an achievement!"

This drive for more and greater achievements continues this year when Sydney celebrates the 200th anniversary not only of its own birth, but also of the founding of modern Australia. Several of the works to be undertaken in 1988—such as the building of a monorail to connect the city with its new entertainment and tourist district, Darling Harbor, and the construction of an underwater tunnel to provide a second "dry crossing" of Port Jackson—will, for better or worse, alter again the fast-changing character of this South Sea metropolis.

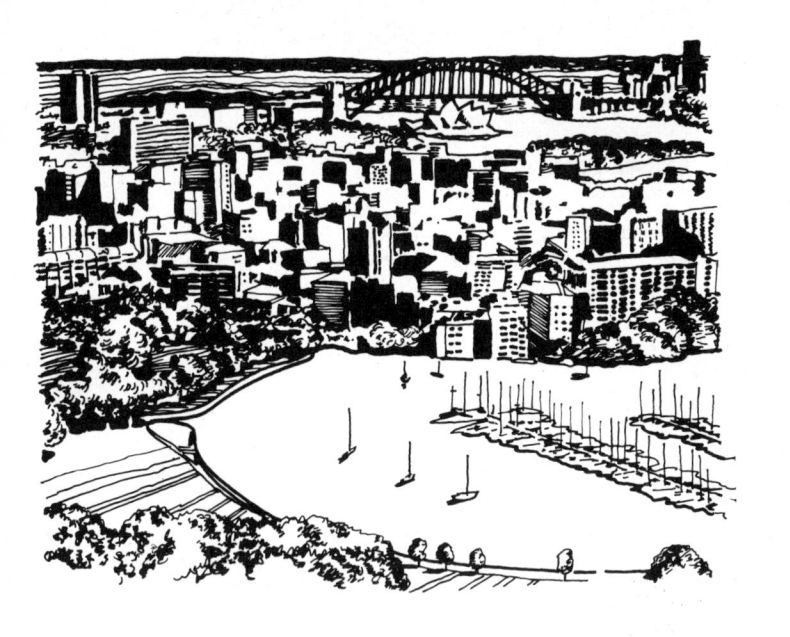

Exploring Sydney

by
DAVID SWINDELL

There can be no doubt that Sydney is one of the world's great cities. With the breathtakingly beautiful harbor, a focal point of life here, the city's appearance is something a visitor won't soon forget.

It's not a difficult place to tour. Many of the attractions are within walking distance of one another, and public transportation is plentiful and uncomplicated. The Sydneysiders themselves are friendly and helpful, and seem genuinely to like tourists.

But the most important thing to remember as you set out to see Sydney is that it's no small town. It's bigger than Vienna or San Francisco, about the same size as Rome. There are an abundance of traffic, plenty of people, and the same somewhat hectic pace you're apt to find in any major world city. So be advised that the best way to tackle seeing this most magnificent city of the Southern Hemisphere is by sections.

Sydney Tower

You may want to orient yourself and plan your touring route by first seeing Sydney from the top, with a trip up Sydney Tower (also called Centrepoint Tower) to the enclosed observation deck a thousand feet above Sydney. It commands a startling 360-degree view of the city, the harbor, the Opera House, the Pacific Ocean, the airport, and all the outlying suburbs. On a clear day you can see all the way to the Blue Mountains in the west. The tower is located on Pitt Street near the Hilton Hotel. You'll have to take the escalator from street level up four floors, through the 200 or so shops in Centrepoint Arcade, to the ticket booth and high-speed elevators that rocket you in seconds up the highest manmade peak in Australia.

After you get your bearings atop Sydney Tower, there are numerous places of interest to visit down below. One of the best ways to see the city is the Sydney Explorer tour bus, operated by the Urban Transit Authority. The red buses travel throughout the city, stopping at more than 20 tourist attractions in town. Riders are free to enter and exit the bus at any of its stops. (See "Tours" under *Practical Information*.)

Perhaps a good spot to embark is at Stop 15 on George Street, in front of Sydney's newest and most exciting shopping and restaurant complex, the Queen Victoria Building. Now extensively renovated, it reopened at the end of 1986. It was originally designed in 1893 to accommodate a fruit and vegetable market. The building occupies an entire city block.

Sydney Harbour

Sydney Harbour frames Sydney in a spectacular panorama that is easily comparable to the beautiful harbor settings of San Francisco, Rio, and Cape Town—but, if anything, Sydney Harbour is more breathtaking and active than those august relatives. The harbor has always been part commercial highway, part navy yard, part playground, and part tourist attraction, and is almost always littered with sailboats, pleasure craft, fishing boats, Australian Navy ships, cruise liners, ferries, freighters, and tankers. Once a ship passes into Sydney Harbour, it must jockey for a safe position until the moment it ties up at its berth. It is a rare moment indeed when Sydney Harbour is still.

Of course, you'll be able to see the harbor from many vantage points in the city, or you can simply walk along its concrete shores from the cruise-liner pier near The Rocks, past Circular Quay and the Opera

EXPLORING SYDNEY

House, to the Royal Botanic Gardens. But without a doubt, the best way to see the harbor is from right in the middle of it on a harbor cruise or by riding one of the public transportation ferries.

Public ferries have been plying Sydney Harbour since 1789, when a sail-and-oar vessel took a week to travel from Sydney to Parramatta. That trip today takes about 45 minutes by train. Modern ferryboats and hydrofoils operated by the city go from Circular Quay to most suburbs that line the harbor. Perhaps the best, and most inexpensive, way to see the harbor is by riding the Manly Ferry from Circular Quay to the suburb of Manly, which lies on the shores of the South Pacific Ocean. The ferry takes 35 minutes and costs $1.40 for adults, 70 cents for children. On the way back, take the Manly Hydrofoil, a 15-minute trip across the harbor costing $2.60 for adults and children. The Manly Ferry leaves from Circular Quay jetty no. 3; the hydrofoil leaves from jetty no. 2.

Since the Manly Ferry is public transportation, you won't get a narrative explaining the sights along the way, as you would on a harbor tour. But what you'll save in money, coupled with the experience of traveling with a boatload of Sydneysiders, makes the voyage well worthwhile.

The first and the most obvious sights you'll see on your trip across the harbor are the Sydney Harbour Bridge and the Sydney Opera House. Almost underneath the bridge on the opposite shore, in North Sydney, is Luna Park, the city's popular amusement park. On the far side of the Opera House are the beautiful grounds of the Royal Botanic Gardens and Farm Cove, where colonists planted the first crops in Australia. Just behind the Opera House, but not directly on the harbor, look for Government House, home of the premier (governor) of the state of New South Wales. Soon, off the port side of the Manly Ferry, you'll see Fort Denison, an early Australian fortress and venue of the nation's first criminal court, organized in 1788. If you're a real history buff, arrange a visit to the fort by calling 240–2111.

Off the starboard side is Garden Island, not very pretty and not open to the public, as it is the Australian Navy depot. In the early days of settlement, almost 200 years ago, the area was farmland. The marina you see next to the navy yard is Rushcutters Bay, home of the Cruising Yacht Club of Australia, which sponsors the annual Sydney-to-Hobart yacht race, one of the sailing world's most important events. The next large inlet you pass is Rose Bay, the largest bay on Sydney Harbour. You will pass several other bays as you sail through the harbor, each a separate Sydney neighborhood. Watson's Bay, the next large inlet after Rose Bay, is the location of Doyle's Seafood Restaurant, one of Sydney's legendary seafood establishments. As you travel keep an eye out for the many mansions that line the harbor, since quite a few of

30   **EXPLORING SYDNEY**

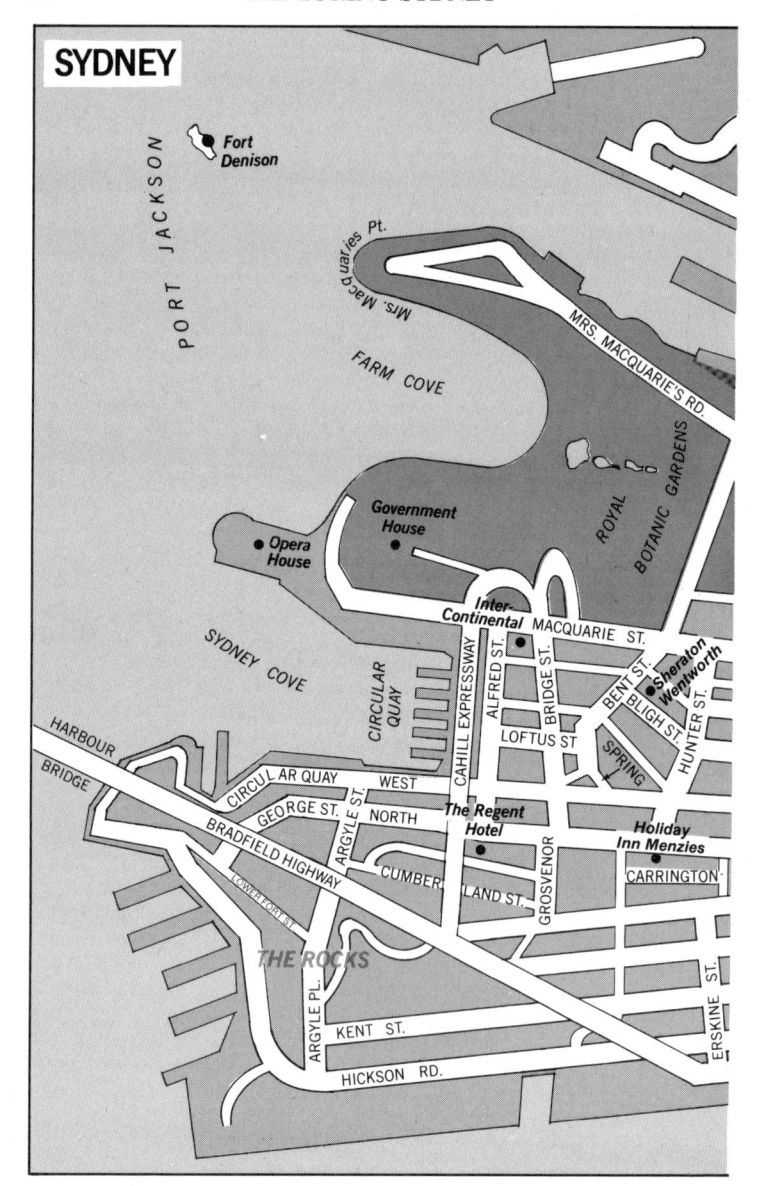

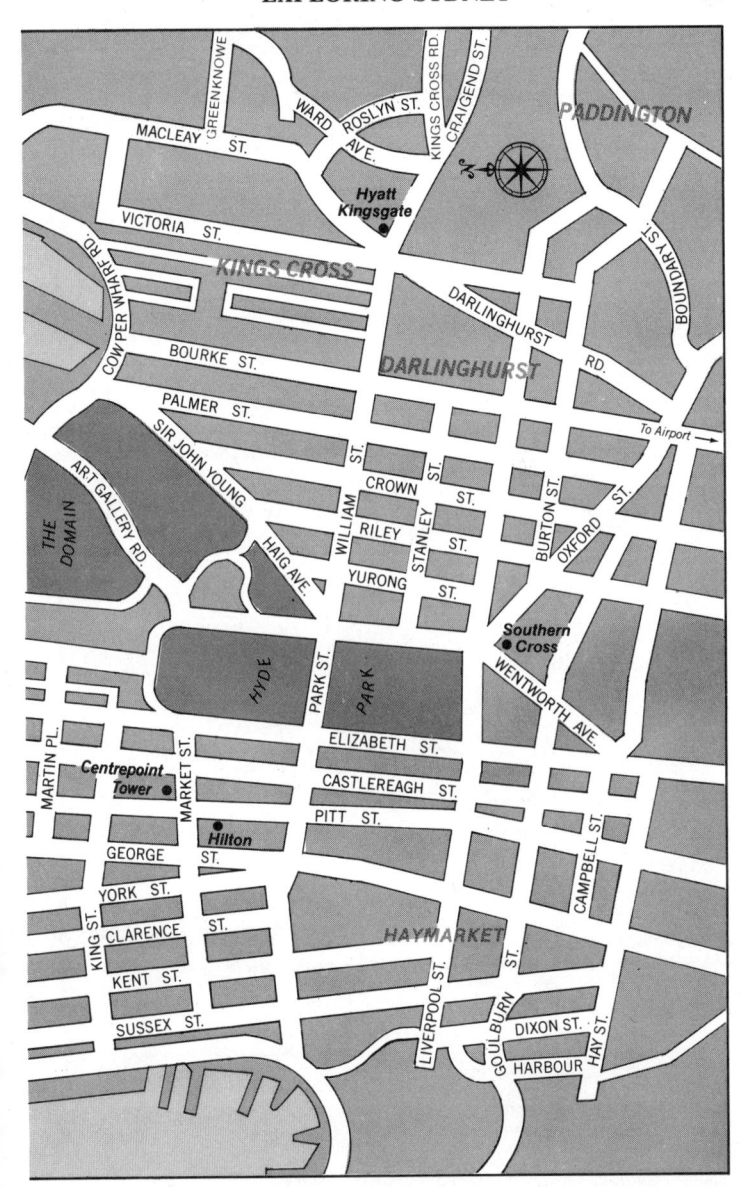

EXPLORING SYDNEY 31

32 EXPLORING SYDNEY

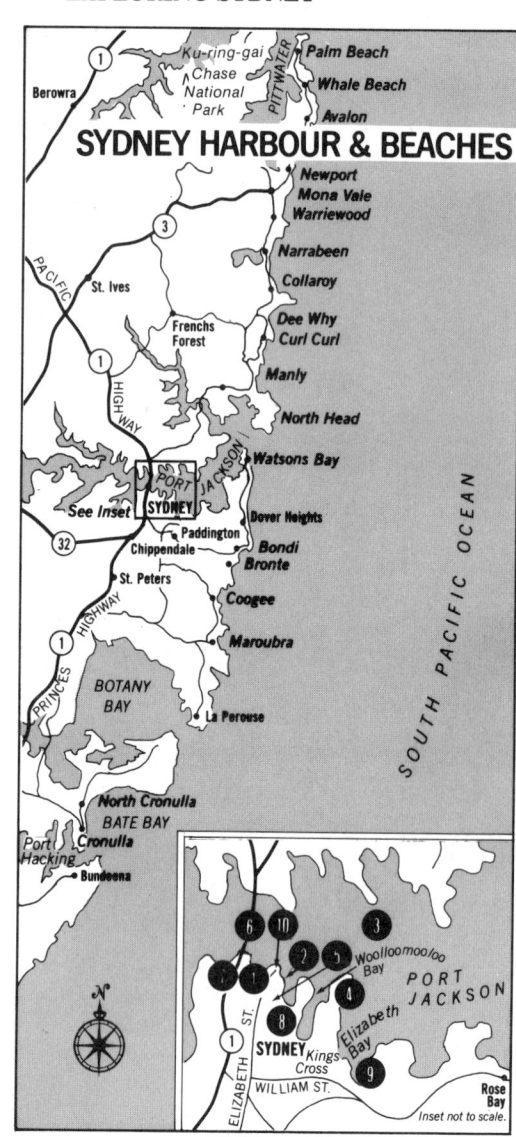

SYDNEY HARBOUR & BEACHES

Points of Interest

1) Circular Quay
2) Farm Cove
3) Fort Denison
4) Garden Island
5) Government House
6) Harbour Bridge
7) The Rocks
8) Royal Botanic Gardens
9) Rushcutter's Bay
10) Sydney Opera House

EXPLORING SYDNEY

them can't be seen from land. Just around from Watson's Bay are the harbor beaches of Camp Cove and Lady Jane, but you'll have to crane your neck to glimpse the nude sunbathers who frequent them.

Reef Beach, on the route to Manly, is another top spot for nude sunbathing. Sydney Harbour National Park, a favorite place for picnics, is nearby. Manly Wharf is next, and there the trip ends. Manly is a very pleasant oceanside suburb with a resort atmosphere. The relatively new Manly Pacific Hotel is a good place to stop for refreshment before heading back to town, and there are several pubs and good seafood restaurants on or near the beach.

You may prefer to take a guided tour of the harbor for an in-depth look at it; if so, there are several choices of tour operators, times, and prices. See "Tours" in *Practical Information.*

Circular Quay

At Circular Quay, from which ferries leave, there are souvenir shops where you can buy postcards, camera film, and Australiana knick-knacks, and restaurants and refreshment stands. Infostar, a computerized tourist information service for Sydney, can be found near Jetty 6.

It may come as a surprise to some readers that Australia is one of the world's leading producers of wines. Displays of select Australian wines are featured at the Australian Wine Centre, 17–21 Circular Quay West. Wine is available for purchase and shipment back home.

Sydney Opera House

Reams of copy have been written about the Sydney Opera House, mountains of books and postcards printed, and no doubt millions of photos taken of Australia's most easily recognized landmark. Like the Statue of Liberty in New York and the Eiffel Tower in Paris, the Opera House is a symbol of its city and its nation as well.

Queen Elizabeth, as head of the British Commonwealth, to which Australia belongs, officially opened the Opera House in 1973. It had been almost 20 years in the planning and building. Thirty sites in Sydney were considered before the final choice of Bennelong Point as the spot to build. Bennelong Point juts right out into Sydney Harbour in the very shadow of that other Sydney symbol, the Sydney Harbour Bridge. The Royal Botanic Garden lies just beside the Opera House.

A worldwide competition to design the Opera House was held, and Sydney's city fathers were swamped with 233 architectural plans from 32 countries before Joern Utzon from Denmark was chosen to build a dream. Utzon's plans caused a headache almost from the beginning. Squabbling, dissension, public disillusionment, not to mention the structural difficulties of actually erecting the building, had to be contended with during the 14 years it took to build the Opera House.

One look at the structure, however, and there is little doubt that it was worth the superhuman effort. Utzon's geometric shells, resembling the sails of the thousands of sailboats that pass the Opera House, were set on a perfect sphere. Each saillike shell is covered with millions of gleaming white Swedish tiles, giving the building a sparkling, luminous look day and night, rain or shine. No wonder Sydneysiders pegged the Opera House the "Eighth Wonder of the World."

Today, the Opera House is more than just a tourist attraction—it is the premier seat of the performing arts in Australia. The Australian Opera (cofounded by Sydneysider Dame Joan Sutherland), the internationally acclaimed Sydney Dance Company, the Australian Ballet, and the Sydney Symphony Orchestra call the Opera House home. Throughout the year, hundreds of other performances and exhibitions are staged in the building's four main halls—the Concert Hall, Opera Theatre, Drama Theatre, and Music Room. Some say that the 10,500-pipe mechanical organ in the Concert Hall is the world's largest musical instrument. In addition to what goes on inside the Opera House, almost as many spectacles take place outside in front of the building, including the annual National Folkloric Festival and free concerts every Sunday afternoon, weather permitting.

There are four restaurants in the Opera House complex. The most posh is the Bennelong, open Monday to Saturday for lunch, pretheater dinner, and dinner. The Harbour Restaurant is a seafood restaurant with spectacular harbor views. Indoor and outdoor tables are available. The Forecourt restaurant also has excellent views across Circular Quay. Before and after the theater, light refreshments and drinks are available at Café Mozart in the box office foyer.

There are daily guided tours of the Opera House complex and backstage tours on Sundays.

It is, of course, necessary to reserve tickets in advance for performances. The hotter the ticket, the earlier the performance should be booked. When hometown favorite Sutherland sings at the Opera House, tickets go fast. Generally, however, tickets can be purchased at the box office up to a day before the performance; phone 250–7111. A package tour called "An Evening at the Opera House" is also available; it includes a tour, dinner at the Bennelong restaurant, and a performance.

The opera season generally lasts from June to October (winter and spring) with additional summer performances in January and February. The ballet season is normally in the autumn months of April and May, with summer performances scheduled for the three weeks before Christmas.

EXPLORING SYDNEY

The Opera House can be reached by foot from most points in the city center, though the hike may prove formidable for some people staying in hotels in the heart of town. The closest terminal for city buses and trains is Circular Quay, adjacent to the Opera House. From there, buses and trains run to all parts of Sydney. Taxis are readily available in front of the Opera House after a performance, or at Circular Quay.

Royal Botanic Gardens

One of the most peaceful places in the inner city, and the pride of Sydney, is the Royal Botanic Gardens, which sit beside Sydney Harbour near the Opera House. The area was the site of the first farm in Australia and today contains a vast collection of exotic trees and plants indigenous to the country, as well as plant and tree species from around the world—all clearly marked with name and country of origin. Plants, flowers, and trees from Australia's tropical rain forests can be seen in the greenhouse. There is free admission to the gardens, which are open daily from 8:00 A.M. to sunset.

Adjoining the Gardens are Government House (the residence of the governor of New South Wales) and the Conservatorium of Music, originally built in 1817 as the Government House stables.

Macquarie Street

If you continue past the Botanic Gardens up Macquarie Street, you'll see the State Library of New South Wales at the Cahill Expressway. The classical-style sandstone building houses the largest existing collection of written records and illustrations related to the development of Australia. In the galleries early manuscripts, maps, and other types of memorabilia are displayed.

Macquarie Street itself is an elegant stretch, originally laid out by Governor Lachlan Macquarie. Many professionals have their offices here, and there are a number of restored buildings. Of particular interest to visitors is the early-19th-century area occupied by the New South Wales Parliament House, Sydney Hospital, the Mint Museum, and Hyde Park Barracks. At one time this was the site of Sydney's notorious "Rum Hospital," so named because Governor Macquarie rewarded the contractors with a monopoly on importing rum, for years virtually a currency, into the colony. (The bronze boar outside the hospital is *Il Porcillino,* a replica of a 15th-century Florentine sculpture; legend has it that it's lucky to rub his nose—which is why his nose has worn away.)

The Mint Museum houses a collection of Australian decorative arts —furniture, costumes, silver, ceramics, and glass; the building has been

36 EXPLORING SYDNEY

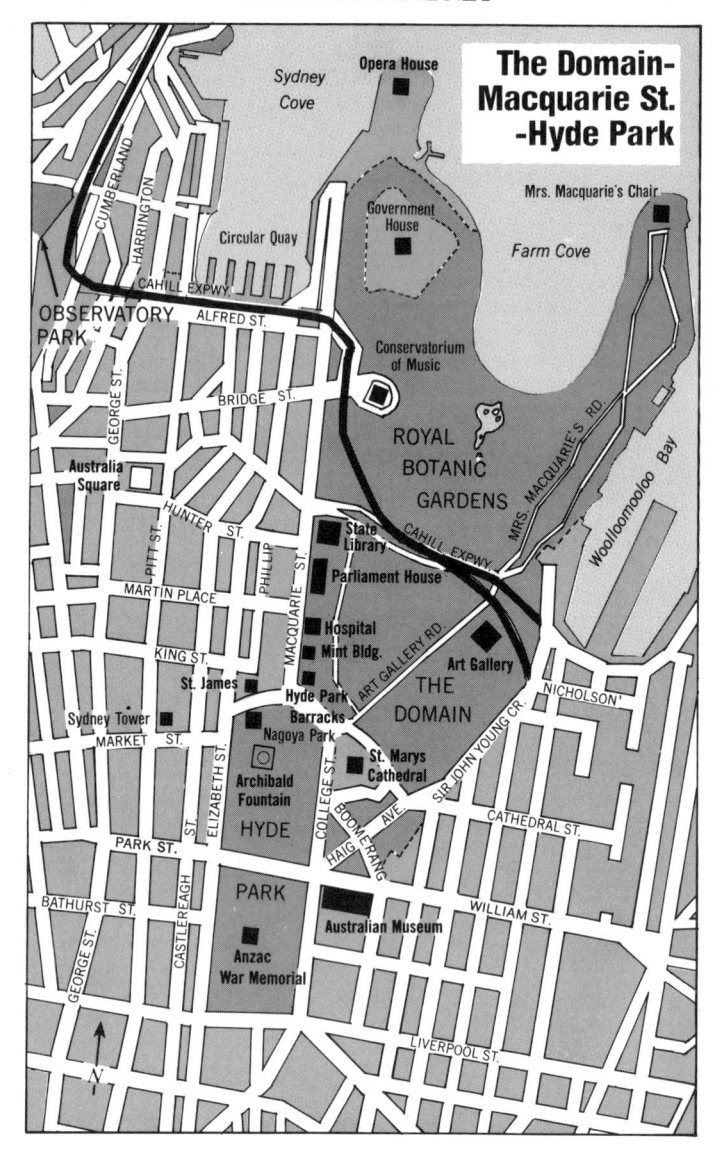

The Domain-Macquarie St.-Hyde Park

EXPLORING SYDNEY

beautifully restored. Beside the Mint is the Hyde Park Barracks, designed by Francis Greenway to house convicts. Greenway himself was a convict, later given his freedom by Governor Macquarie. The Barracks is now a museum of the history of Sydney and New South Wales. If you want some background on Sydney in-a-nutshell, this is the place to get it. There's a pleasant outdoor café next door.

Opposite the Barracks, on the other side of Queens Square, is another of Greenway's buildings, St. James Church. Sydney's oldest church, it is an excellent example of late-Georgian architecture.

Hyde Park

Hyde Park extends from Queens Square to Liverpool Street, between Elizabeth and College streets. It was originally established by Governor Macquarie as a town common, and named by him after London's Hyde Park. In the park's northwest corner is a Japanese garden, Nagoya Park—a tribute to one of Sydney's sister cities. The Archibald Fountain stands in the middle of the northern half of the park. The work of French sculptor François Sicard, the fountain commemorates the French-Australian alliance during World War I. That's Apollo in the middle.

In the southern half of Hyde Park stands the art deco Anzac War Memorial. Even if you have no particular interest in war memorials do stop a minute inside. The statue group (by Rayner Hoff) is a moving one; the theme is sacrifice.

The Australian Museum on College Street houses Australia's largest natural history collection and exhibition of ethnic cultures in Australia. Admission is free.

The Domain

Located behind Macquarie Street, this city park comes alive on Sundays, when it turns into a soapbox forum for citizens to air their opinions and gripes. It is a very entertaining format for public discussion.

The grassy expanse of the Domain extends to to the water's edge. There are some great possibilities here for photographing the Opera House with the Harbour Bridge behind. At the tip of the Domain, harborside, is the stone Mrs. Macquarie's Chair. The story goes that Governor Macquarie's wife used to sit here for hours just absorbing the view.

Located on the Domain and Art Gallery Road, the Art Gallery of New South Wales is not exactly heavy on the European masters, but exhibits a very impressive collection of paintings, sculptures, and collages by Australian artists from the 19th and 20th centuries. Also of interest is the collection of Australian and New Guinea aboriginal primitive art. There is a restaurant in the museum, and a bookshop that sells reproductions, books, and cards.

Martin Place

Martin Place is the city's main pedestrian walking street, running between George and Macquarie streets. Large shade trees, food stands, flower stalls, and fountains give the street a certain European flair and beckon the thousands upon thousands of office workers to leave their skyscrapers and come outside for lunch. Free entertainment is featured at the amphitheater in the middle of the street weekdays, weather permitting, from noon until 2:00 P.M. On Thursdays, at 12:30 P.M. the Cenotaph opposite the General Post Office is the scene of the Australian Army's "Mounting of the Ceremonial Guard" exhibition. The performance of the ceremony is subject to the weather, and not performed during the Christmas holiday break.

The Strand Arcade

This shopping arcade, south of Martin Place, contains more than 80 different shops and boutiques on four levels. It was built in 1891 and refurbished in 1976 as what is perhaps the city's top shopping center. The roof is glass, tinted to give it a golden glow. The arcade runs between Pitt and George streets.

Opal Skymine

Australia is the world's leading producer of opals and the only place on earth where the exotic black opal is mined. However, you won't be anywhere near Australia's opal mines in Sydney, unless you visit the Opal Skymine on the sixth floor of Australia Square Tower, George Street, north of Martin Place. It is a life-size reconstruction of an operating opal mine, the only one in Australia where all the nation's opal types are found in one mine. The Opal Skymine is open Monday–Friday, 9:00 A.M.–5:30 P.M.; Saturday, 9:00 A.M.–12:30 P.M.

The Rocks

Australia began on The Rocks, one might say, when the First Fleet from England landed at Sydney Cove in 1788 with its cargo of some 700 transported convicts. The officers and sailors of the fleet, along with the convicts, were sent ashore at the area now called The Rocks to

EXPLORING SYDNEY

THE ROCKS

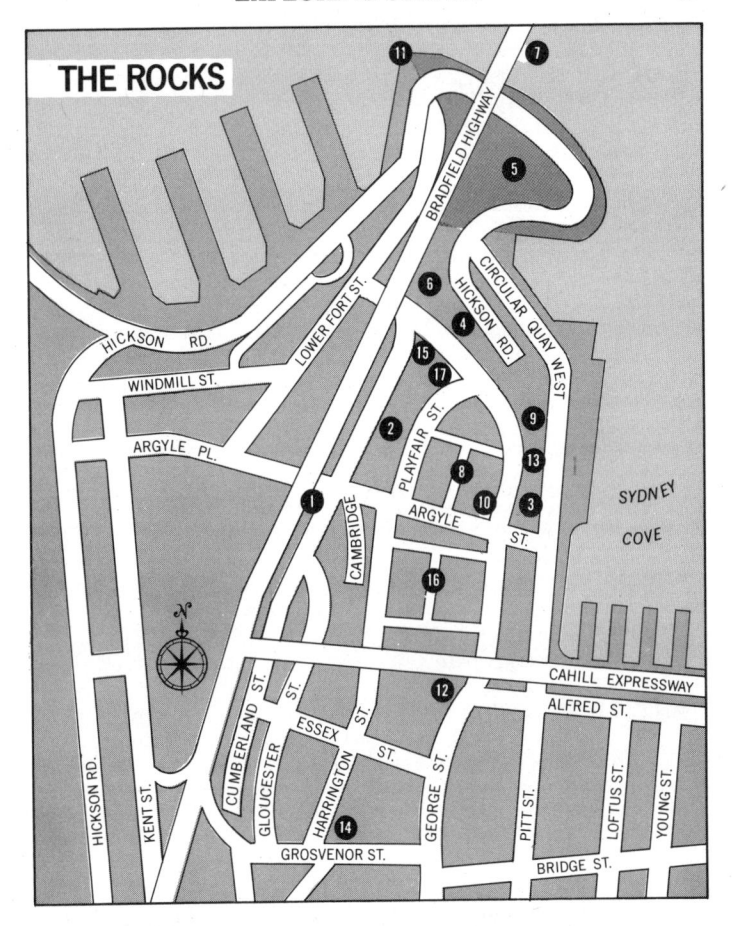

Points of Interest

1) Argyle Cut
2) Argyle Terrace
3) Cadman's Cottage
4) Counting House
5) Dawes Point Park
6) Geological & Mining Museum
7) Harbour Bridge
8) Kendall Lane
9) Old Mariner's Church
10) Orient Hotel
11) Pier One
12) The Regent Hotel
13) The Rocks Visitors Centre
14) St. Patrick's Church
15) Sergeant Majors Row
16) The State Archives
17) Union Bond

EXPLORING SYDNEY

establish what became the first European settlement of Australia. (Australia will celebrate its bicentennial in 1988.) Sydney and, consequently, all Australia had their beginnings at The Rocks. During the young colony's first century, The Rocks was transformed from a pioneering colony to a bawdy sailor's haven. When plague broke out in Sydney in 1900, many old buildings—buildings that told the architectural history of Australia from its beginnings—were summarily burned in hopes of ridding the city of the rats that had come ashore from ships docked in the harbor.

Many buildings that survived the 1900 burning were torn down when the Sydney Harbour Bridge was built in the 1920s, while others were razed as the Cahill Expressway was built in the 1950s. Still others were left to rot. Finally, in 1970, the government of New South Wales acted to preserve the remaining historically significant buildings at The Rocks as a living reminder of Australia's beginnings. Restoration and reconstruction to revive Australia's heritage began that year, and now, 17 years later, The Rocks is one of Sydney's—and Australia's—premier attractions.

The Rocks sits directly on Sydney Harbour and is easily reached on foot from most city hotels, or by train or bus to Circular Quay. The best way to see The Rocks is on foot, as the entire restored area covers only a few city blocks. A good place to begin your walking tour of The Rocks is at the Regent International Hotel, where you might want to have coffee before you set out to explore Australia's past.

Just up George Street from the Regent is The Rocks Visitor Centre (104 George Street), where you can get a free map and brochure to guide you and explain some of the sights you'll see along the way. A free film shown regularly at the center gives a bit more information about the history of Sydney and Australia. The staff on hand at the center will be happy to point you in the right direction and can answer questions you may have. Restrooms are located at the center.

As you leave the Visitor Centre, take a quick look at nearby Cadman's Cottage (1816), Sydney's oldest surviving building. It was built for the governor's boat crew and occupied by John Cadman, superintendent. It's now used as a maritime museum. Then head up George Street toward the Sydney Harbour Bridge. You'll pass the Old Mariner's Church, dating from 1857. Cross the street and walk down the stone steps to Hickson Road, and on your right will be the Australian Steam Navigation Company's headquarters building, which dates from 1883. The tower was built so that company executives could see their ships enter Sydney Harbour. From Hickson Road you can enter Metcalfe Stores (1916), which houses a restaurant and shops, including Lambswool Trader, where you'll find reasonably priced clothing made from quality lambswool, kangaroo leather goods, and other Australian

EXPLORING SYDNEY   41

leather goods. Exit the shops back on George Street and in quick succession you'll pass Union Bond (1841) and Counting House (1848), which were essentially warehouses, and Sergeant Majors Row (1881). The last commemorates Australia's first street. At the end of George Street is the Geological and Mining Museum, housed in an electric light station built in 1902.

If your feet are still holding out, continue into Dawes Point Park underneath the Sydney Harbour Bridge and enjoy some of the most panoramic and breathtaking views of the city skyline and the Opera House. It is perhaps the most ideal outdoor spot in Sydney for photographing the city. But if your feet are beginning to cry for a little relief, turn back at the mining museum and walk back down George Street, away from the bridge and toward the city. Turn onto Playfair Street and continue to Argyle Terrace, a series of workers' cottages that date from the 1870s and now house several shops and Harry's Bar and Restaurant, where you can have refreshments or lunch on the outdoor terrace. Argyle Cut (1843), off Argyle Street, was hewed from solid rock by convicts (and, later, free labor). Nearby are the Argyle Steps. Made before the Cut, they were also carved from the rock.

A few places off the beaten track are well worth a visit in The Rocks, though they are not quite within the bounds of the primary walking area. The State Archives, which can be entered from Globe Street, houses convict transportation journals and memorabilia, passenger lists, and early maps of Sydney; cobbled Kendall Lane has been authentically reconstructed to look just as it did in its heyday a hundred years ago; and St. Patrick's Church on Grosvenor Street is Sydney's oldest Catholic church, dedicated in 1844. There are several small museums and galleries and some other historical buildings listed on the map you'll get at the Visitor Centre, so you can choose what you want to see and do in The Rocks. Keep in mind, however, that not all buildings are open to the public.

Shops at The Rocks are quaint and interesting. The Australian Heritage Bookstore (81 George Street) carries a complete line of Australiana books and Australian history books and a selection of left-handed products, such as knives, scissors, catcher's mitts, can openers, and even boomerangs, all designed for lefties. Close by at the Graphic Factory (75 George Street), brightly woven fabrics with koala, emu, kangaroo, and platypus designs are sold along with stuffed toy Australian animals. Australian artist Ken Done's eccentric and fanciful drawings of such Sydney landmarks as the Opera House and Harbour Bridge are found on postcards, posters, T-shirts, beach wraps, and silkscreen prints at the Sydney Harbour Shop (123 George Street) and the Art Directors Gallery (21 Nurses Walk). His original drawings sell for about $1,500 and paintings from around $4,000, but cards, happily, cost only $2.

If you're ready for lunch, stop in at the Orient Hotel, corner of George and Argyle streets, where you can get a dozen Sydney rock oysters quite reasonably, or grill your own steak or chops outside on the patio. For tonier meals, try the Carriage Brasserie in the Old Sydney Parkroyal hotel on George Street, toward the bridge. Several old pubs have survived the ravages of time around The Rocks and have faithful followings to this day. The Observer Hotel at the corner of George Street and Mill Lane hasn't quite come to terms with women's liberation—the ladies' parlor and lounge is separate from the pub, with its entrance on a side street. But don't let the signs fool you; women will have no problem walking in the front door and drinking up in the main room. The bistro in back of the hotel is a good place to have lunch outside. Also worth a look are the pubs at the Fortune of War Hotel (137 George Street) and the Ox of The Rocks Tavern (155 George Street).

If you've seen enough of The Rocks for one day, and you're rested up after lunch, take a walk around under the Harbour Bridge to Pier One. A collection of souvenir stores, craft shops, and inexpensive places to eat, Pier One is set in a lovely spot on Sydney Harbour, providing a view of the city not often seen by visitors—that part of the harbor beyond the Opera House and the city center. It is a good place to stop for a soft drink and just gaze out across the water. Souvenirs seem no more or less expensive at Pier One than in city shops, but there are certainly plenty of them under one roof.

Chinatown

By the standards of New York or San Francisco, Sydney's Chinatown is not overwhelming. Nevertheless, it is a pleasant diversion while walking around the city, especially if you like Chinese food. Behind every door in Chinatown, it seems, is a Szechuan, Cantonese, or Pekingese restaurant.

Dixon Street is the main thoroughfare in Chinatown. It has been turned into a pedestrian mall between Hay and Goulbourn streets, a distance roughly two blocks long, with a large, easily identifiable Chinese arch at either end of the walking street. The arches are inscribed with all the wisdom of a fortune cookie—"Continue the past into the future" and "Understand virtue and trust"—indicating that you have arrived in the Down Under version of the Orient.

As you walk down Dixon Street, of most interest are likely to be the exotic shops that sell the wares and goods of the Orient. About the only other establishments lining the street are the aforementioned Chinese

EXPLORING SYDNEY

restaurants. The large, modern complex you'll see to the right at the corner of Dixon and Little Hay streets is the new Sydney Entertainment Centre, where indoor sports events, rock concerts, and exhibitions of all kinds are held. Street musicians who work the street almost uniformly are Oriental and play Oriental melodies, a soothing relief from the often jarring tunes played by street performers in other parts of the city.

Darling Harbour

Just to the east of Chinatown, beyond the Entertainment Centre, is Darling Harbour, Sydney's major project to commemorate the Bicentennial. The site was a railway-goods yard and cargo wharves that became run down and decayed. It has now been redeveloped to house a convention and exhibition center, several leisure areas and restaurants, a Chinese garden, theater space, shops, museums, and an aquarium. A casino-hotel is planned for the future. Darling Harbour is linked to the city center by monorail (a controversial project among Sydneysiders). The major components of the development are to open in 1988, and the First State 88 exhibition to be held there during the first half of 1988 should be well worth a visit.

Paddy's Market

Just on the edge of Chinatown opposite the Hay Street end of Dixon Street is Paddy's Market. It is open Saturdays and Sundays only and is a cinch to find—just follow the crowds. The market, the busiest in Sydney, sells everything under the sun, usually at a bargain. Some of the best buys for souvenir hunters are kangaroo skins and belts, T-shirts with all sorts of Australiana painted on them, and stuffed toy koalas, kangaroos, and platypuses. Whatever you may be looking for, odds are it's available at Paddy's Market. Even if you're not in a shopping mood, it's a terrific place to get a good, close-up look at a cross section of Aussies.

Kings Cross

Sydney's Times Square is the somewhat sleazy part of town known as Kings Cross. Sleazy, that is, by Australian standards. Compared to the real Times Square, it is Versailles. True, there seems to be a hooker hanging on every lamppost, and there are dozens of peepshows and "massage parlors" in The Cross, but, to their credit, the Aussies just can't quite pull off sleaziness the sinister way it's done in big-city America. That alone may make it worthwhile to spend a couple of

Kings Cross

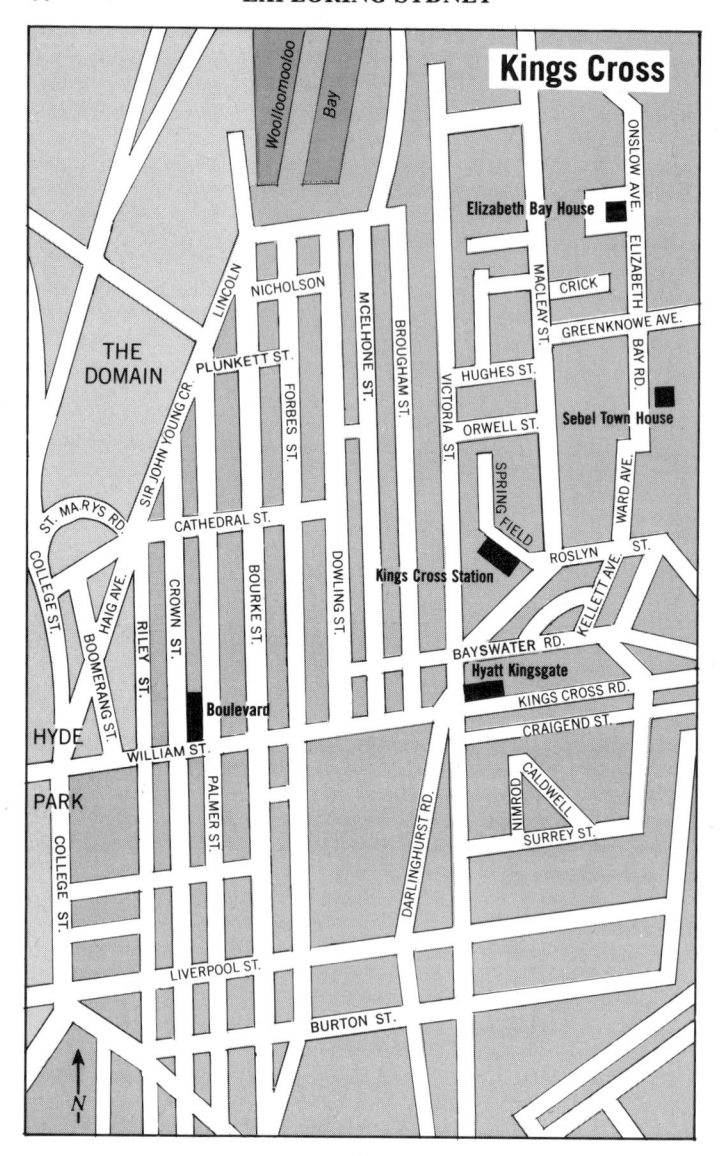

EXPLORING SYDNEY

hours at The Cross—a chance to sample the seamier side of life, with few of the consequences associated with a walk on the wild side.

There's a rail station at Kings Cross, near the McDonald's, and city buses nos. 324 and 325 stop in the area, so The Cross is easily accessible from the city center. A cab ride from the city center to The Cross costs no more than $3.00. And it's possible to walk the distance along William Street in under half an hour.

Aside from the more lurid attractions in The Cross, there are some shops worth a look. On William Street, opposite the Boulevard Hotel, at no. 73, there is a tempting antique shop called Glenleigh, although the beautiful furniture items are a bit large for a suitcase. A little further east is Kabuki, which sells fun Japanese clothes. Just up the street as you near Darlinghurst Road, the main thoroughfare in Kings Cross, stop at the Boomerang School. You can buy a boomerang and get a quick lesson in how to use the thing.

You'll know you're at the heart of The Cross when you see the Hyatt Kingsgate Hotel, at the corner of Darlinghurst and Bayswater roads. Amble down Darlinghurst Road from the Hyatt away from William Street and you'll pass a succession of exotic dance halls (generally covers for brothels), tattoo parlors, pinball and video arcades, strip clubs, "adult" theaters, tax-free shops, bars, pool halls, bistros, cafés, and coffee houses. Unless you're interested, you'll quickly figure out the places to avoid. Establishments like Pink Pussycat, Pleasure Chest, and Sweet Box may not be suitable for the family.

If you like a titillating atmosphere, probably the best time to see The Cross sizzle is at night. Barkers line Darlinghurst Road outside the various clubs, imploring every passerby to come in for a drink and whatever thrills may be behind closed doors. The prostitutes—male and female—are abundant and quite aggressive, and the streets are alive with dumbstruck kids from the country, sailors from the world's navies, and drunks and revelers from all walks of life, hell-bent on having a good night at The Cross. There are a few nightclubs in the area that present a legitimate show, albeit of a risqué nature. The most famous is Les Girls, at the corner of Darlinghurst and Roslyn roads. Its long-running show stars female impersonators, who have been bringing down the house in rollicking good fun for years with their campy renditions of Carol Channing, Barbra Streisand, Bette Davis, and other drag favorites.

Look down the side streets for small, intimate restaurants, where you can find meals of French, Italian, Chinese, or any of a number of cuisines. Two popular Sydney watering holes/restaurants for lunch or dinner are Bourbon and Beefsteak (26–28 Darlinghurst Road) and Bayswater Brasserie, on Bayswater Road next to The Mansions, another of the nightspots popular in The Cross.

Elizabeth Bay House

Elizabeth Bay House is considered by Australia's National Trust one of the ten finest buildings in Sydney. It was built in 1835 as the home for one of Australia's colonial secretaries and, thanks to loving care over the years, remains one of the most splendid examples of Australian colonial architecture. It overlooks the harbor and has been converted into a museum dedicated to life in Australia in colonial days. The house is located on Onslow Avenue in the neighborhood of Elizabeth Bay, which is just down the hill from Kings Cross.

Paddington/Oxford Street

Few examples in the annals of urban rejuvenation match the metamorphosis of Paddington from an ugly duckling into a swan. It wasn't so long ago that this inner-city suburb was a run-down, crime-ridden area where few dared wander at night. Its cheap property values and rents attracted Sydney's artist, gay, and "bohemian" crowd, who slowly went about transforming the area into what is today one of the city's trendiest neighborhoods—an area often called Sydney's Greenwich Village.

Oxford Street, Paddington's main boulevard, is lined with boutiques, coffee houses, antique shops, art galleries, bistros, and bookstores. There are restaurants serving all types cuisine—Italian, French, Greek, Lebanese, Chinese, Balkan, Spanish, German, Thai, Indian, Australian, continental—up and down the street. Afrilanka (237 Oxford Street, Darlinghurst) serves an interesting mix of East African and Sri Lankan specialties.

Turn any corner off Oxford Street in Paddington and you'll find row after row of Victorian terrace houses, many lovingly restored to their original splendor. In fact, Paddington contains the largest number of Victorian terrace houses in Australia. Take city bus no. 389 from Circular Quay on a scenic ride through Paddington if you'd like a close-up look at Australian terrace houses. Suffice it to say, property values and rents are no longer cheap in Paddington.

The best place to begin a walk up Oxford Street is at Taylor Square, which is actually in the neighboring inner-city suburb of Darlinghurst. From the city center, Taylor Square is no more than a ten-minute cab ride. City buses 379 and 380 follow a route from the city center along Oxford Street to and beyond Taylor Square; the fare is about 60 cents. On the Square you'll see the buildings of Darlinghurst Court House, and off the Square on Bourke Street is Kinsela's Brasserie and Cabaret,

EXPLORING SYDNEY 47

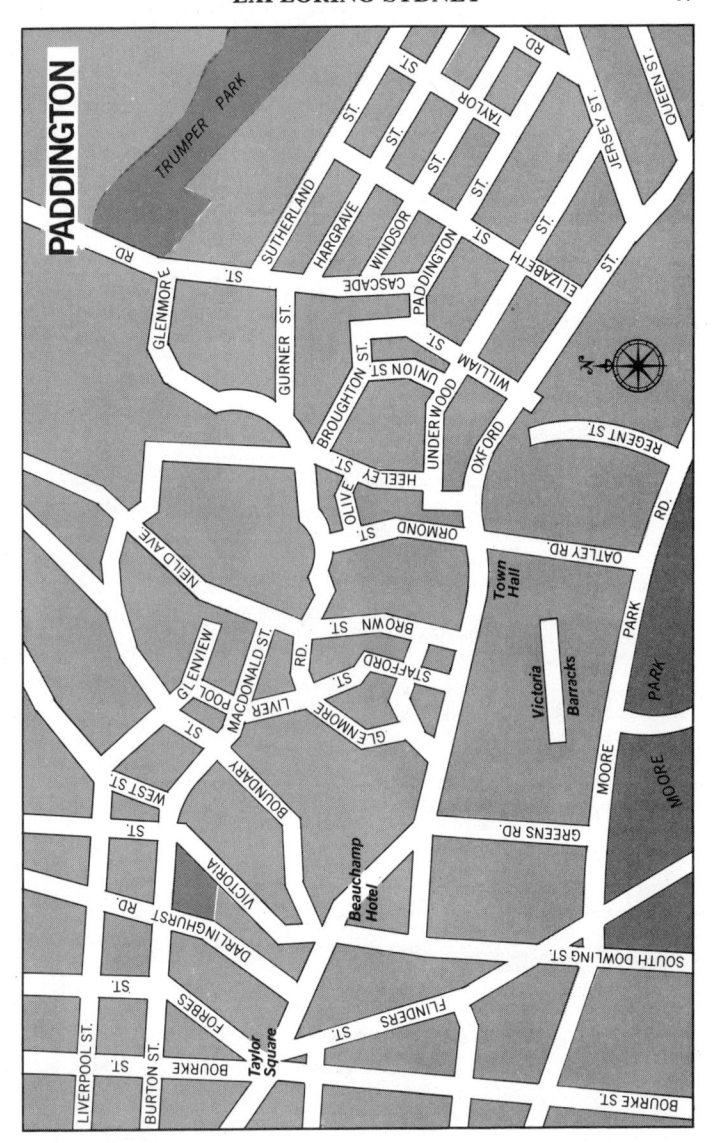

48 **EXPLORING SYDNEY**

where many of Australia's brightest, most talented performers are showcased.

Walk east on Oxford Street to the corner of South Dowling Street, where Paddington begins, and you'll see the venerable old Beauchamp Hotel. The pub there is a good place to wet your whistle before beginning the walk along Oxford Street in Paddington. Those who'd rather have coffee or tea and cake before beginning the trek may want to stop at Cappuccino City (10 Oxford Street) or across the street at Flick's Café.

All along Oxford Street in Paddington are the clothes boutiques where many of Australia's "new wave" designers sell their wares. You will see a colorful display of these clothes, as well as of people, at the Paddington Markets, held every Saturday at the Village Church. Wattle Tree (294 Oxford Street) carries a line of boldly designed women's clothes that are pure Australiana, with fabrics of kangaroo, boomerang, and koala prints. Wildly designed women's clothes and jewelry are also found at Zanoli (52 Oxford Street), or at Rosie Nice (276 Oxford Street), Jazz'd Up (296 Oxford Street), and Studio One (440 Oxford Street). New-wave men's clothing is the thing at Cavalli (428 Oxford Street), Gary Wolff's (270 Oxford Street), and De-Mani (387 Oxford Street).

Numerous bookstores and art galleries are located on Oxford Street, as might be expected in this part of town, where artists and intellectuals congregate. By consensus, the most interesting of the bookstores is New Editions Tea Room and Bookshop (328 Oxford Street), which last year celebrated its twelfth anniversary. It contains an excellent selection of Australiana books and cards and has an intimate café attached, where you can sit and read your purchases. Farther up the street is Book Thrift (414 Oxford Street), with another large selection of Australiana literature. Of the art galleries on Oxford Street, Collage Gallerie (210 Oxford Street) specializes, as the name suggests, in collage as well as in primitive art, while Strokes sells international limited-edition prints and exhibition posters.

As you amble along Oxford Street, you'll see several hotels that are, in the scheme of things, more important as pubs. The Unicorn (106 Oxford Street) and Albury, at the corner of Oxford and South Dowling streets, cater to a gay crowd. Up the street, hotel/pubs that are frequented by a cross section of Sydneysiders are the Paddington Inn, at the corner of William Street (also take a peek in the Sweet William Chocolate Shop, across William Street from the pub); the Imperial Hotel, at the corner of Underwood Street; the Hotel Canberra (384 Oxford Street), with its beer garden; and the Light Brigade Hotel, at the corner of Oxford Street and Jersey Road, where Paddington ends and Woollahra begins.

EXPLORING SYDNEY

Coffee and tea shops, where you can usually order a sandwich or cake and sit in observation for hours, include Passion du Fruit (96 Oxford Street), which has won kudos in the Sydney press for the quality of its food; Anastasia's (286 Oxford Street); Hot Gossip Café (438 Oxford Street); and the Café Giovanni, at the corner of Queen Street in Woollahra, where Centennial Park begins.

Antique' buffs will find plenty of shops to poke around in along Oxford Street, one of Sydney's top antique areas. The Antique Market, a sprawling establishment on South Dowling Street just off Oxford Street, is a treasure trove of Australian antiques. Also worth a stop in are Country Style Interiors (122 Oxford Street) and Gregory Ford Antiques (264 Oxford Street). An Australiana shop on Oxford Street that is well worth a visit if you're looking for a one-of-a-kind souvenir from your trip to Sydney is Coo-ee Australian Emporium (98 Oxford Street), which carries books, clothes, pottery, cards, paintings, and jewelry that are distinctly Australian.

Eastern Suburbs

Sydney's finest homes and many of its trendiest boutiques, along with several of its top restaurants, are found in the sections of town lining the harbor and collectively called the Eastern Suburbs—residential districts like Paddington, Woollahra, Double Bay, Watson's Bay, Darling Point, Bondi, and Rose Bay, to name a few of the larger ones. A good way to see these areas is by city bus 324 or 325, which can be boarded at various points in the city or at Kings Cross. They weave a path through the Eastern Suburbs as far as Watson's Bay. The cost is 60 cents to $1.20, depending on the distance traveled.

Two of the Eastern Suburbs are especially worth leaving the bus to explore; the others are primarily residential. (See the separate section about Paddington, above.) They are Double Bay, Sydney's answer to Beverly Hills, and Watson's Bay, home of the famed seafood restaurant Doyle's. Double Bay, irreverently referred to as "Double Pay" by Sydneysiders who don't happen to live there, is indeed Sydney's mecca of the idle rich—an area of Rolls-Royces, Mercedes-Benzes, Jaguars, done-to-death shop windows, perfectly coiffed matrons in tennis outfits, and, no doubt about it, high prices.

Get off the bus on New South Head Road and you'll be in the midst of the main Double Bay shopping district. There, shops such as Pierre Cardin, Charles Jourdan, Christian Dior, and Gianni Versace, along with shops that are distinctly Australian and more often than not more interesting and appealing, can fill up a few hours of browsing. Explore the side streets—particularly Knox and Cross streets—for out-of-the-way boutiques and tea shops. For lunch, a popular spot is the Cosmopolitan, in the shopping complex of the same name on Knox Street, just off New South Head Road.

After lunch, reboard the bus and ride to Watson's Bay, at the end of the line. Call in at the pub for a drink. Its beer garden features a magnificent view of Sydney Harbour and the city skyline in the background. If you didn't have lunch in Double Bay, have a meal at Doyle's, or get some fresh take-away seafood or fish and chips at Doyle's-on-the-Pier and sit on the grass and lunch. Prices are cheaper at Doyle's take-away than inside the restaurant. Take a short walk around the bay if you're interested in Camp Cove or Lady Jane, two of Sydney's nude sunbathing beaches.

Parramatta

Parramatta is essentially a suburb of Sydney, in that the city's public rail system operates a line there from Town Hall in the city center. Parramatta was founded in 1788, later in the same year that the First Fleet landed at Sydney Cove. In the early years of the colony, it was farming land. Some old buildings have survived in the area and have been restored to their colonial looks. A guide to historical buildings is available from the City of Parramatta Promotional and Tourist Bureau, Prince Alfred Park, Market Street, Parramatta; telephone 630–3703.

Among the colonial buildings to look for are Old Government House, which dates from 1790–99. It is a fine example of Georgian-Colonial architecture and has been fully restored and decorated with period furnishings. Australia's first observatory stood in Parramatta Park, built in 1822, but all that remains of it today is a plaque commemorating its existence. Experiment Farm Cottage (1791) and Elizabeth Farm House (1793) represent two of the earliest efforts to till the land in colonial Australia. Elizabeth Farm House is the oldest house in Australia and the best example in the nation of early colonial farm architecture. It has been restored with period furnishings and is open to the public Tuesday through Sunday and public holidays from 10:00 A.M. to 4:00 P.M. It was on this farm that the earliest experiments in Merino wool production were conducted in Australia. Today, wool is one of Australia's main industries.

Other noteworthy historical buildings in Parramatta are St. John's Church (1803), Church Street, and the attached cemetery, Australia's oldest; Hambledon Cottage (1824), Hassall Street, famous for its English gardens; Harrisford House (1831), 182 George Street, a fine example of a Georgian cottage; and Parramatta Town Hall, Macquarie Street, on whose site the first fair in Australia was held in 1813.

Practical Information for Sydney

HOW TO GET THERE. By air. No matter where on earth you are, you won't have a difficult time finding a flight to Sydney. Thirty major international airlines link Sydney with cities in North America, Europe, Asia, the Middle East, and the rest of the Pacific. From North America, six international airlines connect Sydney with Los Angeles, San Francisco, New York, and Vancouver: *Qantas* (Australia's national airline), *United Airlines, Continental Airlines, Air New Zealand, Canadian Airlines,* and *UTA French Airlines.* On any given day of the week, you'll have several airlines and departure times to choose from for your trip to Sydney.

Flying time between North America and Sydney varies depending on the route taken. En route to Australia most flights stop once or twice, in Honolulu, Fiji, Tahiti, New Caledonia, or New Zealand, but both Qantas and United have nonstop Los Angeles–or San Francisco–Sydney flights several days a week. If your flight stops once en route, the combined flying and ground time between the West Coast and Sydney will be about 16–18 hours. If you fly nonstop, the flight lasts under 15 hours.

All flights to Sydney are operated with jumbo jets, either Boeing 747s, 747-SPs (Special Performance—the long-range jumbo), or DC-10s. All airlines that fly between North America and Sydney offer three classes of service, first, business, and economy (coach). Even if your budget is tight, you may want to seriously consider splurging for business class; the flight is long, and the extra space does make a difference. However, you'll be fed a couple of times and see a couple of movies even in coach, so the long flight time doesn't seem so bad. And spending so much time with your fellow passengers is a good way to meet people.

You'll cross the International Date Line when you fly to Sydney. That means you "lose" a day on the flight down, but "regain" it on the flight home. For example, if you leave North America on Monday, you'll arrive in Sydney on Wednesday morning. On the return flight, if you leave Sydney on Saturday you'll get back to North America on Saturday, often at about the same time you left.

Airfares to Sydney, like airfares to everywhere, can change at a moment's notice, so you must call the airline or ask your travel agent what the fare is for when you want to fly. Fares to Sydney are also seasonal; you'll pay more to fly to Sydney when it's winter in North America and summer in Australia than when it's the other way around. At press time, the lowest airfare from the West Coast to Sydney is an APEX (advance purchase excursion) fare of $1,096 (U.S.) round-trip economy class for travel from April to November (fare subject to change). The APEX fare jumps a few hundred dollars for travel in Nov.-Mar.

SYDNEY

By ship. There are no regularly scheduled ship sailings between North America and Sydney anymore. The jet plane took care of all that 20 years ago. However, there are cruises that include Sydney as a port of call. The unfortunate thing about a cruise is that you'll be able to stop in Sydney only for a day, overnight, or at most a couple of days before it's back to sea. The cruise lines that do sail periodically to Sydney are *Cunard, P&O Cruises, Sitmar Cruises,* and *Royal Viking Line.* Your travel agent is the best source of information about cruises to Australia from North America.

From elsewhere in Australia. Domestic airlines link all capital and major cities in Australia with Sydney. *Ansett Airlines, Australian Airlines* (TAA), and *East-West Airlines* are the trunk carriers, while *Air New South Wales* provides services within the state. Your travel agent can reserve seats and issue tickets on any domestic Australian airline.

For travel by rail, the *State Rail Authority of New South Wales* operates trains within the state. High-speed trains are used on the most heavily-traveled routes, while most other services are operated with commuter trains. Reservations can be made at any rail station in New South Wales. *Railways of Australia* operates passenger trains from many cities in Australia to Sydney's Central Railway Station. Your travel agent can book passage on the Railways of Australia before you leave home, or you can buy tickets at any rail station in the country.

Ansett Pioneer and *Greyhound Australia* provide express motorcoach services from interstate and some country towns to Sydney. Tickets can be purchased through your travel agent prior to departure, or at any bus station in Australia.

HOTELS AND MOTELS. Having plunged into a competitive spending spree during 1985–86, Sydney's leading hotels have spent the past 12 months consolidating. The Regent and the Inter-Continental remain the newest and the best, but the Sheraton-Wentworth is also excellent. Room rates have gone through the roof, although with the decline in the Aussie dollar this has not been a problem for American or Japanese travelers. Hotel rates are based on double occupancy. Categories by price are *Deluxe,* $215–$290; *Expensive,* $150–$200; *Moderate,* $100–$150; *Inexpensive,* $70–$90.

AIRPORT AREA

Expensive

Hilton International Sydney Airport. 20 Levey St., Arncliffe; (02) 597–0122, toll-free 008–222255. The Airport Hilton is the only hotel at the airport. All rooms and restaurants are being completely renovated. Excellent workout facilities (two tennis courts, two squash courts, swimming pool, jogging track, fitness club), where jaded travelers can overcome their jet lag. Free city bus shuttle every hour, 8:00 A.M.–11:00 P.M.

HOTELS AND MOTELS

SYDNEY

Deluxe

Inter-Continental. 117 Macquarie St.; (02) 230–0200. Completed late 1985. Sydney's newest, most luxurious hotel. Incorporates the handsome sandstone façade of the colonial treasury building. The sensitive restoration evokes the opulence and high-Victorian splendor of the 1850s, when gold rushes made this the hub of the bustling colony of New South Wales. Gourmet dining in the *Treasury* restaurant. Magnificent harbor views, in particular from the 31st-floor rooftop cocktail lounge, which overlooks the Royal Botanic Gardens. Extensive new business center equipped with the latest personal computers and electric typewriters. Upgraded executive suites. A five-minute stroll to the Opera House and all city shopping. Convention facilities.

Regent. 199 George St.; (02) 238–0000. Completed in 1984. Ultramodern and elegant, inside and out. Fine dining, especially at *Kable's* where nouvelle cuisine is the specialty. The multilingual staff is efficient and courteous. Situated at the western end of Circular Quay and close to the Sydney Opera House and the historic Rocks area. Most rooms enjoy panoramic views of one of the world's most beautiful harbors. Convention facilities.

Expensive

Cambridge Inn. 212 Riley St.; (02) 212–1111. Five-minute walk from city center. Good hotel/motel-style accommodation. Recently refurbished. New conference facilities. Surrounded by some of Sydney's most popular restaurants.

Camperdown Travelodge. 9 Missenden Rd., Camperdown; (02) 516–1522. Handy to airport, the city, Sydney Cricket Ground, Randwick Racecourse, Harold Park trotting and greyhound track, and several golf courses. Health club and fitness center, outdoor pool, restaurant, function facilities.

Chateau Commodore Sydney. 14 Macleay St., Potts Point; (02) 358–2500. Extensive views of city and harbor. Good motel/hotel-style rooms. Recently refurbished. Close to Kings Cross and city. Licensed restaurant and pool. Free parking.

Florida Motor Inn. 1 McDonald St., Potts Point; (02) 358–6811. Situated in unusually quiet and green area only minutes from the bustle of Kings Cross and city. Good motel-style rooms and apartments accommodating up to six. Pool, sauna. Continental breakfast.

Gazebo Ramada. 2 Elizabeth Bay Rd., Kings Cross; (02) 358–1999. Two hundred plush new rooms were added to the distinctive white tower block late in 1984. All rooms in the older wing have been refurbished and now offer comfort as well as stunning harbor views. Conference facilities. Rooftop pool.

Hilton International Sydney. 259 Pitt St.; (02) 266–0610. Central City. All rooms and restaurants recently upgraded. Conference facilities. *Juliana's* disco. *San Francisco Grill* offers fine gourmet food. Arcade with over 50 shops.

Holiday Inn Menzies. 14 Carrington St.; (02) 2–0232. One of Sydney's older hotels, the Menzies has just spent many millions of dollars on a face-lift. Although its rooms are still not as big and bright as those of the newest hotels, the central-city location puts guests very close to all the major shops. Choice of restaurants.

Hyatt Kingsgate. Kings Cross Rd., Kings Cross; (02) 357-2233. Favored by celebrities, not least because of its location close to the heart of the city's nonstop and often notorious Kings Cross. Rooms are bright and cheery, and have been recently renovated. Harbor views. Conference facilities.

Hyde Park Plaza. 38 College St.; (02) 331-6933. Opposite glorious Hyde Park and very close to city center. All rooms are being refurbished. Rooftop pool, spa, sauna, sun deck.

Koala Park Regis. 27 Park St.; (02) 267-6511. Basic motel-type accommodations. Rooftop pool. Panoramic views of city and harbor.

Macleay Street Travelodge. 26-34 Macleay St., Potts Point; (02) 358-2777. Good basic motel-style rooms. Close to the heart of Kings Cross, yet far enough away to be quiet. Only minutes to city center by subway and bus. Pool, free parking.

Manly Pacific Parkroyal. 55 North Steyne, Manly; (02) 977-7666. Five years old, spacious, and very pleasant if you want a change from central-city living. Situated opposite magnificent surfing beach. A 24 km journey from airport by road, but only 11 km from city by hydrofoil, which travels the length of the harbor in just 15 minutes. Nice bright rooms with balconies overlooking the beach. Rooms available for handicapped.

North Sydney Travelodge. Blue St., North Sydney; (02) 92-0499. Big comfortable rooms, all with spectacular views of the city (from across the Sydney Harbor Bridge) and the harbor itself. Pool, poolside barbecue. Ten minutes by road or rail to city center. Conference facilities.

Northside Gardens. 54 McLaren St., North Sydney; (02) 922-1311. In the heart of the North Sydney business district. Twenty-five minutes from airport; ten minutes from city center; courtesy bus to and from city. Twenty-four-hour room service. Attractive garden setting.

Old Sydney Parkroyal. 55 George St., The Rocks; (02) 2-0524. Old stone warehouse has been turned into a very pretty atrium-style hotel in the heart of The Rocks. Handsome rooms; those with views of the harbor and Opera House are worth requesting. (If you're going to want to get to sleep before 11:00 P.M., be sure you don't get a room on a low floor facing the Observer Hotel; the pub gets quite loud at night.) A full service hotel with a friendly, if somewhat relaxed, staff. Rooftop pool and sauna overlook Opera House. Restaurants serve adequate food.

Rushcutter Travelodge. 110 Bayswater Rd., Rushcutter's Bay; (02) 331-2171. The usual high Travelodge standard hotel/motel accommodation, with the added distinction of glorious views over Rushcutter's Bay Park and Sydney's biggest marina complex, in the Bay itself. Five-minute walk to Kings Cross and the city. Double Bay with its high-quality boutiques and excellent restaurants is also five minutes away by buses that stop right out front. Also close to Paddington, with its own distinctive restaurants, art galleries, and antique shops.

HOTELS AND MOTELS 55

Sebel Town House. 23 Elizabeth Bay Rd., Elizabeth Bay; (02) 358-3244. A modern smaller hotel popular with overseas performers and celebrities. Attentive service. Good, bright rooms with spectacular harbor views. Fifteen-minute walk to city center through Kings Cross. VIP limousine service. Picnic lunches prepared.

Sheraton–Wentworth. 61-101 Phillip St.; (02) 230-0700. Solid, dependable. One of the nicest things about the Wentworth is the thorough professionalism of its multilingual staff. The *Garden Court* is one of the best restaurants in town. "Civilized" is the word for the Wentworth. Popular with country visitors.

Shore Inn. 450 Pacific Hwy., Artarmon; (02) 427-0144. Seven km north of the city center. Good standard motel-type rooms. Two restaurants, pool, sauna.

Southern Cross. Elizabeth and Goulburn sts.; (02) 2-0987. Recently completed. Good big rooms, nicely appointed. Sauna, sun deck, pool.

Sydney Boulevard. 90 Williams St.; (02) 357-2277. Having spent over a million dollars on a major face-lift in 1984, the Boulevard is once again back among Sydney's better hotels. Very popular with Japanese visitors—no doubt because of its Japanese bathhouse. Easy walking distance to both city center and Kings Cross.

Sydney Ramada. 220 Pacific Hwy., Crow's Nest; (02) 922-1199. Ten-minute cab ride north of the city. Large convention facilities. Rooftop pool and garden. Good standard motel/hotel rooms.

Wynyard Travelodge. 9 York St.; (02) 2-0254. Large comfortable rooms with views of the city and harbor. Good central location close to city shops, Circular Quay ferries, and historic Rocks area. Two licensed restaurants. Pool.

Moderate

Artarmon Inn. 472 Pacific Hwy., Artarmon; (02) 412-1644. Basic motel. Twenty-minute bus ride north of city center. Pool, conference facilities.

Bronte Inn. 107 Macpherson St., Bronte Beach; (02) 389-2222. Located in Sydney's eastern suburbs 6 km (about 4 mi) from the city center. Good standard rooms close to an excellent surfing beach. Convention and leisure facilities.

City Gardens Luxury Serviced Apartments. 1 Myrtle St., Chippendale; (02) 690-9100. Located one and a half km (1 mi) from city, eight minutes from airport. All apartments fully self-contained. Restaurant. Heated spa.

Clairmont Village Motor Inn. 5 Ward Ave., Kings Cross; (02) 358-2044. Located in a quiet area near the center of Kings Cross; five minutes to city center by public transportation. Good motel-type rooms recently refurbished. Licensed restaurant and bar. Pool, spa, sauna. Conference facilities.

Cosmopolitan Motor Inn. Knox St., Double Bay; (02) 327-6871. Good standard rooms and all the usual facilities. There is nothing exceptional about this hotel/motel, but it is right in the middle of all the very best Double Bay boutiques, restaurants, shops, and galleries.

Cosmopolitan Motor Inn–Bondi Beach. Campbell Parade and Roscoe St., Bondi Beach; (02) 211-1122. Right on Sydney's most famous surfing beach. Bright, airy rooms with all facilities. Room for up to 600 conference delegates.

Koala Oxford Square. Oxford Square, Darlinghurst; (02) 269-0645. Good standard rooms. Upgraded recently. Heated rooftop pool. Conference facilities.

New Crest Hotel. 111 Darlinghurst Rd., Kings Cross; (02) 358–2755. Pool, duty-free shop, arcade.

Rushcutter Village Motor Inn. 85–97 New South Head Rd., Rushcutter's Bay; (02) 328–7044. Good motel-style rooms that overlook either the harbor and Rushcutter's Bay Park or Paddington and the famous White City Tennis Courts. Conference package rates. Bar and restaurant.

Top of the Town. 277 Victoria St., Kings Cross; (02) 33–0911. Good rooms with magnificent views of city and harbor. Many rooms feature individual spa baths.

Inexpensive–Moderate

Central Plaza. George and Quay; (02) 212–2544. Situated opposite the Central Railway Station, in what has long been the less-developed end of Sydney. A new hotel with comfortable modern facilities, including pool and sauna. Licensed restaurant.

The Russell. 143a George St.; (02) 241–3543. The Russell is one of the real gems of Sydney. Built in 1887, its delightful turreted façade looks very much like the intimate little fairy-tale hostelries in Amsterdam. It's a small, not to say tiny, hotel, but bursting with geniune character and situated in the historic Rocks area to the west of Circular Quay, close to the Opera House, harbor ferries, and all city shops. Its 14 rooms (which can accommodate only 25 people) are all smartly decorated with French provincial wallpaper and feature brass bedsteads. The rooms share five modern and well-appointed bathrooms. Price includes continental breakfast. The Russell offers an intimate charm no large hotel can match. Three new suites and a self-contained apartment at the rear are due for completion in July 1985. Rates range from $42 a night for a single room to $73 for one of the three double rooms that feature marble fireplaces. Most highly recommended.

Inexpensive

Astoria Hotel. 9 Darlinghurst Rd., Kings Cross; (02) 356–3666. Private facilities in all rooms. Darlinghurst Rd. cuts through the center of The Cross and is always busy.

Barker Lodge Motor Inn. 32 Barker St., Kingsford; (02) 662–8444. Ten minutes to airport and city. Opposite University of NSW. Adjacent to Randwick Race course. Good motel-style accommodations. Pool, licensed restaurant.

Camelot Inn Motel. 358 Victoria St., Darlinghurst; (02) 331–7555. Close to Kings Cross. Serviced apartments, fully equipped.

Canberra Oriental. 223 Victoria St., Kings Cross; (02) 358–3155. Rooms with and without private facilities. Located in the heart of Kings Cross.

Centre. 14 Frances St., Randwick; (02) 398–2211. Single, twin, and family rooms. Motel-style accommodations in landscaped gardens. Pool, conference facilities.

Cross Country. 25 Hughes St., Kings Cross; (02) 358–1143. Single, double, and family rooms in the heart of The Cross.

Manhattan. 8 Greenknowe Ave., Kings Cross; (02) 358–1288. Older-style hotel situated in the quieter part of The Cross. Standard facilities.

HOW TO GET AROUND 57

Oxford Towers. 194–198 Goulburn St.; (02) 267–8066. Basic rooms with all the usual facilities. Rooftop pool, licensed restaurant. Opposite interstate bus terminal.

Parramatta Travelodge. Great Western Hwy. and Marsden St., Parramatta; (02) 635–7266. Twenty km (12.4 mi) west of Sydney. Overlooks historic Old Government House and Parramatta Park. Close to golf course and local shops.

Plainsman Motor Inn. 40 Bayswater Rd., Kings Cross; (02) 356–3511. Close to Kings Cross and Rushcutter's Bay. Good standard motel-style accommodations.

Ryde Travelodge. 1118 Victoria Rd., West Ryde; (02) 858–5333. Motel with pool. All rooms overlook golf course. Close to public transportation; 30 minutes from city center. Licensed restaurant.

Studio Apartments. 7 Elizabeth St.; (02) 48–3851. Self-contained apartments in the heart of the city, adjacent to Martin Place. Fully equipped kitchen, linen included. Minimum stay four nights. Maximum four per unit.

Trade Winds Travel Inn Maroubra. 200 Maroubra Rd., Maroubra; (02) 344–5555. Twelve minutes from city center; within easy reach of city beaches, golf courses, and sporting facilities. Views over Botany Bay. Conference room, pool, gymnasium, restaurant, bars, coffee shop.

Twin Towers Motor Inn. 260 Pacific Hwy., Artarmon; (02) 439–1388. Good standard motel-style accommodations. Twenty minutes from city center. Good restaurant, pool.

University Motor Inn. 25 Arundel St., Broadway; (02) 660–5777. Opposite main gate of University of Sydney. Twenty minutes to airport and seven minutes by bus to city center. Good fully serviced motel-style rooms. Licensed restaurant.

HOW TO GET AROUND. Sydney has a well-developed transportation system, which includes buses, trains, taxis, and ferries. Several firms rent cars, with or without chauffeur. Getting about is fairly simple so long as you don't venture beyond the city proper. Finding your way is more complicated in outer suburbia. A visitor who wishes to tour the suburbs would be well advised to invest in two detailed directories: *Gregory's Street Maps* and *Gregory's Sydney by Public Transport,* available at most bookstores and newsstands.

Getting from and to the airport. Kingsford Smith Airport is less than 5 mi from downtown. The government's *Urban Transport Authority* (UTA) operates buses on five routes to the domestic air terminal at Mascot: nos. 303 and 322 from Circular Quay (via Kensington), 385 from Wynyard, 044 from Sydenham Station, 064 from Bondi Junction.

Other buses head to and from the domestic and international terminals. The no. 300 "Airport Express" starts from jetty no. 2 at Circular Quay, stops on George St. opposite the Regent Hotel, then at Hunter St. (Wynyard), Market St., Town Hall, and Eddy Ave. (near Central Station), and from there heads directly for domestic and international terminals. "Airport Express" operates seven days a week. The buses leave the international terminal every 30 minutes

58 SYDNEY

between 6:15 A.M. and 10:00 P.M. (weekdays, every 20 minutes from 7:00 A.M. to 5:00 P.M.), stop at domestic terminals, then proceed directly to the city stops. Fare $2.20, children $1.10. For additional information phone 29–2622.

A private company operates the *Kingsford Smith Airport Bus Service*. Its buses, on request, pick up passengers from any hotel or motel, within the City, Kings Cross, or Double Bay area between 6:00 A.M. and 8:00 P.M., seven days a week. They serve all airline terminals. Reservations must be made at least an hour prior to departure. Buses also meet all major incoming flights. For reservations phone 667–3221, 667–0663, 669–3111. Fare $3.00, children $1.50.

There are plenty of taxis at the ranks outside the airport terminals. The fare to the city, about 10 km (6 mi) away, is around $12. For getting a taxi to the airport, see "By taxi," below.

Some airways accept reservations inflight for chauffeur-driven cars, which are between 50 and 100 percent more expensive than taxis. See "By rental car," below.

Rental cars are available at the airport if reserved in advance through *Avis, Budget,* or *Hertz*. See "By rental car," below.

By taxi. Except when the weather is bad, it is no problem to find a taxi in the city at cab stands or outside the busier suburban railway stations. Cruising taxis can be hailed in the streets. All cabs are metered, and the Department of Motor Transport sets the rates. Tipping is customary; about 10 percent of the fare is sufficient. The charge is $1.10 plus 65 cents per km. The waiting charge is $16.60 per hour. Taxis can be ordered by telephone or radio, but a small surcharge is added to the metered cost. A toll of 20 cents is charged to cross the Harbour Bridge. It is quite usual for any passenger to sit next to the driver. Some of the main taxi companies sending telephone-ordered cabs are *Legion Cabs,* 2–0918; *Taxis Combined Services,* 339–0488; and *RSL Cabs,* 699–0144.

By rental car. There are several drive-yourself and chauffeur-driver rental car firms. Standards of maintenance and service are usually high, and the cost for self-driven cars is moderate: $50 a day for a small car. Not all overseas driver's licenses are accepted by the Australian authorities, so it is advisable to have an international driver's license. Rent-a-car firms include *Avis:* in U.S. 800–331–2112, in Sydney 922–8181; *Budget:* in U.S. 800–527–0700, in Sydney 339–8888; *Hertz:* in U.S. 800–654–3131, in Sydney 669–0066. Chauffeur-driven hire cars: *Astra,* 699–2233; *Legion,* 211–2844; *Prestige,* 923–1011; *VIP,* 357–1193. Most chauffeur-driven car rental firms have a fleet of top-ranking luxury cars, including Rolls-Royces, Mercedeses, and Lincolns.

In Australia, traffic keeps to the left. Seat belts are mandatory for drivers and *all* passengers. Drunk-driving laws are very strict, and the police carry out spot checks to ascertain whether a driver's blood alcohol content exceeds the legal .05 percent. (According to expert opinion, this gives a person a chance to consume a small whiskey and a glass of wine an hour before driving.)

By bus. These operate between 4:00 A.M. and 11:30 P.M. Service from the city to the suburbs is quite efficient and, except for rush hours (7:30–9:30 A.M., 4:30–7:30 P.M.), when all traffic is heavy, they are fast. *UTA* buses connect the

HOW TO GET AROUND

heart of the city with main suburbs within the area of Palm Beach, Frenchs Forest, East Lindfield, Chatswood, and Lane Cove to the north; Epping, Carlingford, Lidcombe, and Bankstown to the west; Beverly Hills, Sans Souci, La Perouse to the south; and Bondi and Bronte to the east. Minimum fare is 60 cents. Call 29–2622.

UTA also provides two free buses. Number 777, which runs 9:00 A.M.–3:30 P.M. Mon.–Fri. at 10-minute intervals, services the main inner-city shopping areas. No. 666 runs every 30 minutes between Wynyard Station and the Art Gallery, Mon.–Sat., including public holidays (except Christmas Day and Good Friday), 10:00 A.M.–5:00 P.M.

A unique and very worthwhile service is UTA's Sydney Explorer. This consists of a fleet of bright red buses that stop at 20 of Sydney's most important tourist attractions. Passengers can alight or join the bus at any of the marked Explorer stops. See "Tours," below.

By train. Sydney has an extensive above- and below-ground electric train system controlled by the State Rail Authority. The area serviced by it is bounded by the suburbs of Otford, Campbelltown, Emu Plains, Richmond, and Cowan and includes 160 stations. There are eight main lines and several branch lines. All services pass through the Central Railway Station in the city proper. Other city stations are Wynyard, Town Hall, Circular Quay, St. James, and Museum. A separate line connects Central with Town Hall, Martin Place, Kings Cross, Edgecliff, and Bondi Junction. Trains run frequently: every 15 minutes during the day, much more often during the morning and evening rush hours, when carriages are filled to capacity like the proverbial boxes of sardines. On the whole, outside rush hours, train travel is fairly comfortable and reasonably fast, though some of the rolling stock suffers from age and perhaps even more from vandalism. They operate from 4:30 A.M. to 12:30 A.M. Fares are fairly high: 60 cents minimum for a couple of stations. Tickets must be purchased at the station. Traveling without a ticket is considered a fairly serious offense, punishable by a fine of up to $200. For directions, ask at the booking offices. For more information call 29–2622.

By ferry. A pleasant and cheap way to explore Sydney Harbour and other Sydney bays and waterways is ordinary commuter ferry services, though some of them tend to be—to put it mildly—"temperamental": They may break down, or their crew may go on strike for one reason or another. It is advisable to telephone the operator to find out whether there is a hitch or it will be a day of easy sailing.

Ferry services on Sydney Harbour start from Circular Quay. Signs here clearly mark which ferry leaves from where. UTA runs ferries to Cremorne, Mosman, Kirribilli, Neutral Bay, Taronga Zoo, Balmain Greenwhich, Cockatoo Island, Woolwhich, and Hunters Hill. Single fare to each of these suburbs is $1.10; children 55 cents. For information: 29–2622. To Manly: by ferry $1.40 and 70 cents; by hydrofoil $2.60. For Manly ferry information phone 29–2622. A private company, Hegarty & Son Pty. Ltd. (27–6606), operates ferries to McMahon Point, Lavender Bay, Milsons Point, Kirribilli, Balmain, and Luna Park. There are also ferry services that connect Sydney, via bus and train, with points farther away from the city. For information about timetables and connections for services on Pittwater call 918-2747, 918-9533, or 99-3492; for Hawkesberry River, 455-1566; for Port Hacking, 523-2990.

A water taxi service, *Aqua Cab,* 929-0477, covers all of Sydney Harbour. The company has four motorboats and picks up passengers at any public wharf. (A popular pickup point is the Man O'War Steps, Opera House). Minimum charge is $120 per hour. To cross the Harbour would be about $15.

Economy fares. An economical way to get about is to buy a daily or weekly UTA concession ticket. The *Day Rover,* $6, is a one-day ticket valid from 9:00 A.M. on weekdays, anytime on weekends. It entitles the holder to travel within the Sydney area on trains, buses, and ferries (except the hydrofoil, cruise boats, and the Sydney Explorer bus). The ticket can be bought at railway stations, bus depots, or Circular Quay terminals. *The Purple Travel Pass,* $23.90, is a ticket for seven consecutive days with the same conditions. Call 29-7614 for details.

TOURIST INFORMATION. There are several tourist information bureaus in Sydney with expert staffs who can answer practically any visitor query. These services are free of charge and include:

Travelers' Information Service, Sydney International Airport Terminal, arrivals level (02) 669-1583. In addition to providing information, it helps with hotel, tour, and transportation reservations. Open seven days a week, from 6:00 A.M. until the arrival of the day's last plane. Telephone information provided every day, 8:00 A.M.-6:00 P.M., (02) 669-5111.

Travel Centre of New South Wales. Corner Pitt and Spring sts., in the city (02) 231-4444. A state government organization. It also accepts reservations for accommodations, transportation, and tours. Open Mon.-Fri., 9:00 A.M.-5:00 P.M.

Visitor Information Service. Martin Place between Castlereagh and Elizabeth sts. in the city; (02) 235-2424. Open Mon.-Fri., 9:00 A.M.-5:00 P.M.

Tourist Newsfront. 22 Playfair St., The Rocks; 27-7197. Open daily, 9:00 A.M.-5:00 P.M. except Christmas Day and Good Friday, for information and bookings.

N.S.W. Infostar, Circular Quay. Open daily 9:00 A.M.-5:00 P.M.

National Roads and Motorists Association (NRMA), 151 Clarence St., in the city; 260-9222. Emergency Road Service, 632-0500. Road Condition Report (recording), 1-1571. Open during business hours. Members of overseas auto clubs who present their membership card can get free goods and services, including a comprehensive accommodations list, accommodations reservations, detailed road maps, legal and technical services, and insurance.

There are a number of free weekly theater, movie, concert, etc., programs, such as *This Week in Sydney, Sydney's Top Ten,* and the *Sydney Tourist Guide,* which can be picked up at most of the better hotels and/or at visitor centers. Among the newspapers, the *Sydney Morning Herald* and the *Daily Telegraph* publish daily entertainment pages.

TOURS

TOURS. A wide variety of organized tours—by bus, foot, boat, and even helicopter—are available in Sydney. They may take as little as an hour (by helicopter) or a full day. Several of them have free additional pickup service from the main hotels and motels, to which customers can be returned at the end of the tour.

Bus tours. See the city on the *Sydney Explorer* tour bus, operated by the Urban Transit Authority. The red buses travel throughout the city, stopping at more than 20 tourist attractions in town. Riders can get off and on the bus at anytime at any of the stops.

The price is $7.50 for the day, $3.75 for children under 16. The bus runs seven days a week, except Christmas and Good Friday, approximately every 25 minutes from 9:30 A.M. to 5:00 P.M. Distinctive "Sydney Explorer" bus-stop signs located throughout the city indicate where you can board. Pay for your ticket on the bus. The price includes a guidebook that tells you where the bus stops and gives detailed information about attractions along the route. Tickets also allow discounts at several of the attractions. Among the stops are the harbor, Opera House, Royal Botanic Gardens, Art Gallery of New South Wales, King's Cross, Australian Museum, Chinatown, Centrepoint Tower, The Rocks, Elizabeth Bay House, and Pier One.

Some of the main standard tour operators are: *Ansett Pioneer,* Corner Oxford and Riley Sts., Darlinghurst; 268–1881. *Australian Accommodation & Tours,* 46 Kent Rd., Mascot; 669–5444. *Australian Pacific Tours,* 109–123 O'Riordan St., Mascot; 693–2222. *Clipper Coaches,* 9 Alma Rd., North Ryde; 888–3144.

These standard tours are designed to provide enough time at each attraction for passengers to absorb the sights and the commentaries (provided by the driver/guide) and take photos. Tipping the driver or (if there is one) guide is not expected. Between all of these, a choice of more than a dozen half-day tours of the city, suburbs, national parks, beaches, etc., are offered. The usual times of departure are 9:00 A.M. and 2:00 P.M. These tours take about 3 hours 15 minutes. The cost is about $18; children $12–15. There are about two dozen all-day tours also available; some include Sydney Harbour cruises with lunch on board. Other tours take the visitor farther afield—to the Blue Mountains and even to the national capital, Canberra, for the day.

Sydney nightspot tours are also offered by the main tourist operators throughout the year, five nights (Tues.–Sat.) a week. They include a visit to Sydney Tower, The Rocks, "naughty" Kings Cross, and a nightclub or two. Dinner and a glass of champagne are usually served and are included in the cost. Night tours cost around $55–$60. There are a few rules for joining: Minimum age is 18, men must wear a jacket, no jeans or thongs allowed, tickets must be reserved in advance and paid for before the tourist enters the tour bus. There are also tours to show off the city by night that are suitable for families and do not include dinner or nightspots; cost is around $19.

Chauffeur-driven tours (maximum four persons per car) are also available. *Astra,* 699–2233, half day $180, all day $360. *Hughes Chauffeured Limousines,* 332–3344, half-day Sydney City Sights, $32 per hour.

SYDNEY

Walking Tours. These are guided tours in different parts of Sydney for those who like sightseeing at a leisurely pace, on foot. Operators include: *Australian Pacific Tours,* 693-2222. Tours depart daily from Circular Quay at 9:15 A.M. and return 12:15 P.M. Price ($18, children $15) includes admission to Opera House, ferry fare, and tour of The Rocks. Tour does not operate in wet weather. *Captain Cook Cruises, "Harbourside Sydney in a Day,"* 27-4416 ($41.50 adult, includes lunch) is one of the most popular tours. Includes walking in The Rocks, 2½-hour cruise on Sydney Harbour, tour of the Opera House, lunch at the Opera's Bennelong Restaurant. *Sydney Opera House Walking Tours,* 250-7111. Daily guided tours of the Opera House ($3.50, children $1.80) begin at 9:00 A.M. and last about an hour. The last walk leaves at 4:00 P.M. *Tours of Royal Botanical Gardens,* 231-8111. Free guided tours leave from the Visitors Centre (gate nearest the Art Gallery) Wed. and Fri., except public holidays, at 10:00 A.M.

Air Tours. *Aquatic Air Services,* 919-5966, operates De Havilland Beavers. Sydney Harbour (about 30 minutes): minimum of 4 people, at $25 each, or $100 per hour. *Heliflite,* 680-1511, offers sightseeing flights from $75 and charters from $255 per hour from Castle Hill. *Airship Pacific,* 234-4000, operates 75-minute sightseeing flights over Sydney in a blimp: $200.

Cruises. The Sydney Telephone Directory (yellow pages) lists 11 pages of boats for hire, for charter, and organized cruises. One can but name some of the best-known operators among them. *Captain Cook Cruises,* 27-4416, runs four large vessels. Daily excursions include: Coffee Cruise, 10:00 A.M.-12:30 P.M. and 2:00-4:30 P.M. Cost $16, children $10. Luncheon Cruise, 12:30-2:00 P.M. Cost $22, children $19, includes the meal. Sydney Harbour Budget Cruise, four times a day for about 1¼ hours each, starting at 9:30 A.M., 11:00 A.M., and 2:30 P.M. Cost $9, children $5. Candlelight Dinner Cruise, 7:00 P.M.-9.30 P.M. or 11:00 P.M. Cost $40. All cruises leave from Circular Quay jetty no. 6. Reservations not necessary for budget cruise, but recommended for the others.

Hawkesberry River Ferries, 455-1566. Historic Mail Boat Run. Accompany the last riverboat postman in Australia as he delivers mail and supplies to isolated river-dwellers. Mon.-Fri., 9:30 A.M., returns 1:15 P.M. Cost $14, children $7.

Urban Transport Authority Harbour Ferry Cruise; 29-2622. Daily except Christmas Day. Refreshments available on board. Depart at 10:00 A.M. and 1:30 P.M. Adults, $6; children, $3.

Fort Denison Cruise; 240-2111. As a permit is required, this is the only way you will be able to land on Fort Denison (or Pinchgut) and have a guided tour of the historic island. Tues.-Sat. and Sun.

John Cadman's Cruising Restaurant, 922-1922 or 27-4416, offers a nightly dinner cruise that also departs from Circular Quay jetty no. 6. Call for reservations. Other dinner cruises are listed in the "Dining Out" section, below.

Sydney Harbor Explorer, 27-4416, also operates from jetty no. 6. Cost $12; children $6, for cruises to The Rocks, Opera House, Watson's Bay, Pier One, and Taronga Park Zoo.

In addition to guided tours, the commuter ferries offer a great way to see the harbor. You'll save money and be spending time with real Sydneysiders. A

PARKS AND GARDENS 63

self-guided tour is available on cassette from *Headset Tours*. Call 22-5537 or 27-7197. The trip to Manly affords the best sightseeing (see the Sydney Harbour section under "Exploring Sydney," above); it takes about 45 minutes and costs $1.40, children 60 cents. The Manly ferry leaves Circular Quay jetty no. 3. Call 27-9251.

A sailing cruise is available on a 65-foot schooner through *Sydney Harbour Sailing Cruises*, 669-6066 or 524-1605. Lunch and wine or beer are included in the $45 price. Cruises depart from Man O' War Steps, Opera House Wharf, Wed., Fri., Sat., at 11:00 A.M., returning at 4:00 P.M. Reservations essential.

SPECIAL-INTEREST SIGHTSEEING. Sydney Opera House walking tour. Daily guided tours begin at 9:00 A.M. and last about an hour. The last walk leaves at 4:00 P.M. Cost $3.50, children $1.80. Backstage tours are conducted Sun. only, 9:00 A.M.–5:00 P.M. Cost $5; children under 12 not permitted. There's no need to book in advance (unless you're traveling with a group); tours tend to leave when enough interested people have gathered in the foyer.

A package tour called "An Evening at the Opera House" includes a tour, dinner at the Bennelong Restaurant, and a performance. The package, with one opera ticket, costs about $70 per person, or around $86 for gala performance or opening night. Packages that include a ticket to the ballet or symphony cost less, beginning at about $50 per person. The package can be reserved by calling the Opera House box office, 250-7341, or through your travel agent before you leave home.

Royal Botanic Gardens tours, 231-8111. Free guided tours leave from the Visitors Centre (gate nearest the Art Gallery) at 10:00 A.M. Wednesday and Friday (except public holidays).

PARKS AND GARDENS. Sydney is blessed with three of the world's largest and most beautiful manmade parks (Hyde Park, Centennial Park, and the Royal Botanic Gardens), most of which are all the more attractive because of their proximity to Sydney's glorious harbor. All the parks are well served with facilities, and picnickers are welcome to spread a blanket or simply loll on the grass. As well as the very big parks, there are many much more intimate parks, each with its own character, and each featuring its own monumental sculpture. The smaller parks are often dominated by enormous, ancient Port Jackson or Moreton Bay fig trees. Sydney's office workers make good use of their shade in summer, while in winter they are often the place for chess games. Joggers abound in Sydney, and when the weather warms up every park seems to swarm with the seminaked young (and not so young).

Centennial Park. Opened in 1888 to commemorate Australia's first centenary, the park, which is less than ten minutes from the city center, stretches over 220 hectares (528 acres). It features many playing areas for cricket, rugby football, and soccer. There are lakes, grasslands, wooded areas, horse riding tracks, bicycle paths, and walking tracks, as well as roads for motor vehicles only.

Dawes Point Park. Surrounding the pylons at the southern approaches to the Sydney Harbor Bridge, the park is often overlooked by Sydneysiders and tourists alike, despite the fact that it commands extraordinary views of the Opera House and the harbor from Lavender Bay to Bradley's Head.

Hyde Park. This is the city center's major park and the site of the annual Festival of Sydney each January. Shaded by enormous fig trees and many varieties of other native Australian trees, the park stretches over four city blocks from historic Queen's Square at the southern end of Macquarie St. all the way south to Liverpool St. The park is sliced in two by Park St. At the northern end of the park is the magnificent Archibald Fountain, while down toward Park St., near William, are the lovely Sandringham Gardens, created for and dedicated by her Majesty Queen Elizabeth II (who is also Queen of Australia). In the southern half of the park is the imposing pink granite War Memorial, which commemorates Australians killed in conflicts from the Boer War to Vietnam. The colorful changing of the guard ceremony is held here every Thurs. at 12:50 P.M.

Ku-Ring-gai Chase National Park. About 30 km (19 mi) north of the city, at Bobbin Head (457–9322). Wooded areas and beautiful beaches fill this park, too. Broken Bay, Pittwater, and the Hawkesbury River within the Park are favorite spots for boating and fishing enthusiasts.

Observatory Park. A delightful park surrounding the southern approaches to the Harbor Bridge. Easy access can be obtained by stairs that climb up from Argyle St. opposite the historic Garrison Church in The Rocks. Stop here to rest after a walking tour of The Rocks; it commands spectacular views—particularly of the western reaches of the harbor, and also a most unusual, almost telescopic, view of the great coat-hanger arch of the bridge. In Sydney's hot summer months the park's elevation, the shade of the giant figs, and the cooling sea breeze offer a refreshing refuge.

Royal Botanic Gardens. Opened in 1816, "The Gardens," as they are known to all Sydneysiders, are far and away the most beautiful of all the Sydney parks. Not only are the lawns, flower beds, and trees from all over the world magnificently laid out and maintained, they also overlook the harbor at Farm Cove, a delightfully symmetrical bay fringed by a low sandstone wall. Special attractions include a palm grove, a pyramid-shaped glass house, and a very fine collection of Australian rain forest trees. Located behind the Opera House and Government House, the gardens are open every day, 8 A.M.–sunset. Guided walks are conducted every Wed. and Fri. (except public holidays) at 10:00 A.M. The visitors' shop is open Tues.–Fri., 10:00 A.M.–4:00 P.M.; weekends, 1:00–5:00 P.M. The gardens have an excellent restaurant, the Kiosk, which serves first-class salads and simple lunches.

Royal National Park. About 30 km (19 mi) south of Sydney, off the Princes Hwy. (521–5422). A small fee is charged for entering motor vehicles. Wooded areas and lakes cover much of the park and rugged cliffs drop down to sandy beaches. (Watch the hang gliders here.) Snacks and row boats are available. The

PARKS AND GARDENS

13 mi of coastline make popular beach spots. Campers must get a permit from the Visitors' Centre. Trains from Sydney's Central Station will get you to the Park.

Rushcutter's Bay Park. Embracing the blue waters of Rushcutter's Bay, just east of the city, this lovely area of lawn and ancient Port Jackson figs is a favorite spot for yachtsmen, who wash and dry their sails here after an arduous ocean race. The Cruising Yacht Club of Australia stands at the easternmost tip of the park.

Shark Island and Clark Island. Two delightful hideaway islands in the middle of Sydney Harbor (actually part of Sydney Harbour National Park; see below) seem to be off the tourist-beaten track, although they are beautifully maintained and provide coin-operated gas-fired barbecue grills. Access is by private boat only, and prior arrangements must be made through the administrating agency, the National Parks and Wildlife Service, 237-6500. Well worth the trouble to get there if you want to spend a completely carefree day in the middle of one of the world's most beautiful harbors.

Sydney Domain. On the eastern side of the Royal Botanic Gardens and separated from it by Mrs. Macquarie's Rd., the Domain is an extensive area of lawn that sweeps down to Mrs. Macquarie's Point, one of the harbor's best and most accessible vantage points. It was here that Mrs. Macquarie, wife of the early colonial governor, used to repair on hot summer days to sit under the shade of the great figs (which still dominate the point) and take her ease in the cool northeast breeze. The Domain is still a great favorite with Sydneysiders—not least because in its upper reaches, between Hospital Rd. and Art Gallery Rd., the great Australian tradition of soapbox oratory is still carried on. Here on Sun. anyone with something to say can stand up and say it, whether pro- or anti-nuclear, about women's liberation, or merely on the state of local politics.

Sydney Harbour National Park. Phone 960-1413. This is in fact many lovely harborside parks lumped under an umbrella title. One of the biggest and most spectacular of these is near Manly, atop *North Head,* the great sandstone cliff that guards the harbor's opening to the Pacific. The park offers dramatic views all the way up the harbor to the bridge and is an ideal spot from which to view the spectacular start of the annual Sydney–Hobart Yacht Race, which begins at noon on Boxing Day. Visitors are asked to keep to carefully marked paths and roadways to avoid the dangerous cliffs; the plunge to the surf below is over 300 feet. If you take the ferry or a bus to Manly, it is a mile-and-a-half walk (mostly uphill) along Darley Rd. and out to the end of North Head Scenic Dr.

Other parks in this group include *Ashton Park,* an area of bushland that sweeps down to the harbor at Bradley's Head (near Taronga Zoo Wharf; you can take the Taronga Zoo ferry), where there are excellent views from grassy observation areas and from the sandstone rocks at the water's edge; *Clifton Gardens,* (between Chowder Bay and Taylors Bay) with a major picnic area and harborside swimming; and George's Heights through Obelisk Bay to Middle Head. Best access to all these parks is by car.

SYDNEY

Enterprising young enthusiasts have started an excellent walking-tour-guide business in Sydney Harbor National Park. The 4 km walk, which takes in the inspection of the historic fortifications at Bradley's Head, costs $10, children $5. Lunch can be provided, for a total of $26, children $16. They also provide guided walking tours around Greater Sirius Cove and Little Sirius Cove, two of the nicest bays on the harbor. Telephone Harbor Walks, 95-1755.

Wynyard Park. Tucked in just behind busy York St. on the western side and Carrington on the east, this wedge-shaped park is a genuine oasis for jaded city office workers in summer.

Yarranabbe Park. Opposite New Beach Rd. and running right along the eastern arm of Rushcutter's Bay, Yarranabbee Park is another favorite spot on hot summer days. The sea breeze makes it delightful, and it commands wonderful views across crowded yacht moorings to Elizabeth Bay with its luxury apartment buildings and the great naval dockyard at Garden Island.

THEME PARKS. *Luna Park,* located at Milson's Point, across Sydney Harbour from The Rocks, is a permanent carnival, featuring rides, games, and a variety of amusements for everyone. It's famous "laughing face" can't be missed. Open Friday night, Saturday and Saturday night, and Sunday, as well as public and school holidays. Call 922-6644.

See also *Old Sydney Town* in the chapter "Outside Sydney."

ZOOS. Featherdale Wildlife Park. 217-229 Kildare Rd., Doonside (41 km/25 mi west of Sydney); 622-1705. Open seven days a week (except Christmas Day), 9:00 A.M.-5:00 P.M. Home of the Qantas koala. Boasts Australia's largest private collection of native fauna, including over 200 species of birds as well as koalas, emus, wallabies, Tasmanian devils, tiger cats, possums, kangaroos, and wombats. There are also many exotic animals and birds, including African antelope, deer, and monkeys. Refreshments, barbecue-equipped picnic area, gift shop. Admission $3.50, children $1.50.

Koala Park. Castle Hill Rd., West Pennant Hills (25 km/15 mi from Sydney); 84-3141. Every day except Christmas, 9:00 A.M.-5:00 P.M. A very popular small zoo specializing in Australian native flora and fauna, particularly koalas, kangaroos, emus, dingoes, echidna, wombats, and colorful parrots. The Koalas are on display all day. Visitors may pose with them and hand-feed and pet kangaroos and wombats. Opened in 1930, Koala Park was the first private koala sanctuary in New South Wales. Preservation of the koala is the park's major theme. Picnic area with barbecue grills. Gift shop. Admission $4, children $1.50.

Taronga Zoo and Aquarium. Bradley's Head Rd., Mosman; 969-2777. Open daily, 9:30 A.M.-5:00 P.M. Situated on the shores of magnificent Sydney Harbour, Taronga Zoo exhibits more than 4,000 native and exotic mammals, birds, reptiles, and fishes. Taronga has the world's finest collection of Australian fauna. Special exhibits include koala, platypus, reptile, and nocturnal houses, where Australia's unique animals are seen to their best advantage. There is also a Seal

BEACHES

Theatre and the world's largest captive colony of chimpanzees. Picnic in the zoo's gardens and enjoy panoramic views of the city skyline, the Opera House, and the harbor. The best way to reach the zoo is by ferry. A 12-minute ride from Circular Quay jetty no. 5 brings you to the zoo's front door. Guided tours, refreshments, gift shop. Wheelchairs and children's push-chairs available. Admission $3.60, children $1.80.

Waratah Park Wildlife Reserve. Namba Rd., Duffy's Forest (30-minute drive from Harbour Bridge); 450–2377. Open every day, 10:00 A.M.–5:00 P.M. A small sanctuary specializing in Australian native flora and fauna, and home of Australian TV's Skippy the Bush Kangaroo. Visitors are encouraged to wander through natural enclosures where they can feed and pet animals such as kangaroos, wallabies, and emus. The park also features koalas (there are opportunities to pet them, too), dingoes, foxes, and eagles and many other native birds. Light food and refreshments, gift shop. Admission $5, children $2.50.

BEACHES. If you visit Sydney in the summer, you won't miss the fact that everyone is very, very tan. Water sports and beaches are a large part of life, and there is plenty of sand and sun here. You'll have your choice between ocean beaches and the calmer waters of the harbor.

A few precautions, however. The sun is strong, so protect your skin—more than you would on North America's beaches; Australia has the world's highest rate of skin cancer. As for sharks, helicopters do patrol for them, but they are not a major concern for Sydneysiders. Netted ocean beaches are considered very safe; unmeshed harbor beaches are thought to be more risky—though not very. Flags are set up on ocean beaches to keep swimmers out of dangerous currents; you must swim between these markers.

Most beaches are accessible by public transportation. For information phone the Urban Transit Authority, 2–0543, or the State Rail Authority, 219–4517. For a map showing the location of beaches, see "Exploring Sydney."

NORTHERN OCEAN BEACHES

The beaches north of the harbor are beautiful. One follows another as you move north along Barrenjoey Rd. to Palm Beach.

Manly (9½ mi north of Sydney). Consists of three beaches: Manly, North Steyne, and Queencliff. A popular, commercial beach, sandy, with a length of 1 mi. Patrolled in season. Dressing sheds, swimming pool, and rock pool. Shops are adjacent to beach and pool. Parking available, with a time limit in some areas. Surf-o-Planes are available from kiosk. Surfboard riding is permitted in defined areas. Easily accessible from Sydney by ferry. Manly Pacific International Hotel is across the street from the beach allowing a beach and city vacation combination.

Harbord (11½ mi). Beach is sandy, with a length of ½ mi. Patrolled in season. Dressing sheds and a rock pool. Shops are adjacent, and a parking area is available for a fee in season. Surfboard riding is permitted in defined areas, although waves are rather gentle, making this a favorite beach for body surfing.

Curl Curl (13 mi). Beach is sandy, with a length of 1 mi. Patrolled in season. Dressing sheds, rock pool, and snack bar. Off-street parking available for a fee in season. Surfboard riding is permitted in defined areas.

Dee Why (13 1/3 mi). Beach is sandy, with a length of 2 mi. Patrolled in season. Dressing sheds only. Off-street parking is available for a fee in season. Surfboard riding is permitted in defined areas, and body surfing is good here.

Long Reef (14 mi). Beach is sandy, with a length of 2 mi. Patrolled in season. Dressing sheds only. Off-street parking is available for a fee in season. Surfing is considered consistently good here.

Collaroy (14½ mi). Beach is sandy, with a length of 4 mi. Patrolled in season. Dressing sheds, rock pool, and snack bar. Off-street parking is available for a fee in season. Surfboard riding is permitted in defined areas.

Narrabeen (16 mi). Beach is sandy, with a length of 4 mi. Patrolled in season. Dressing sheds, rock pool, and snacks. Off-street parking is available for a fee in season. North Narrabeen is a favorite surfing beach.

Warriewood Beach (17½ mi). Beach is sandy, with a length of 1 mi. Patrolled in season. Snack bar. Off-street parking available for a fee in season. Surfboard riding is permitted within defined areas.

Mona Vale Beach (18½ mi). Beach is sandy, with a length of 1 mi. Patrolled in season. Dressing sheds, swimming pool, and shops. Off-street parking available for a fee in season. Surfboard riding is permitted in defined areas.

Newport Beach (21 mi). Beach is sandy, with a length of ½ mi. Patrolled in season. Dressing sheds and shops. Parking available for a fee in season. Surfboard riding is permitted in defined areas.

Bilgola Beach (22½ mi). Beach is sandy, with a length of ½ mi. Patrolled in season. Dressing sheds, swimming pool, and snack bar. Off-street parking available for a fee in season. Surfboard riding permitted in defined areas.

Avalon Beach (22 8/10 mi). Beach is sandy, with a length of 1 mi. Patrolled in season. Dressing sheds, rock pool, and shop. Parking area available for a fee in season. Surfboard riding is permitted in defined areas.

Whale Beach (23½ mi). Beach is sandy, with a length of ½ mi. Patrolled in season. Dressing sheds, rock pool, and snack bar. Off-street parking available for a fee in season. Surfboard riding is permitted in defined areas.

Palm Beach (27 mi). This fashionable beach is beautiful and sandy, with a length of 1½ mi. High-priced houses look out over the Pacific. Patrolled in season. Dressing sheds, rock pool, snack bar, and shops. Off-street parking available for a fee in season. Surfboard riding is permitted in defined areas.

SOUTHERN OCEAN BEACHES

Bronte Beach (5 mi east). Beach is wider and more open than Tamarama, sandy, with a length of a ¼ mi. Patrolled in season. Dressing sheds, swimming pool, rock pool, snack bar, first-aid room. Parking area available for a fee in season. Beach equipment for hire. Surfboard riding permitted in defined areas.

BEACHES

Coogee (5 mi south) Family beach, sandy, with a length of a ¼ mi. Patrolled in season. Dressing sheds, rock pool, and parking area. Beach equipment for hire in season. Surfboard riding permitted in defined areas.

Bondi Beach (5½ mi east of Sydney). Sydney's most famous beach, with the archetypal bronzed surfers everywhere. Very busy and commercial. Beach is sandy, with a length of 1 mi. Patrolled in season. Dressing sheds, swimming pool, rock pool, snack bar, first-aid room, and children's playground. Parking area available for a fee in season. Beach equipment for hire.

Tamarama (5½ mi east). Beach is quieter than Bondi, surrounded by cliffs, sandy, with a length of a ½ mi. Patrolled in season. Dressing sheds, snack bar, and first-aid room. Surfboard riding is *not* permitted.

Maroubra (7 mi south). Family beach is sandy, with a length of a ½ mi. Patrolled in season. Dressing sheds and parking area both available for a fee. Beach equipment for hire in season. Surfboard riding permitted in defined areas.

Malabar (8 mi south). Beach is sandy, with a length of ⅛ mi. Patrolled in season. Dressing sheds and rock pool. Surfboard riding permitted.

Cronulla Beaches: Cronulla, North Cronulla, Wanda, and Elouera Beach (18 mi south). Beaches are sandy, 2 mi long. Patrolled in season. Dressing sheds, rock pools, snack bar, and parking areas. Surfboard riding permitted outside patrolled area.

Garie Beach (32 mi south). Fifty-cent entrance fee to Royal National Park. Beach is pretty, surrounded by cliffs, and popular, sandy, with a length of 1 mi. Patrolled in season. Dressing sheds, toilets, snack bar, and parking area. Surfboard riding is permitted within defined areas.

Stanwell Beach (35 mi south). Beach is sandy with a length of 1 mi. Patrolled in season. Parking area available for a fee. Surfboard riding is permitted outside patrolled area.

Coalcliff Beach (37 mi south). Beach is sandy, with a length of 1 mi. Patrolled in season. Rock pool and parking area. Surfboard riding is permitted in defined areas.

Scarborough Beach (40 mi. south). Beach is sandy and 1 mi long. Patrolled in season. Dressing sheds, rock pool, and parking area. Surfboard riding is permitted in defined areas.

Coledale Beach (42 mi south). Beach is sandy, with a length of 1 mi. Patrolled in season. Dressing sheds, rock pool, and parking area. Surfboard riding is permitted in defined areas.

Austinmer Beach (44 mi south). Beach is sandy, with a length of a ¼ mi. Patrolled in season. Dressing sheds, rock pool, and snack bar. Parking area available for a fee. Surfboard riding permitted in defined areas.

Sandon Point (45 mi south). Beach is sandy and 1 mi long. Patrolled in season. Parking area available. Surfboard riding is permitted outside swimming area.

Thirroul Beach (45 mi south). Beach is sandy, with a length of 1 mi. Patrolled in season. Dressing sheds and snacks available. Swimming pool and parking area available for a fee. Surfboard riding permitted in defined areas.

Bulli Beach (46 mi south). Beach is sandy and 1 mi long. Patrolled in season. Dressing sheds, rock pool, snack bar, and parking area. Surfboard riding is permitted outside swimming area.

Woonona Beach (46 mi south). Sandy beach is 1 mi long. Patrolled in season. Dressing sheds. Rock pool, surf club, snack bar, and parking area. Surfboard riding is permitted outside swimming area.

Bellambi Beach (48 mi south). Beach is sandy and 1 mi long. Patrolled in season. Dressing sheds, rock pool, surf club, snack bar, and parking area. Surfboard riding is permitted outside swimming area.

Corrimal Beach (49 mi south). Beach is sandy and 1 mi long. Patrolled in season. Dressing sheds, snack bar, camping area, and parking area. Surfboard riding permitted outside swimming area.

Towradgi Beach (49½ mi south). Beach is 1 mi long and sandy. Patrolled in season. Dressing sheds, rock pool, and parking area. Surfboard riding is permitted outside swimming area.

Fairy Meadow (50 mi south). Beach is sandy, 1 mi long. Patrolled in season. Dressing sheds and parking area. Surfboard riding is permitted outside swimming area.

North Wollongong (51 mi south). Sand beach is 1 mi long. Patrolled in season. Dressing sheds and snacks available. Parking area available for a fee. Surfboard riding is permitted outside swimming area.

Wollongong (52 mi south). Beach is sandy, 1 mi long. Patrolled in season. Dressing sheds, snack bar, and parking area. Surfboard riding permitted outside swimming area.

Port Kembla Beach (58 mi south). Sand beach, 1 mi long. Patrolled in season. Dressing sheds, snack bar, and parking area. Swimming pool available for a fee. Surfboard riding is permitted outside swimming area.

HARBOR BEACHES

Balmoral is on the north side of the harbor and a very pretty beach (with shark net), a good place to watch yachts on weekends. Shops, restaurant nearby. Popular with families.

Camp Cove is a small beach at Watsons Bay, in front of houses, with a grassy headland. Snack bar. Topless bathing is popular here. Usually crowded with families on weekends.

Lady Jane. Popular nude beach at Watsons Bay. You must descend ladders down a cliff face to get here.

Nielson Park, on the south side of the harbor in Vaucluse. A narrow sandy beach, with grassy headlands, and a large park behind it. Snack bar and dressing sheds. A favorite spot for watching the Sydney-to-Hobart yacht race.

SPORTS

SPORTS. Life in Sydney is life outdoors. A wonderful climate (hot summers and mild winters) means that on weekends and, indeed, often during working weekdays many people are throwing themselves into their favorite sporting activity. If your favorite sport is in season when you visit Sydney you are almost certain to find opportunities for either playing or watching it. Information is published in the five daily newspapers. All sporting clubs are listed in the Yellow Pages. Sports results can be obtained by phoning 1–187.

PARTICIPANT SPORTS

Boating: Boats-for-hire on Sydney Harbor tend to be big launches with professional crews. *Flagship Charters d'Albora Marine,* New Beach Rd., Rushcutter's Bay, 328–7666. *VIP Cruises,* 5 Gresham St. 241-1008. On Pittwater try *Clipper's Anchorage* at Akuna Bay in the Kuringai National Park, 450–1888, or *Halvorsen Cruisers,* 457–9011. (See "Sailing," below.)

If you like **fishing**, ocean beaches and coastal cliffs will be a paradise for you. Mullet, sole, snapper, and whiting are caught in those waters, while bream, flathead, snapper, whiting, blackfish, and crabs are caught in the waters of Sydney Harbour, Botany Bay, and the nearby Georges and Hawkesbury rivers. You'll need a fishing license, obtainable from the New South Wales State Fisheries. The organization also has additional information about fishing in the Sydney area, and the Travel Centre of New South Wales can tell you about fishing charters and equipment rental.

Golf: There are 40 public golf courses in and around Sydney and all of them welcome overseas visitors. Book a day in advance. *Bondi Golf Links,* 30–1981; *Castle Cove Country Club,* Deepwater Rd., Castle Cove, 406–5444; *Ku-Ring-Gai Golf Course,* 361 Bobbin Head Rd, Turramurra, 44–5110; *Moore Park Golf Course,* Anzac Parade, Moore Park, 663–3960; *Northbridge Golf Club,* Sailors Bay Rd., Northbridge, 95–2169.

Hang Gliding: If you'd like to see what it's like to fly, hang gliding is for you. Beginners start at Kurnell Sand Dunes and the very adventurous can be watched at the coastal cliff areas south of Sydney. For lessons, equipment included, contact *Stanwell Soaring Centre,* 5 Sheridan Cr., Stanwell Park, (042) 94–2648. Advance booking is necessary. Cost of a day's lesson is around $50. These are also the people to contact for **sail plane gliding** information.

Sailing: Sydney is the sailing capital of Australia and on weekends every arm of the harbor is alive with thousands of sailboats of all shapes and sizes. Charter companies abound. *Abob Bob Schooner Cruises* sail from Clontarf and provide both food and drink. Phone 94–6254. *Adam's Executive Charters* run the luxuriously appointed 18-meter ketch *Sydneysider* and provide food and drink for up to 33 people, 25 Sugarloaf Cr., Castlecrag, phone 958–1964. Or contact *Sail Australia,* 23A King George St., North Sydney, 957–2577.

Surfing: All the Sydney beaches provide excellent surfing facilities. Bathers are expected to know what they are doing in the water although there are life guards on duty at every beach. Red and yellow flags mark the safe swimming areas. Surfboards are not rented, however, rubber surf floats are available at Bondi and Manly.

Tennis: There are hundreds of tennis courts all over Sydney with most of them available at minimal rates. A call a day in advance should secure a court. Courts close to the city center include *Rushcutter's Bay Tennis Centre,* open seven days and nights, Waratah St., Rushcutter's Bay, 357-1675 and *Ridge Street Tennis Centre,* North Sydney, open seven days, 7 A.M. to 11 P.M., 929-7172.

Windsurfing: Best location is Middle Harbor, well out of the way of commercial shipping and the crush of yachting on the main harbor. The boards can be hired at *The Spit Marina,* Mosman.

SPECTATOR SPORTS

Cricket: *Sydney Cricket Ground,* Moore Park (357-6601), is the venue in the summer months (October–March) for international test matches and Sheffield Shield cricket matches. (The Sheffield Shield is a series of matches between the Australian states.) Admission to matches ranges from $8 for open Hill seats ($3, children) to $10–20 for sheltered stands. Sydney's first grade cricket competition is played on various city and suburban grounds.

Football: The four football codes—rugby league, rugby union, soccer, and Australian rules—are played in Sydney. Rugby Union is strictly amateur: Thirteen men on a side can score touchdowns (tries) and kick goals between uprights. Its offshoot, the intensely popular Rugby League, is professional. Fifteen men on a side do much the same thing. Club sides play fast and furious throughout the winter months. Australian Rules has 18 men a side and is a very fast moving, open game featuring spectacular high kicks and leaps. Soccer is European football. All four codes are played on dozens of suburban grounds, which are all on public transport routes. Admission is usually no more than $2. Tickets available at grounds. Details of club matches are published in the daily newspapers.

Greyhound Racing: These events are held at *Wentworth Park,* Wentworth Park Rd., Glebe, 713-1955; *Harold Park,* Ross St., Glebe, 660-5313.

Harness Racing: Trotting meetings, regularly at *NSW Trotting Club,* Ross St., Glebe, 660-3688.

Horse Racing: This is one of Sydney's most popular year-round spectator sports and regular meetings are held at the *Australian Jockey Club,* Alison Rd., Randiwick, 663-8400; *Sydney Turf Club,* King St., Canterbury, 799-8000; *Rosehill,* Grand Ave., Rosehill, 682-1000; and *Warwick Farm,* Hume Hwy., Warwick Farm, 602-6199. The most important events are the autumn Doncaster Handicap and Sydney Cup and spring Epsom and Metropolitan Handicaps. Races are held each Saturday throughout the year. Admission $4–$5.

Motor Racing: This has a strong year-round following with stock-car, racing-car, "drag," and motor cycle events held in various city and out-of-town locations such as the *Amaroo Park,* Annangrove Rd., Annangrove, 679-1122, and the *Oran Park Raceway,* Oran Park Rd., Narellan, (046) 46-1004.

SITES

Sailing: Sydney has dozens of small boat and yacht clubs, and at weekends the harbor is alive with all manner of sailing boats competing in dozens of races. One of the most spectacular of all the racing classes is the world-famous eighteen-footers, which carry preposterous amounts of sail while their two- and three-man crews struggle to keep them upright. The eighteens often travel at over 20 knots and are frequently airborne in a good blow. Excellent spectator sports include Bradley's Head, Mosman (known as Scotchman's Point because there's no need to pay to watch from here) and ferries, which follow the racing boats as they career around the harbor. On Saturdays between September 22 and March 31 the eighteens race from the Sydney Flying Squadron (Australia's oldest open boat club), and a ferry leaves the clubhouse at 76 McDougall St., Milson's Point at 2:15 P.M. On Sundays the ferry leaves the NSW eighteen-foot Sailing League clubhouse at the foot of Bay Street, Double Bay at 2:15 P.M. The same admission charges (about $2 a person) apply. Highly recommended as a way of not only seeing spectacular sailing action but a good deal of the harbor as well.

Surfing Carnivals: These colorful, spectacular displays are held at ocean beaches from November to March. For information contact NSW Centre of the Australian Surf Life Saving Association on 663-4298.

Tennis: *The Davis Cup* and the *NSW Tennis Championships* are played between November and December at White City Courts, 30 Alma St., Paddington, 331-4144. Covered stands and open areas both $15 for NSW men's and women's semifinals and finals.

SITES OF ARCHITECTURAL AND HISTORIC INTEREST. See also "Museums," below. **Sydney Harbour.** The city of Sydney is, of course, superimposed on a harbor of surpassing beauty. When he first saw the harbor in January 1788, Captain Arthur Phillip, the penal colony's first governor, wrote, "a thousand sail of the line may ride in the most perfect security." The harbor abounds with its own historic sites, and the best way to see them is to get aboard one of the many cruise boats that depart from Circular Quay. (See "Tours," above.)

Admiralty House. Kirribilli Ave., Kirribilli. Built by Lieutenant-Colonel J. G. Gibbes in 1842. Enlarged in 1900. The residence for admirals of the British squadron in Australia until 1913. Now the Sydney residence of the governor-general of Australia.

Australia Square. George St. between Bond and Hunter sts. Designed by Harry Seidler and opened in 1967. The circular tower is still one of Sydney's tallest buildings. A skywalk on the 48th floor is open daily, 10:00 A.M.–10:00 P.M. There is a revolving restaurant, the *Summit,* on the 47th floor.

Bare Island Historical Site. Anzac Parade, La Perouse (15 km/9 mi south of city center); 668-9548. Open daily, 9:00 A.M.–5:00 P.M. Closed Good Friday and Christmas Day. The fortress was built during the 1880s as naval defense for the colony against a feared Russian invasion. The collection includes four gun batteries, an armor-encased room, and an 18-ton gun. Parking, bus service, nearby picnic areas. Demonstrations by prior arrangement. Admission free.

Captain Cook's Landing Place. See "Museums."

Church Hill. Near the approaches of the Harbour Bridge around Lang Park, bordered by York, Lang, and Grosvenor sts., is Church Hill, a traditional site for churches. Old St. Philip's Church was built there before 1800, and in 1848 a new stone church was begun to a design by Edmund Blackett, one of the colony's best architects. Blackett's Gothic Revival–style St. Philip's was completed in 1856.

Circular Quay. The Quay has been realigned several times since the early colonial days, when a stream of fresh water known as the Tank Stream trickled down to drain the marshes in what is now Centennial Park. Built by British military engineer Colonel George Barney (1792–1862), the Quay was for many years the very hub of the infant colony. Indeed, it was here, on a site just to the west of the Customs House, that Governor Phillip and his Royal Marines first raised the British flag, on January 21, 1788.

Colonial Secretary's Building. Corner Bridge and Macquarie sts. Designed by colonial architect James Barnet in 1878. Later additions by W. L. Vernon.

Conservatorium of Music. Conservatorium Rd., Royal Botanic Gardens; 27-4206. Francis Greenway, architect (1821). Former Government House stables, designed for Governor Macquarie. It has been a conservatorium since 1915. Visitors are advised to call ahead. Schedule of concerts available.

Customs House. The dignified stone Customs House on Circular Quay bears a carved royal coat of arms and a clock spelling out the hours. Begun in 1844 as a smaller building on the same site, it was rebuilt in 1855 by colonial architect James Barnet, who was responsible for many of the other great stone buildings of colonial Sydney.

Darling Harbor Development. The State Government and private enterprise are combining to spend over $1 billion on what will be the biggest, most expensive, and most imaginative bicentennial development in Australia at Darling Harbor, just to the west of the city center. It will include a major convention center, an exhibition complex, and an international marketplace similar to that on the Boston and Baltimore waterfronts. There will also be a new $30 million National Maritime Museum, which will be the central repository for the nation's considerable maritime heritage. All this is to be open in October.

Darlinghurst Jail and Courthouse. Forbes and Oxford sts., Darlinghurst. The great colonial architect Mortimer Lewis designed both the jail and the courthouse facing Taylor Square. The jail was started in 1841, only a few years before the transportation of convicts from England was stopped. The courthouse in the Greek Revival style was completed in 1835. Building the jail took a long time, since much of the construction was carried out by unwilling inmates. The jail was, in fact, notorious for its harshness; its public hangings used to attract large crowds in the 19th century. After 1921 it was converted into the East Sydney Technical College and its Arts School.

Elizabeth Bay House. (See "Museums.")

SITES

Elizabeth Farm. 70 Alice St., Parramatta; 635–9488. Built by John Macarthur in 1793, this is the oldest existing building in Australia and a prototype of the early colonial farmhouse, with its roof sheltering the walls to form shady verandas. Built on Macarthur's first land grant, it was his family home for nearly 40 years. Here Macarthur planned the overthrow of Governor Bligh in 1808. The farmhouse has been meticulously restored by the state government and is now administered by the state's Historic Houses Trust. Tues.–Sun., 10:00 A.M.–4:30 P.M. Admission $2, children 80 cents.

Fort Denison. The magnificent stone fort with its dintinctive Martello tower was built by a nervous colonial administration during the Crimean War, when it was thought that Sydney might be a Russian invasion target. It was here, on what was known as Rock Island, that the worst of the convicts were chained and fed bread and water. The island's colloquial name, Pinchgut, is believed to stem from its prison-island history. Fort Denison lies in Sydney Harbour opposite the great arc of Farm Cove and not far from the Opera House. Guided tours operate Tues.–Sat., irrespective of weather conditions, departing from Circular Quay jetty no. 6 at 10:15 A.M., 12:45 P.M., and 2:15 P.M. Tours last about 90 minutes. Admission $5.50, children $3.50. Well worth the visit. Phone 240–2111.

Government House. Bennelong Point. Designed by Edward Blore in Gothic Revival style (1845). The residence of the governor of New South Wales, it is not open to the public.

Great Synagogue. 166 Castlereagh St. Byzantine and Georgian (1878). The synagogue fronts Elizabeth St., but the wrought iron gates are kept locked except during services; general entry is from Castlereagh St. A museum focusing on Australian Jewish life is housed within (see "Museums").

Intercontinental Hotel. Corner Macquarie and Bridge sts. Due for completion in 1985, the Intercontinental is a radical idea in modern Sydney architecture. It is being built on the site of the historic old Treasury Building and Premier's Office and will incorporate the façades of these buildings into a multistory hotel.

Kirribilli House. Kirribilli. Gothic Revival (1854). Official guest house for distinguished visitors and used by the prime minister when in Sydney. Not open to the public.

Lancer Barracks. Smith St., Parramatta. The Lancer Barracks were completed in 1820. *Linden House,* the stone building in the compound, contains a military museum. Sun., public holidays, 10:00 A.M.–4:00 P.M. Admission free. 635–7822.

Macquarie Place. In Loftus St. to the right of the Customs House stands a tiny, well-shaded park with memorials to the earliest settlement. A stone obelisk was erected here in 1818 according to a design by distinguished convict-forger-turned-architect Francis Greenway. Distances to the then-known extent of the colony were marked on it. Bathurst, 221 km away across the Blue Mountains, was the farthest settlement at the time. Near the obelisk is the anchor of the *Sirius,* the flagship of the First Fleet, wrecked off Norfolk Island in 1790. The anchor was retrieved a hundred years later. A statue of Sir Thomas Mort, the colony's refrigeration and shipping pioneer, also stands here, together with a small fountain commemorating the fallen in the Great War of 1914–18. Opposite Macquarie Place on Bridge St., the brown sandstone bulk of the Lands Department (1876–91) features statues of the famous inland explorers, many of whom perished in the Outback.

Macquarie St. Macquarie St., perhaps more than any other in the city, reflects the growth and development of Sydney. Only six blocks long, it was laid out by Governor Lachlan Macquarie, who named it and capped its southern end with the magnificent greenery of Hyde Park. Near the park Macquarie placed two symbolic buildings, a jail (*Hyde Park Barracks*) (see "Museums," below) and a church (*St. James*), which face each other in Georgian splendor across Queens Square. Both these historic buildings were designed by convict architect Francis Greenway, who was subsequently given his freedom by Macquarie. On the western side of Macquarie St., opposite the Royal Botanic Gardens and the government buildings, lie the professional rooms of specialist doctors and lawyers. One of the few remaining 19th-century town houses on Macquarie St. is no. 133. Built by newspaper magnate John Fairfax, it is the present home of the *Royal Australian Historical Society,* 27–4461. The society keeps a library and exhibition area open Mon.–Fri., 10:00 A.M. to 5:00 P.M. Tours by appointment only. Admission is free.

Martin Place. Designed as a grand way through the heart of the city, Martin Place runs downhill through a succession of public walkways from Macquarie St. right through to George. Its major building is also its oldest: the General Post Office (GPO), designed by James Barnet, was built in the Italian Renaissance style between 1866 and 1886.

Old Government House. Parramatta Park; 635–8149. A must for any visitor interested in Australia's colonial past. Old Government House is the oldest remaining public building in Australia. It was closely associated with all the early governors of New South Wales prior to the granting of responsible government in 1856. The building was begun in 1799 as a house for Governor Hunter and enlarged in 1815 for Governor Macquarie. By an act of Parliament it was vested in the National Trust in 1967. Following extensive restoration, it has been furnished in the period of occupation as a viceregal residence and includes a fine collection of Australian colonial furniture and paintings of the early 19th century. Open Tues., Wed., Thurs., Sun., public holidays, 10:00 A.M.–4:00 P.M. Closed Good Friday, Christmas, Boxing Day and February. Gift shop, restaurant, parking, close to buses. Admission $2.50, children 50 cents.

Opera House. Bennelong Point. Sydney's most famous landmark, completed in 1973 at a cost of $102 million. Designed by Danish architect Jørn Utzon. Guided tours of the theaters leave from the Exhibition Hall daily except Christmas and Good Friday, 9:00 A.M.–4:00 P.M. Tours of large backstage areas on Sun., 9:00 A.M.–4:00 P.M. There is an á la carte restaurant, the *Bennelong,* and an outdoor snack bar on the harbor's edge.

Paddington area. Sydney's most attractive 19th-century suburb. Rows of predominantly Victorian-style terrace houses with cast-iron lacework, many beautifully restored.

SITES

Parliament House. Macquarie St.; 230–2111. Recently stripped back to its original sandstone façade, the imposing Georgian structure with its deep, shaded, colonnaded verandas embodies within one of its wings one of the earliest colonial buildings in Australia. Once part of the notorious Rum Hospital (1811–16), it was built for Governor Macquarie in return for a monopoly on the importation of rum. Visitors are welcome Mon.–Fri. Tours are generally held at 10:00 A.M., 11:00 A.M., and noon; when Parliament is sitting, shorter tours are available and the visitors' gallery is open. What was originally the south wing of the Rum Hospital is now the *Mint Museum* (see "Museums").

Queen Victoria Building. George St. between Market and Park. The QVB was begun in 1893 in an American-influenced Romanesque-Byzantine style, capped by a great copper dome surrounded by clusters of smaller domes, and guarded on either side by imposing white marble monumental sculptures. The enormous sandstone building, originally designed as a vast fruit and vegetable market with many shops surrounding a grand "Galleria," is undergoing a multi-million-dollar restoration, which will see it returned to its former glory late in 1985.

The Rocks. Named originally for the towering sandstone cliffs and rocks on the western side of Sydney Cove, The Rocks was the home of brawling seamen, Chinese opium dens, teeming pubs, and the gangs who roamed the streets during the halcyon days of the great sailing ships. Saved from wholesale destruction and redevelopment in the mid-1960s, The Rocks now contains some of the best examples of early colonial architecture as well as quite a bit of the flavor of those early years. An excellent starting point for any tour of Sydney. Tourist information for the area is available at 104 George St.; 27–4972; Mon.–Fri., 8:30 A.M.–4:30 P.M.; Sat., Sun., holidays, 10:00 A.M.–5:00 P.M. The Visitors Centre building used to be the Coroner's Court. Lower George St. (now simply George St.), running parallel to the western shore of Sydney Cove, was earlier known as High St., Spring Row., and Serjeant Major's Row, and was once the beginning of the main thoroughfare of Sydney Town—a road that started here and ran through to Parramatta and then on to the Blue Mountains and Bathurst on the Western Plains. Wharves and shipping terminals flank the street still, and buildings dating back to the 1830s and 1840s stand along it. The oldest of these is Cadman's Cottage (see below). Other major points of interest are also listed below.

Cadman's Cottage. 110 George St., The Rocks; 27–7971. Close by the rather ugly 1950s functionality of the Overseas Passenger Terminal (soon to be torn down and replaced) is a simple little stone building erected in 1816, in which lived Governor Lachlan Macquarie's Superintendent of Boats, John Cadman. The cottage, Sydney's oldest dwelling, once stood at the water's edge. It is now open to the public as a maritime museum, free of charge, and has a gift and souvenir shop. Open Mon.–Fri., 9:30 A.M.–4:30 P.M.; Sat., Sun., 10 A.M.–4:30 P.M.

Old Police Station. 127 George St., The Rocks; 27–7156. A James Barnet design. Built of stone in 1882, the police station with its forbidding cells has been restored and turned into a sales and exhibition area for Australian artisans. Tues.–Sat., 10:00 A.M.–5:00 P.M.; Sun., noon–4:00 P.M. Admission free.

SYDNEY

Argyle Arts Centre. The Rocks. From George St., Argyle St. runs at a right angle past the Argyle Arts Centre on the right. A former warehouse complex, known as the Argyle Bond, it was built in 1828 by Captain John Piper and later sold to Mary Reiby, the penal colony's most successful emancipist businesswoman. Now a multilevel exhibition and sales area for Australian crafts. Mon.-Sat., 10:00 A.M.–5:00 P.M.

Argyle Terraces. A row of workers terraces on Playfair St., The Rocks (c. 1875), now featuring crafts, art galleries, and souvenirs. Open seven days, 10:00 A.M.–5 P.M.

Argyle Cut and the Garrison Church. The Rocks. Convict gangs were set to work carving a pass through the solid sandstone, and in 1843 they broke through what is now known as the Argyle Cut to Argyle Place, a grassy, tree-lined sanctuary, which features an excellent row of early colonial terrace houses. At the end of Argyle Place stands the Holy Trinity or Garrison Church. It was here that the various British regiments on duty in the colony were mustered for Sunday prayers.

Observatory Hill. The Rocks; 241-2478. Looming directly above the Garrison Church are the sandstone ramparts of Observatory Hill. Stone steps lead up to a lovely, secluded park shaded by ancient figs. It was here that anxious lookouts watched distant South Head for signals of incoming ships. Observatory Hill provides one of the harbor's finest vantage points. The old stone observatory buildings recently ceased operating as timekeeper and observer of the southern skies—a role they have filled since 1858. Long-term plans for the Observatory include displays of major items of unusual interest, including a working radio telescope, a heliostat, and a large sundial. Mon.-Fri., 10:00 A.M.–noon; Wed., 10:00 A.M.–5:00 P.M.; Sat., Sun., 1:00-5:00 P.M. Admission free.

National Trust of Australia. The Rocks; 27-9222. Also on top of Observatory Hill is the grand and imposing office of the National Trust of Australia. Begun as a hospital in 1815, the building served for many years as the home of one of Sydney's most prestigious schools, Fort Street Girls High School. Bookshop and gift shop. Admission free. Mon.-Fri., 8:30 A.M.–5:30 P.M.; Sat., Sun., 2:00-5:00 P.M.

Lower Fort Street. The Rocks. A neighborhood of cozy terraces that still house waterfront workers. The wedge-shaped Hero of Waterloo Hotel serves cold beer and counter lunches. Its thick sandstone walls make it a cool haven for walking tourists.

Circular Quay West. The Rocks. Campbell's Bond store once secured the colony's precious gold and rum stocks. Now the solid stone warehouses have been converted into a series of restaurants, close to the water's edge and with views overlooking the Opera House.

St. Andrew's (Anglican) Cathedral. On the other side of the town hall, on George St., rise the towers and pinnacles of St. Andrew's Cathedral. First projected by Governor Macquarie, its foundation stone was relaid by Governor Bourke in 1837. It was eventually consecrated in 1868.

State Theatre. Market St.; 264-2431. Originally built in 1929 by Henry E. White, this grand and ornate Gothic-style picture palace was restored in 1980.

SITES

Strand Arcade. 193–5 Pitt St. and 408–10 George St. Designed by J. B. Spencer. C. 1891. Edwardian classical shopping arcade. Reconstructed to original splendor after a disastrous fire in 1976.

Sydney Hospital. Macquarie St. Nurses' wing at the back originally designed to the requirements of Florence Nightingale.

Sydney Tower. Above Centrepoint, corner Pitt, Market, and Castlereagh sts. 231–6222. The Tower rises 305.4 meters above Sydney and is Australia's highest structure. Two observation decks provide magnificent views of the whole city and far beyond. Decks are open Mon.–Sat., 9:30 A.M.–9:30 P.M.; Sun., public holidays, 10:30 A.M.–6:30 P.M. Entry is through the Centrepoint shopping center. Tickets for the observation deck cost $3.50, children $1.50. The Tower has two restaurants, with the same superb views. Reservations for lunch or dinner at the top of the tower can be made on Level 3 of Centrepoint Arcade at the top of the escalator.

Sydney University. South from the center of the city and along Paramatta Rd. rise the graceful gothic towers of Sydney University. The magnificent main quadrangle was begun in 1854, and its fine stone buildings took form from plans by Edmund Blacket. Today they represent Sydney's greatest group of Gothic Revival buildings. The Great Hall, with its high stone walls and hammer-beamed roof, was based on Westminster Hall in London, but generally the dominant influence on the quadrangle was that of the medieval colleges of Oxford.

Town Hall. Like an elaborate wedding cake carved in stone, the flamboyant French Renaissance-style town hall sits at the corner of George and Margaret sts. Begun in 1868, it was known as the Centennial Hall when finished in 1889. A token of rising civic pride, it was said to be "the largest town hall in the world" at its opening. It still boasts one of the world's biggest organs. The magnificent stained glass windows are well worth seeing. Admission free; guided 1½-hour tours at 11:00 A.M. Tues. and Thurs. Call 265–9333 for information on additional free entertainment.

Vaucluse House. Wentworth Ave., Vaucluse (9 km/5½ mi east of city center); 337–1957. This historic colonial house was built betweeen 1829 and 1847. William Charles Wentworth, the statesman and father of the Australian constitution, lived here. The delightful colonial building surrounded by gardens has recently been restored and the interiors have been refurnished to represent a mid-19th-century house. Much of the original furniture, bric-a-brac, and china of Wentworth's era remains. The stables and coach house contain examples of carriages used in NSW. Tues.–Sun., 10:00 A.M.–4:30 P.M. Closed Mon., Good Friday, and Christmas Day. Restaurant, picnic area, parking. Guided tours. Admission $1.50, children 50 cents, free admission first Thurs. of each month.

Victoria Barracks. A little farther along Oxford St., southeast of Darlinghurst Courthouse, are Victoria Barracks. A bus can be taken there from Circular Quay, Elizabeth St., or Taylor Square, Darlinghurst (nos. 379 and 380). Victoria Barracks was begun in 1841 after it was decided to move the military from their old George St. Barracks in the middle of the city. Designed by Colonel George Barney (architect of Circular Quay and Fort Denison), the beautiful sandstone

80 SYDNEY

buildings with their deep verandas form a precinct behind massive stone walls. Arranged around a wide, level, smoothly grassed parade ground, they possess a conspicuous air of military neatness and precision. Visitors are invited to attend the changing-of-the-guard ceremony on Tues., 10:30 A.M. Military museum. Conducted tours can be arranged. Telephone 339-3543.

MUSEUMS. Australia is 200 years young. But that does not mean that Australians are not fierce protectors of their heritage. Sydney in particular is blessed with a great variety of museums of all descriptions, and more are being built. The state government is currently spending many millions of dollars on the expansion of the Museum of Applied Arts and Sciences, whose vast collection has for years lain mostly hidden in scattered warehouses because of a lack of central space. The Power House Museum, in the gutted and restored former Pyrmont Power House, is to now hold a grand collection of mainly mechanical bits and pieces. Under the same state government, many of the city's most important historic buildings have also been rescued and lavishly restored to their colonial glory. The Mint and the Hyde Park Barracks are two prime examples, next door to each other on Macquarie St. The museums are listed here in alphabetical order: first those in Sydney and its immediate environs, then those farther from the city.

Art Gallery of New South Wales. Art Gallery Rd.; 221-2100. Mon.–Sat., 10:00 A.M.–5:00 P.M.; Sun., noon–5:00 P.M. Closed Christmas Day and Good Friday. Permanent exhibition of works of art from the gallery's collection of Australian, European, Asian, and Primitive art, prints and drawings, tribal and contemporary art, and photography. Temporary exhibitions from overseas and Australian sources. Film screenings and art lectures by professional staff. Guided tours, bookshop, and restaurant. Special facilities for the disabled. Admission free, although there may be charges for major exhibitions.

Australian Centre for Photography Ltd. Dobell House, 257 Oxford St., Paddington; 331-6253. Wed.–Sat., 11:00 A.M.–6:00 P.M. (winter, 5:00 P.M.); Sun., 1:00–5:00 P.M. Changing exhibitions on Australian photography, historic and modern. Gift shop. Admission free.

Australian Fishing Museum. 45 Murray St., Pyrmont, 660-6144. Mon.–Sun., 10:00 A.M.–4:00 P.M. Closed Good Friday and Christmas Day. This is believed to be the only museum in the world devoted entirely to recreational fishing. There are displays of fishing methods, aboriginal fishing artifacts, sport fishing tackle from the 1800s. Life-size replicas of all common fish, including a 1,365-pound black marlin caught by golfer Jack Nicklaus. Display of NSW State Fisheries Department tag-and-release research program. Videotapes on amateur fishing activities and even on how to cook fish according to one of Sydney's best-known seafood restaurateurs, Peter Doyle. Well worth the visit if you happen to be a fishing nut. Gift shop. Restaurant, picnic areas, parking, close to buses. Guided tours. Nearby facilities for disabled. Admission is free.

Australian Museum. 6–8 College St.; 339-8111. Sun., Mon., noon–5:00 P.M.; Tues.–Sat., holidays, 10:00 A.M.–5:00 P.M. Closed Good Friday and Christmas

MUSEUMS

Day. A natural history museum with exhibits of Australian native birds and mammals, artifacts from Pacific and aboriginal cultures, fish, shells, reptiles, insects, and more. The Hall of Life describes the process of life on Earth using 3-D models and audiovisual displays. The Arid Zone Gallery describes Australia's heartland. Newer galleries include: Mammals in Australia, Birds, and the Abelam People of Papua New Guinea. The Marine Gallery includes life-size dioramas of underwater habitats and a small theatre. Well worth a visit. Admission is free. There are guided tours and a good gift shop on the ground floor. Facilities for the disabled.

Colonial House Museum. 53 Lower Fort St., Dawes Point.; 27–6008. Daily, 10:00 A.M.–5:00 P.M. Closed Good Friday and Christmas Day. Comprehensive pictorial display of Sydney during the 19th century. Aims (and by and large succeeds) at re-creating the atmosphere of a living urban residence. Well worth a visit, especially since the museum is set in the heart of the Rocks area, which contains some of Australia's earliest buildings and reminders of the colonial-convict past. Admission 90 cents, children 40 cents.

Don Bank Museum. 6 Napier St., North Sydney; 929–3026. Sun., 1:00–4:00 P.M.; Wed., noon–4:00 P.M. Anyone interested in early Australian colonial architecture will be fascinated by this little cottage tucked away amid the tower blocks of busy commercial North Sydney. The building materials include magnificent cedar slabs, some of which are thought to have been from the district's first homestead, Crows Nest Farm, c. 1823. Three of the eight rooms have been left unplastered to show the original wall and ceiling structure. Early pieces of colonial wallpaper are on display. Photographic displays of early North Sydney and buildings. A costume display and an old furnished kitchen. Gift shop. Nearby picnic area. Parking, close to buses. Guided tours by arrangement. Facilities for disabled. Admission free. Fun to visit.

Elizabeth Bay House. 7 Onslow Ave., Elizabeth Bay (3 km/2 mi east of city center; take Bus 3121 from Hunter St., near Wynyard Station); 358–2344. Tues.–Fri., 10:00 A.M.–4:00 P.M.; Sat., 10:00 A.M.–5:00 P.M.; Sun., noon–5:00 P.M. Closed Mon., Christmas Day, Good Friday. If you are interested in colonial architecture, this is a must, built in 1835 by architect John Verge for Alexander Macleay, the colonial secretary. Restored to its original condition as "the finest house in the colony." The ground floor includes elegant rooms luxuriously furnished and decorated in the 1835–50 style. The first floor features changing exhibitions on Australian colonial history and the history of Australian architecture, society, and the decorative arts. Gift shop, nearby picnic area, parking. Admission $2, children 80 cents; free on first Tues. of each month.

S. H. Ervin Museum and Art Gallery. The National Trust Centre, Observatory Hill; 27–5374. Tues.–Fri., 11:00 A.M.–5:00 P.M.; Sat., Sun., 2:00–5:00 P.M. Closed when changing exhibitions. The building was constructed in 1857 as Georgian-style classrooms for Fort Street School. The Gallery specializes in changing exhibitions of Australian art and architecture with a historical emphasis. Gift shop, restaurant, parking, close to buses. Admission 50 cents.

Geological and Mining Museum. 36 George St., The Rocks; 251–2422. Mon.–Fri., 9:30 A.M.–4:00 P.M.; Sat., 1:00–4:00 P.M.; Sun., public holidays, 11:00 A.M.–

SYDNEY

4:00 P.M. Originally built as Sydney's first power station, the building was never used as such. It was transferred to the Department of Mines for use as a museum. Fascinating collection of gold and gemstones, mineral resources, geology, and fossils of NSW. Excellent systematic and interpretive displays supported by models, dioramas, maps, and films. Guides also offer personal tours. Gift shop, picnic area, close to public transportation. Facilities for disabled. Admission free.

Hall of Champions. First floor, Sports House, 157 Gloucester St.; 241-3122. Mon.-Fri., 1:00-4:00 P.M.; weekends and public holidays, noon-5:00 P.M. Closed Good Friday and Christmas Day. Originally built as Science House, in 1933 the building won the coveted Sulman Award for excellence in Australian architecture. The Hall is meant to be a tribute to the state's sporting heroes from 1876 to the present. Photographs and biographies of over 200 famous sportsmen and women, including the legendary Australian cricket captain Sir Donald Bradman, the great Olympic swimmer Dawn Fraser, World Squash Champion Heather McKay, Olympic rower Mervyn Wood, and innumerable tennis greats. Also featured is a sports museum with trophies, medals, and equipment. Admission free.

Hunters Hill Historical Society Museum. Hunters Hill Town Hall, Alexandra St., Hunters Hill. 20 minutes by ferry (no. 5 jetty, Circular Quay) to Valentia St., Woolwich, then a 5-minute bus ride. Open second and fourth Sun. of each month, 2:00-4:00 P.M., except holiday weekends. The main town hall was opened in 1903. In 1963 the building was extended to house the museum. Consists of objects of local interest, photographs, and archives. Admission free but by prior arrangement.

Hyde Park Barracks. Macquarie St.; 217-0111. Governor Lachlan Macquarie left Sydney with a legacy of magnificent Georgian architecture. The barracks, which are both elegant and austere, were designed by the convict Francis Greenway. Open seven days, 10:00 A.M.-5:00 P.M., except Tues., noon-5:00 P.M. Admission free.

Ivan Dougherty Gallery. Corner Albion Ave. and Selwyn St., Paddington; 331-5066. Mon.-Fri., 10:00 A.M.-5:00 P.M., all public holidays, weekends, and all January. This building, originally a public school c. 1894, now houses an exhibition of contemporary fine art and student work from Australia and overseas. Admission free.

Macleay Museum. University of Sydney; 692-2274. Tues.-Fri., 8:30 A.M.-4:30 P.M. Sydney's first fireproof building. Built in 1888, it houses the collection of Alexander Macleay, the first colonial secretary. There are anthropological and zoological displays as well as technical and scientific instruments of historical interest. Gift shop, parking, close to public transportation. Guided tours. Facilities for disabled. Admission free.

Manly Art Gallery. West Esplanade, Manly; 949-2435. Tues.-Fri., 10:00 A.M.-4:00 P.M.; weekends and public holidays, noon-4:00 P.M. Closed Mon., Good Friday, and Christmas Day. Established in 1924, the gallery contains a permanent collection of Australian paintings and ceramics supplemented by loan,

MUSEUMS

traveling, and historical exhibitions. Adjoins Manly Museum. Picnic areas. Gift shop. Facilities for disabled. Admission $1, children 50 cents.

Manly Museum. West Esplanade, Manly; 977-3411. Tues.-Sun., 10:00 A.M.-4:00 P.M. Closed Good Friday and Christmas Day. Opened in September 1982, the museum concentrates on subjects of local interest, including Sydney Harbour. Gift shop. Facilities for disabled. Admission $1, children 50 cents.

National Maritime Museum. Darling Harbor; 27-9111. Due for completion in October 1988, this spectacular building, with soaring wing-like roofs that echo the billowing sails of a clipper ship, is the national repository for Australia's maritime heritage. Open seven days. Admission $5.

Nicholson Museum of Antiquities. University of Sydney; 692-2812. Mon.-Thurs., 10:00 A.M.-4:30 P.M.; Fri., 10:00 A.M.-4:15 P.M. Closed on public holidays. Located in the Main Quadrangle building on the southwest side. Completed in sandstone in 1909. Founded by Sir Charles Nicholson in 1860, this is now one of the most comprehensive archaeological museums in Australia. Collections include pottery and sculpture and artifacts of wood and metal from Near Eastern, Egyptian, Cypriot, Greek, Southern Italian, Etruscan, Roman, and prehistoric European areas. Highlights include an Egyptian 7th-century B.C. painted wood mummy case, 8th-century B.C. funerary urn, the 3rd-century B.C. sculpture, the Nicholson *Hermes,* and 250,000-year-old stone axes. Gift shop, nearby café, no parking, close to buses. Guided tours. Facilities for disabled. Admission free.

Museum of Fire. Castlereagh Rd., Penrith; 047-31300. Sat., Sun., public holidays (except Christmas), 10:00 A.M.-5:30 P.M. The collection includes firefighting and related equipment. Over 40 fire engines (hand-drawn, horse-drawn, steam-powered, and motorized) dating from the 1870s. Communications, uniforms, documents, photographs. Gift shop. Guided tours, demonstrations. Admission $1, children 60 cents.

Power Gallery of Contemporary Art. Madsen Building, City Rd. entrance, University of Sydney; 692-3170. Mon.-Sat., 2:00-4:30 P.M.; Wed., 10:30 A.M.-4:30 P.M. Closed public holidays and University Christmas holidays. Dr. John Power, a graduate of the university, was the benefactor. Established in 1967 to make available to the people of Australia the latest ideas and theories in the plastic arts through the purchase of some of the most contemporary art in the world, excluding Australia. Here are paintings, drawings, sculptures, photographs, collages, gouaches, water colors, kinetics, and wall pieces; works by Henry Moore, Barbara Hepworth, Christo, and Marcel Duchamp. Café and nearby facilities for disabled. Admission free.

Power House Museum. Mary Anne St., Ultimo; 217-0111. Mon.-Sun., 10:00 A.M.-5:00 P.M. Closed Good Friday and Christmas Day. Locomotive Number One (c. 1854), a Bleriot monoplane (c. 1915), an Australian Six vintage car (c. 1923), a bicycle wall display, Australian, European, and Oriental decorative arts, and a range of Australian gadgets and inventions. Many millions of dollars have just been spent on a complete facelift that makes the Power House one of the finest museums in Australia. Gift shop, restaurant, picnic areas, close to public transportation. Guided tours. Facilities for disabled. Admission free.

SYDNEY

Randwick and District Historical Society. 194 Avoca St., Randwick. Tues., Wed., Thurs., 10:30 A.M.–4:30 P.M.; Sat. morning. Items of interest relating to local history are housed in a lovely vernacular-style homestead c. 1890. Nearby parking. Guided tours by arrangement. Admission by donation. Randwick is 8 km (5 mi) east of the city center.

A. M. Rosenblum Jewish Museum. 166 Castlereagh St.; 267-2477. Tues., Thurs., Sun., noon–4:00 P.M. Closed Jewish holidays, Christmas Day, Boxing Day, New Year's Day. The museum is housed in the Great Synagogue, a vast sandstone edifice built in 1878. There is a changing exhibition program depicting the Jewish way of life, with emphasis on Australian Jewish culture, customs, literature, etc. Admission 80 cents, children 40 cents.

Royal Mint. Queens Square, Macquarie St.; 217-0111. Mon.–Sun., 10:00 A.M.–5:00 P.M.; Wed., noon–5:00 P.M. Closed Christmas Day and Good Friday. Glorious restoration of one of Australia's oldest buildings. Built in 1811 and used for a variety of purposes: first as a wing of the old Rum Hospital and later for minting the colony's coins; eventually it was part of the District Court system; currently a museum of Australian decorative arts, housing displays of furniture, costume, silver, ceramics, and glass. Each room has a distinctive theme. Well worth a visit. Gift shop. Guided tours. Admission free.

State Library of NSW: Mitchell and Dixson Galleries. Macquarie St.; 221-1388. Mon.–Sat., 10:00 A.M.–5:00 P.M.; Sun., 2:00–6:00 P.M. Closed Good Friday and Christmas Day. The library building is a sandstone modification of the Italian Renaissance style. Special features are the great bronze doors depicting aboriginals, explorers, and navigators, stained glass windows, marble Tasman Map of 1644, and the enormous public reading room. Exhibitions in the galleries on the first floor include paintings, drawings, original documents, and rare books on aspects of Australian and Southwest Pacific history. Gift shop. Facilities for disabled. Admission free.

Sydney Centre for Educational and Social History. Glebe Primary School, Derwent St., Glebe. (3 km/2 mi west of city center); 660-4549. Open schooldays, 9:00 A.M.–4:00 P.M. Museum of the history of education in NSW. Houses NSW Department of Education's 1980 centenary photographic exhibition, Glebe Primary School Local History Museum, and a reconstruction of an early-20th-century classroom. Parking. Guided tours. Admission free.

Sydney Maritime Museum. Birkenhead Point, Drummoyne; 81-4374 (6 km/4 mi west of Sydney). Mon., 1:30–5:00 P.M.; Tues.–Sun., 10:00 A.M.–5:00 P.M. Closed Good Friday and Christmas Day. An outstanding feature is the collection of historic ships moored in the harbor at the museum's own piers. The museum, housed in a converted factory at the water's edge, also displays an extensive collection of ship models, paintings, photographs, and thematic exhibits with special reference to Sydney's maritime heritage. Well worth the visit. Gift shop, restaurant, picnic areas. Parking, close to buses. Ferry service from Circular Quay offers ideal way to see some of the western reaches of the harbor en route. Facilities for disabled. Admission $2 for a family, $1 for single adults, 50 cents for children.

MUSEUMS

Sydney Observatory. Observatory Park (near southern approaches to Sydney Harbor Bridge); 241-2478. Wed., 2:00–4:00 P.M.; evenings by appointment. Built in 1858, the Observatory contains telescopes and working models of solar system clocks, historical objects from Parramatta Observatory, and other astronomical displays. Guided tours, demonstrations. Admission free.

OUTSIDE SYDNEY

Captain Cook's Landing Place. Captain Cook Dr., Kurnell (32 km/20 mi south of city center); 668-9923. Mon.–Fri., 10:30 A.M.–4:30 P.M.; Sat., Sun., 10:30 A.M.–5:00 P.M. Closed Good Friday and Christmas Day. Contains exhibits covering the April 29, 1770, discovery of Botany Bay by Captain James Cook on board his Majesty's barque *Endeavour*. Among the major exhibits is a cannon from the *Endeavor*, recovered from the Great Barrier Reef, where it was dumped by Cook after the ship hit the coral reef. Restaurant, parking, bus service. Gift shop. Nearby facilities for disabled. Admission $3 per car, buses $14.

Carss Cottage Museum. Headland, Carss Park, Blakehurst (about 13 km/8 mi from city center); 546-7314. Open Sun. and public holidays, 1:00–5:00 P.M. Closed Christmas Day. Groups by prior arrangement. Built in 1863 of stone quarried on the estate by William Carss, a Sydney tavern keeper, the museum features the same beautiful workmanship as Sydney University. Now a historical museum for the suburban Kogarah District containing many local and general displays, including photographs. Picnic areas, nearby parking, close to bus. Guided tours by arrangement. Admission 30 cents, children 10 cents; free last Sun. in Aug.

Collingwood House. 13 Birkdale Crescent, Liverpool (31 km/19 mi, southwest of city center); 602-1315. Tues., 11:00 A.M.–4:00 P.M.; Sat., 1:00–4:00 P.M.; Sun., 11:00 A.M.–4:00 P.M. Other times by arrangement. The original home was built in 1810 for Captain Eber Bunker, father of Australian whaling. It has been restored with authentic furnishings to c. 1865 and contains displays of local interest. Parking, close to buses. Guided tours by arrangement. Admission 50 cents, children 20 cents.

Concord Historical Society Museum. 3 Alexandra St., Concord; 76-8713. Wed., Sat., Sun., 2:00–5:00 P.M. Closed Good Friday and Christmas Day. Concord is 15 km (9 mi) west of Sydney. Museum is situated on beautiful grounds. Constructed from the Thomas Walker Estate, the collection includes antique and heritage articles, photographs, old dresses, books, and other assorted memorabilia. Gift shop, picnic area, parking, close to buses. Guided tours. Admission 40 cents, children 20 cents.

Hills District Historical Society Museum. Old Castle Hill Rd., Castle Hill; 639-3343. Mon., Tues., Wed., 9:00–11:30 A.M.; Sun., 1:00–3:00 P.M. Closed on public holidays. Other days and times by prior arrangement. Castle Hill is 30 km (19 mi) northeast of Sydney. The collection includes domestic goods, entertainment memorabilia, clothing, some office equipment, medals, furniture, books, and agricultural tools. Picnic areas, nearby restaurant, parking, close to bus. Guided tours by arrangement. Admission 30 cents, children 10 cents.

Lewers Bequest and Penrith Regional Art Gallery. 86 River Rd., Emu Plains; (047) 35-1448. Displays works of the Australian abstract expressionists of the 1850s–1970s, among whom Margot and Gerald Lewers were prime movers. The site was originally the home and garden of the Lewerses. It has been extended to include a newly constructed regional art gallery, concentrating on presenting work of high quality by artists past and present working in a variety of media. Exhibitions change about once a month. Restaurant, parking, gift shop. Admission $1. 30 minutes by train from Sydney, then a pleasant walk along Nepean River to the gallery.

Lydham Hall. 18 Lydham Ave., Rockdale; 59-4259. 30 minutes by train from Sydney. Built in 1855 and furnished 1860-90 by Master Butcher Joseph Davis. Childhood home of Australian author Christina Stead. The museum includes photographs and relics of the suburban St. George District and a display of over 400 pieces of willow pattern china. Commands sweeping views of Botany Bay. Gift shop, picnic area, handy to buses. Guided tours.

Monarch Historical Society. 92 McIntosh Rd., Dee Why (18 km/11 mi north of Sydney); 98-5519. Open by appointment only. Comprehensive collection of militaria and colonial exhibits. Early Australian pre-Federation uniforms and foreign uniforms from countries linked with Australian history. Firearms. Japanese and early European armor, helmets, colonial artifacts, a Japanese tank, and letters from Sir Charles Kingsford Smith, Australia's most famous aviator. Guided tours and demonstrations. Admission $2, children $1.

Parramatta: Experiment Farm Cottage. 9 Ruse St., Parramatta (23 km/14 mi, west of city center); 635-5655. Sun., Tues., Wed., Thurs., and public holidays, 10:00 A.M.–noon, 1:30–4:00 P.M. Closed Christmas Day and Good Friday. Magnificent Georgian-style cottage built c. 1835 for Surgeon Lieutenant John Harris (of the Second Fleet, which arrived in 1790). The site of James Ruse's Experiment Farm. This was the first land grant made in the colony by Governor Phillip, and it was here that Ruse sowed Australia's first wheat crop. The cellars contain farm implements of Ruse's time. The house, which features beautiful cedar joinery, has been restored and furnished, each room representing a different colonial period. Guided tours. Admission 60 cents, children 25 cents.

Steam Train and Railway Museum. Parramatta Park. Open third Sun. of each month, 1:30–4:30 P.M. Australia's oldest operating steam train conveys passengers on a 1 km journey around the park. Other railway steam engines are usually exhibited. Gift shop, restaurant, picnic area, close to buses (no. 325 will get you there). Guided tours. Admission (including train ride) 80 cents, children 60 cents.

FILM. Australian film has a good international reputation—but you won't find only Australian films showing in Sydney. Many of the movies an American might have seen back home will be showing at the commercial theaters here.

MUSIC 87

Sydney has a large number of commercial cinemas, most of which are multicinema complexes in the George and Pitt sts. area. Programs for all cinemas are widely advertised, particularly in the Friday afternoon papers and Saturday's *Sydney Morning Herald*. There are several "art" cinemas that show foreign, political, and art films, as well as classics. The main ones are:

Academy Twin Cinema. 3a Oxford St., Paddington; 33–4453.
Chauvel Cinema. Oatley and Osford sts., Paddington; 33–5398. Devoted to Australian films, new and old.
Dendy Cinema. Martin Place, Central City; 233–8166.
Roma Cinema. 628 George St., Central City; 264–3321.
Sydney Opera House Cinema. Bennelong Point; 20–525.
Valhalla. 166 Glebe Point Rd., Glebe; 660–8050.

MUSIC. To understand the Sydney music scene, it is useful to realize that it is dominated by two nationwide organizations: the Australian Broadcasting Corporation and Musica Viva. The ABC is the national, government-subsidized television and radio broadcaster, in competition with commercial TV and radio. It also is a large entrepreneur, with a symphony orchestra in each capital city. Each year the ABC organizes hundreds of concerts. Its role is historical: The orchestras were set up in the early days of radio to provide broadcast material; the ABC's dominance in music is declining. Musica Viva is a private organization, which receives subsidies and organizes chamber and other smaller ensemble concerts.

Tickets: Bass is a large booking office in Sydney that sells tickets for most major musical performances. There are nine agencies as well as offices in 12 Grace Bros. department stores. A visit to one of the offices is worthwhile to look at brochures on current and forthcoming concerts. Phone 266–4848; credit-card bookings, 266–4800.

Information: Information about concerts and performances in Sydney is readily found in the *Sydney Morning Herald* newspaper. Fri.'s "Metro" supplement has listings for the following week's classical, jazz, and rock performances. Sat.'s paper generally has a big entertainment guide containing advertizements for classical and other concerts. It gives details of Opera House concerts, and can be a useful source of information on coming events.

Australian Broadcasting Corporation. Most orchestral performances feature the *Sydney Symphony Orchestra* with international and Australian guest artists and conductors.

The main series of concerts is in the Concert Hall of the Sydney Opera House, Bennelong Point. Others are the Recital Series and the Saturday Afternoon Great Classics. All tickets are sold on a subscription basis, but there are generally seats available for individual concerts. For all information phone ABC Concert Department, 264–9466, or the Opera House box office, 20–525.

Conservatorium of Music, Macquarie St., City, holds concerts by its own students as well as the *Sydney Youth Orchestra, Pan Pacific Music Camps,* and other musical groups. Call 230–1263 for information.

Musica Viva. Formed in 1946, Musica Viva presents concerts by distinguished overseas ensembles and groups of leading Australian musicians. The emphasis is on chamber music but includes music theater groups and choral ensembles.

Musica Viva runs a series of subscription concerts at the Opera House and the Seymour Centre, City Rd. and Cleveland St., Chippendale. Seymour Centre performances are often fully booked through subscription, but tickets for individual concerts at the Opera House are always available. Another series of concerts, featuring international and Australian artists, is presented at the Opera House and St. James Church, 173 King St., City. For all information about Musica Viva concerts and activities, phone 29–8165.

Sydney University Music Department. The department is active in presenting concerts, recitals, and other performances. During term students give free lunchtime recitals in the Great Hall at the university and in the Old Darlington School on Thurs. evenings at 5:15 P.M. Several music groups are associated with the university, including the *Renaissance Players,* the *Seymour Group,* and the *Sydney University Chamber Choir.* They all perform generally on campus in the Great Hall or the Seymour Centre, but sometimes at other locations. Concerts are not usually advertised outside the university, so for information phone 692–2923.

CHAMBER MUSIC

Australia Ensemble. This chamber music ensemble is run under the auspices of the University of New South Wales. It presents a subscription series of concerts in the Sir John Clancy Auditorium at the university from March to October. Tickets are always available for single performances. Phone 697–4873.

CHORAL

Collegium Musicum Choir. Also run by the University of New South Wales Music Department, the Collegium Musicum Choir gives choral concerts, generally at the Sir John Clancy Auditorium on campus. Phone 697–4873.

Conservatorium of Music, Macquarie St., City, is often the site of performances by various choral groups. Phone 230–1222.

Sydney Philharmonia Society. The society runs a series of concerts featuring the *Philharmonia Choir* (Sydney's largest, with 180 choristers) and the *Motet Choir* (35 members). The Philharmonia Choir presents a subscription series of concerts with the *Australian Chamber Orchestra* at the Concert Hall of the Opera House. It also appears with the Sydney Symphony Orchestra in ABC concerts. For information about programs and bookings, phone 29–6075.

JAZZ

Jazz in Sydney covers a range from traditional to mainstream, modern, and beyond. The *Sydney Morning Herald*'s Fri. "Metro" section gives a listing of the coming week's performances. The *Jazz Action Society,* 232–1419, will provide further information and welcomes calls from overseas visitors. Call Wed., 11:00 A.M. to 3:00 P.M., otherwise you will get an answering machine.

There are **jazz picnics** every third Sunday afternoon at *Berry Island Reserve,* Shirley Road, Wollstonecraft. Phone 452-5831 for information. Bring along your picnic basket, throw a steak or some fish on the barbecue, and listen to a jazz band outdoors.

On the northern broadwalk of the *Sydney Opera House* there are some great **Sunday afternoon outdoor concerts,** usually jazz, starting at 2:30 P.M. There is no charge for the music, or for the great harbor view.

During summer, the *Bondi Pavilion Courtyard,* Queen Elizabeth Dr., Bondi Beach, is the site for **deck chair concerts.** The music is usually jazz and very good. Phone 30-3325 for details.

For major jazz spots see "Nightlife," below.

OPERA

The Australian Opera. The *Australian Opera,* formed in 1956, gives a summer and a winter season in Sydney at the Opera House. Some performances are heavily committed because of subscription tickets, but there are usually some seats available for most performances. Opera season is usually June–Oct., with the summer season in Jan. and Feb. The Opera House box office is open Mon.–Sat., 9:00 A.M.–8:30 P.M.; Sun., 9:00 A.M.–4:00 P.M. Qantas offices can also book advance tickets for visitors. The Australian Opera, 319-1088, will give program details and ticket information, or phone the Opera House box office, 20-525.

Conservatorium of Music. The students stage two operas each year, often with guest artists. The Conservatorium is in the city on Macquarie St.; for information phone 230-1263.

University of New South Wales Opera. This is a semiprofessional company that presents early opera and also music theater works. Two productions are staged each year at the Science Theatre on campus. Phone 697-4873.

ROCK/POP

Pubs and clubs are the main places for local rock bands. A large number are located in the suburbs but are generally accessible by public transport. Some have a cover charge, ranging between $1 and $6, but others are free. The *Sydney Morning Herald*'s "Metro" section on Fri. gives a guide to what is on and where.

Major overseas and local artists generally perform at the *Entertainment Centre,* Harbour St., Haymarket (211-2222), or the *Hordern Pavilion,* Driver Ave., Paddington (33-3769). Tickets and information available through Mitchell's Bass, 266-4848.

See "Nightlife," below.

FREE MUSIC

Conservatorium of Music, Macquarie St., City. When school is in session, free lunch-hour concerts are given by students every Wed. The Fri. twilight concerts (6:00 P.M.) are sometimes free. Phone 230-1263.

Martin Plaza, City. Free lunchtime concerts (noon and 1:00 P.M.) are given each day. For information phone Town Hall entertainment officer, 265-9333.

St. Andrew's Anglican Cathedral, Sydney Square. Different organists give free performances every Thurs. at 1:15 P.M. Phone 265-1555.

St. Stephen's Uniting Church, 197 Macquarie Street, City. Free lunchtime recitals are held each Mon. (Mar.–Nov.) from 1:10 P.M. Phone 221-1688 for details.

See also the jazz section, above.

DANCE. The dance scene in Sydney is active and interesting. A variety of companies perform throughout the year—with programs that range from classical to modern.

Australian Ballet. The Australian Ballet was established in 1962 and is the national classical company. It performs in most major Australian cities—a mixture of the classics, lighter, full-length works, and short ballets. There are two Sydney seasons, Mar.–May and Nov.–Dec., mostly in the Opera Theatre at the Opera House, but also at the Regent Theatre. Tickets are sold on a subscription basis, but single tickets are available for most performances. For information phone the Australian Ballet, 357-1133, or the Opera House, 20-525.

Dance Exchange. This small professional company was established in 1976. It presents a varied program of contemporary dance, usually at the Cell Block, East Sydney Technical College, Forbes St., Darlinghurst, but also elsewhere. For information phone 264-2525.

One Extra Dance Company. This young company, formed in 1976, is under the direction of Malaysian-born former architect Kai Tai Chan. It performs at various venues and many of its ballets have an Asian influence. For information phone 29-5783.

Sydney Dance Company. Established as a small education dance group in 1965, the company became a full-time professional group in 1972. It presents contemporary dance and modern ballet programs, many choreographed by the artistic director, Graeme Murphy. The company has a policy of using Australian designers and composers wherever possible in creating new works. Sydney seasons (July/Aug. and Nov.) are at the Opera House. Information and tickets from the Opera House (20-525), Bass (266-4848), and Sydney Dance Company (358-4600).

THEATER

THEATER. Theater in Sydney is interesting and diverse, with productions to suit most tastes. The emphasis is on Australian works, but classics and foreign plays are also staged regularly.

Groups range from the larger, government-subsidized companies and other professional groups to a number of nonprofessional and fringe companies. There are also a number of theaters without resident companies, used for dramas, musicals, cabaret, etc.

The *Sydney Morning Herald* on Sat. has an "Entertainment Guide" that is the best source of information for current productions and forthcoming performances. Tickets can be booked through Bass (266–4848) for many shows, but phone numbers for individual theaters are included in the following guide.

THEATER COMPANIES

Ensemble Theatre. 78 McDougall St., Milsons Point; information 929–8877, box office 929–0644. Sydney's oldest professional theater company, the Ensemble presents a wide range of plays, both dramatic and lighter, comic works, by Australian, American, British, and Canadian playwrights.

Griffin Theatre Company. The Stables, 10 Nimrod St., Kings Cross; information and box office, 33–3817. The Stables Theatre is the home for this energetic young company. Productions are mainly new Australian works, but the company usually does a few classics each year.

Marionette Theatre. The Rocks Theatre, 106 George St. North; information and box office, 27–3274. Presents puppet shows for children in schools and during holidays; also several adult productions every year.

New Theatre. 542 King St., Newtown; 519–3403. For more than 50 years this nonprofessional company has been presenting modern classics, revues, and contemporary Australian and foreign plays with a social message. Performances are Fri. and Sat. nights, and Sun. at 5:30 P.M.

Nimrod Theatre. Seymour Centre, corner City Rd. and Cleveland St., Chippendale; information 692–0555, box office 692–3511. The Nimrod has three theaters at the Seymour Centre—Everest, York, and Downstairs. The emphasis is on Australian works, but contemporary foreign plays and classics are also done.

Northside Theatre Company. 2 Marian St., Killara; information and box office, 498–3166. A well-established professional company, the Northside Theatre presents a commercial program of drama, musicals, thrillers, and comedy.

Phillip Street Theatre. 169 Phillip St., City; information and box office, 232–4900. The company presents a broad range of plays—contemporary Australian and foreign as well as classics. Children's pantomimes are staged during school holidays.

Q Theatre. Railway St., Penrith; information and box office, (047) 21–5735. The only professional theater company in Sydney's western suburbs. The Q's program encompasses drama, classics, comedies, and Australian works.

Rocks Players Theatre. 2 Marion St., Leichhardt; 569-0223. A nonprofessional group with a great interest in community theater, the Rocks Players stage Shakespeare, modern classics, and new Australian plays.

Sydney Theatre Company. Information and box office, 250-1777. The STC has two homes—one in the Opera House drama theater and other a new complex called the Wharf, Pier 4, Hickson Rd., Walsh Bay. It is the state drama company and presents a mixture of classics and modern Australian plays.

THEATERS

Bay Street Theatre. 75 Bay St., Glebe; 692-0977. Presents a wide range of plays from classics to contemporary Australian.

Belvoir Street Theatre. 25 Belvoir St., Surry Hills; 699-3273. Two theater spaces present diverse theater ranging from avant-garde to classics, including drama, cabaret, and musicals.

Footbridge Theatre. Parramatta Rd., Glebe; 692-9955. Situated in Sydney University, the Footbridge has productions as diverse as musicals, rock 'n' roll, and drama.

Her Majesty's Theatre. Railway Square, 107 Quay St.; information 212-3411, box office 212-1120. Commercial plays and musicals, drama, one-man shows, and cabaret.

The Performance Space. 199 Cleveland St., Redfern. Bookings, 698-7235; information 698-7235. A venue for experimentation in all art forms, including theater, dance, visual arts, and literature.

Seymour Centre. Corner City Rd. and Cleveland St., Chippendale; 692-3511. Now the home for the Nimrod Theatre Company, the Seymour Centre plans to continue as a location for other drama and musicals.

State Theatre. 49 Market St., 264-7186. An elaborate old picture palace, the State Theater now houses musicals and other stage shows.

Theatre Royal. MLC Centre, King St., City; 231-6111. With Her Majesty's, the Royal is one of Sydney's main theaters for commercial plays and musicals.

ART GALLERIES. Sydney is a fine city for gallery browsing, although these days you may not find too many bargains. If you intend to buy and are not familiar with what is likely to be available, it could be useful to go to the Art Gallery of New South Wales first. This has collections of colonial paintings, the Australian impressionists and others of the late 19th and early 20th centuries, and the works of most contemporary Australian painters. The Art Gallery of New South Wales and the Australian Museum also have collections of Australian aboriginal and of Pacific art and artifacts.

As in most countries these days, there are restrictions on the export from Australia of aboriginal art and artifacts; most countries of the Pacific have similar laws. These apply particularly when objects are of historical and, of course, religious significance. It is worthwhile to check the provenance of any-

ART GALLERIES

thing you buy and be sure of the credentials of the person you deal with. The galleries listed are established and have a reputation to maintain.

The suburbs of Paddington and Woollahra, where many galleries are located, adjoin. They are attractive, if a trifle hilly, with many restored 19th-century terrace houses. A pleasant day or half day can be spent on foot moving from gallery to gallery and taking in the sights.

Aboriginal Art Centre. 7 Walker Lane, Paddington; 357-6839, and Argyle Centre, The Rocks; 27-1380. Aboriginal arts and crafts. Tues.-Sat., 11:00 A.M.-6:00 P.M.

Aboriginal Artists' Gallery. 477 Kent St.; 261-2929. Current and traditional work. Mon.-Fri., 10:00 A.M.-5:00 P.M.; Sat., 10:00 A.M.-1:00 P.M.

Art of Man Gallery. 13 Gurner St., Paddington; 33-4337. Permanent exhibition of primitive art from Australia, New Guinea, and surrounding islands. Phone for appointment.

Bloomfield Galleries. 118 Sutherland St., Paddington; 326-2122. Australian contemporary art. Tues.-Sat., 10:30 A.M.-5:30 P.M.

Bonython-Meadmore Gallery. 95 Holdsworth St., Woollahra; 327-5411. Australian contemporary. Tues.-Sat., 10:00 A.M.-5:00 P.M.; Sun., 2:00-5:00 P.M.

David Jones Art Gallery. David Jones department store, Elizabeth St., City; 266-5544. Wide range of the arts, including painting, antique furniture, sculpture. Mon.-Wed., 10:00 A.M.-5:00 P.M.; Thurs.-Fri., 10:00 A.M.-7:00 P.M.; Sat., 10:00 A.M.-3:00 P.M.

Galleries Primitif. 174 Jersey Road, Woollahra; 32-3115. Aboriginal art; Melanesian, Polynesian, Micronesian, and Eskimo art. Tues.-Sat., 11:00 A.M.-6:00 P.M.

Robin Gibson Galleries. 278 Liverpool St., Darlinghurst; 331-6693. Contemporary Australian paintings, lithographs, tapestries, and crafts. Tues.-Sat., 11:00 A.M.-6:00 P.M.

Eddie Glastra. 44 Gurner St., Paddington.; 331-7322. Mainly Australian art. Tues.-Sat., 11:00 A.M.-5:00 P.M.

Hogarth Galleries. 7 Walker Lane, Paddington; 357-6839. Contemporary art, mainly Australian. Tues.-Sat., 11:00 A.M.-6:00 P.M.

Holdsworth Galleries. 86 Holdsworth St., Woollahra; 331-7161. Contemporary Australian art, chiefly paintings. Mon.-Sat., 10:00 A.M.-5:00 P.M.; Sun., noon-5:00 P.M.

Irving Sculpture Gallery. 144a St. Johns Rd., Glebe; 692-0773. Modern and contemporary sculpture from Australian and overseas artists. Tues.-Sat., 11:00 A.M.-6:00 P.M., or by appointment.

Rex Irwin. 38 Queen St., Woollahra; 32-3212. Contemporary Australian art; some European and English graphics. Tues.-Sat., 11:00 A.M.-5:30 P.M.

Josef Lebovic Gallery. 294 Oxford St., Paddington; 332-1840. Original prints, mainly by Australian artists; Australian colonial photography. Mon.-Fri., 1:00-6:00 P.M.; Sat., 10:00 A.M.-6:00 P.M.

Richard King, incorporating The Print Room. 141 Dowling St., Woolloomooloo; 358-1919. Australian and European prints, drawings, and photography, 1850–1940. Tues.–Sat., 11:00 A.M.–5:00 P.M. during exhibitions; otherwise, by appointment.

Macquarie Galleries. 204 Clarence St., City; 264–9787. Contemporary Australian art, including painting, limited-edition prints, ceramics, and sculpture. Tues.–Fri., 10:00 A.M.–6:00 P.M.; Sat., noon–6:00 P.M.

Roslyn Oxley Gallery. 13–21 Macdonald St., Paddington; 331–1919. Contemporary Australian paintings. Tues.–Sat., 11:00 A.M.–6:00 P.M.

Prouds Gallery. Corner King and Pitt Sts., City; 233–4488. Traditional Australian, mainly living, artists. Paintings, graphics, and sculpture. Mon.–Wed., Fri., 9:00 A.M.–5:25 P.M.; Thurs., 9:00 A.M.–9:00 P.M.; Sat., 9:00 A.M.–2:00 P.M.

Stadia Graphics. 85 Elizabeth St., Paddington; 326–2637. Original graphic works from 19th and 20th centuries, contemporary Australian and overseas artists. Mon.–Fri., 10:00 A.M.–5:00 P.M.

Barry Stern Galleries. 19 Glenmore Rd., Paddington, and 12 Mary Place, Paddington; 357–5492. Contemporary Australian art. Mon.–Sat., 11:30 A.M.–5:30 P.M.

George Styles Gallery. 50 Hunter St., City; 233–2628. Traditional oils and watercolors, some contemporary art; all Australian works. Mon.–Fri., 9:00 A.M.–5:30 P.M.

Wagner Art Gallery. 39 Gurner St., Paddington; 357–6069. Landscape and figurative art by well-known Australians. Tues.–Sat., 11:00 A.M.–5:30 P.M.; Sun., 1:00 P.M.–5:00 P.M.

Watters Gallery. 109 Riley St., East Sydney; 331–2556. Contemporary Australian painting and sculpture. Tues.–Sat., 10:00 A.M.–5:00 P.M.

SHOPPING. Driving into Sydney across the great span of the Harbour Bridge at night, one is struck again and again by the dramatic similarity between this city's soaraway skyline, ablaze with a million lights, and that of New York. It's a comparison that holds up on many fronts. This is an aggressive, go-get-'em town where anything and everything is available—at a price. Shopping in Sydney can be every bit as much fun as in New York. It's all here, in a profusion of high-class department stores, trendy boutiques, intimate arcades, and high-tech towers. In the city center, George, Pitt, and Castlereagh sts. run parallel, north–south, and contain the bulk of the really good stores. International credit cards are accepted in virtually every shop. Long ago it used to be said that Australian stores stocked last season's fashions from Europe and North America. Not anymore. Australian fashion designers can and do hold their own against the world's best, and you will find their creative designs and fine-quality clothes in many of the big stores as well as the ritzier boutiques of Double Bay.

SHOPPING

DEPARTMENT STORES

David Jones has long been Sydney's premier department store, all the more so now that the Market St. store has just undergone an $8 million facelift. David Jones is to Sydney what Saks is to New York or I. Magnin to San Francisco. There are in fact three DJs stores in the city center. The Elizabeth St. store (which occupies almost an entire block between Market and Castlereagh) is known as the women's store because it specializes in everything a woman could want, as well as many items of general merchandise. On the sixth floor, *Georges of Melbourne* (perhaps the most exclusive clothing and accessories retailer in Melbourne) has set up its own little store-within-a-store. DJs' men's store is right across the street on the corner of Castlereagh and Market, and once again the store takes a particular pride in stocking a man's every need. The men's store also stocks a wide range of home furnishings. In the basement of the men's store is a newly renovated Harrods-style gourmet food hall, known as *Food, Glorious Food*. It carries the best of imported as well as Australian-made food products. They bake their own bread, and there are half a dozen cozy little sit-down bars selling everything from cake and coffee to fish, oysters, and chilled Australian wines. The third DJs store is on the corner of George and Barrack sts. and features mainly men's wear.

Myers. Not far down Market St. is Myers, another very big department store, which is very much a part of the inner-city retail landscape. It sells general merchandise, although not quite the range or quality of DJs.

Gowings, Lowes, and Waltons are smaller department stores that stock budget items.

SHOPPING AREAS

Arcades. Sydney is blessed with some marvelous old-fashioned arcades. Far and away the best of them is the *Strand Arcade,* between Pitt and Castlereagh. Built in the late 1880s, it was once described as "undoubtedly the finest public thoroughfare in the Australasian Colonies." The Strand has been beautifully restored and today offers a basement and five galleried floors crammed with a delightful array of tiny shops and boutiques selling everything from jewelery to antiques and men's and women's fashion. There's also a profusion of eateries and health food shops. The *St. James Arcade* (between Elizabeth and Castlereagh, just north of DJs), much more modern, also features some very elegant boutiques and jewelery shops.

Centrepoint. In the heart of the city is an enormous steel tower capped by a revolving restaurant. Beneath the tower is a shopping complex, which features scores of outlets for everything from bikinis to bread rolls. A pedestrian walkway links Centrepoint with two David Jones stores and offers a convenient way to move around without having to suffer the fits and starts of traffic.

Double Bay. Although Sydney is full of trendy, designer boutiques, people seem to attach a special aura to the same merchandise when it is sold in Double Bay. Double Bay (also known as Double Pay) is just a few minutes' ride out of the city center along New South Head Rd. The shopping here really is excellent. The affluent middle class who inhabit the swank eastern suburbs don't hesitate to pay top dollar for the finest products, and that goes for everything from meat, poultry, and fish to the latest Italian and French clothing and shoes. There are also some very good restaurants and small eateries in Double Bay. Well worth the visit.

Mid-City Centre. On four levels between George and Pitt, King and Market. Dozens of trendy boutiques plus four good coffee shops on the Gallery level. On the Pitt St. level restaurants offer Asian, Lebanese, Mexican, and Italian delights.

MLC Centre. *Gucci* is here, and so are a lot of other top-quality shops. At the base of the giant white granite cylinder known as the MLC Centre between Martin Place and Castlereagh and King sts. Good eateries, including take-out.

Queen Victoria Building. Sprawling over an entire city block between George, York, Market, and Druitt streets, the QVB has been restored to its 1898 grandeur with dozens of new shops and arcades offering every imaginable shopping convenience. Well worth a visit if only for the architectural experience and the beauty of its stained-glass windows.

ABORIGINAL ART PRODUCTS

Overseas visitors sometimes embark on trips to Outback Australia to purchase aboriginal artifacts, without realizing that the very best of these products are more often than not available in Sydney. The Aboriginal Arts Board of the Australia Council, the Australian government's agency for the support of the arts, has established Aboriginal Arts and Crafts Pty. Ltd., a nonprofit organization to market traditional aboriginal artifacts in the cities. There are two outlets in Sydney, which are highly recommended. The *Collectors Gallery of Aboriginal Art* is at 40 Harrington St., The Rocks, and the *Argyle Primitive Art Gallery* is at 18 Argyle St., The Rocks (27–8492). The *Coo-ee Australian Emporium* at 98 Oxford St., Paddington (332–1544), also has a beautiful range of traditional Tiwi designs hand printed in the batik style on fabrics suitable for either soft furnishings or stylish garments. The Tiwi tribe inhabit Bathurst and Melville Island off the far north coast of Australia.

TAILORS

There is only one in Sydney worth mentioning. In fact, *J. H. Cutler* is the very best tailor in Australia. The fact that 1984 was its centenary year says a good deal for the uncompromising attention to detail and styling that have enabled it to survive where others have gone under. In a trendy, mass-produced world, Cutler sticks to painstaking hand stitching, and of course this is reflected in the prices. A three-piece suit fashioned from the finest-quality English worsted will set you back around $1,500. Well worth a visit to the delightful old-world shop on the mezzanine level of Kindersley House on Bligh St.

CRAFTWORKS

See also "Galleries." *Australian Craftworks* on George St. in The Rocks (27-7156) displays and sells a wide variety of distinctive Australian crafts in a wide range of prices. The store is housed in the Old Police Station, a converted 19th-century sandstone building; some of the old jail cells are now used as exhibit space. It is also possible to arrange for private showings of the collection. Usually open Mon.–Sat., 10:00 A.M.–5:00 P.M.

OPALS

Over 95 percent of the world's opal come from Australia, and the prices these gems sell for in Sydney vary widely. Do shop around first, and you may want to buy one of the inexpensive little books on the gems, easily available.

Significantly cheaper than solid opals are doublets, a thin slice of opal backed with a less precious stone, and triplets, similar to doublets, but with clear domes over the opals.

By showing your passport when you buy, opals can be purchased tax-free. In Sydney, you may want to browse or buy at *Flame Opals,* 119 George St., The Rocks, 27-3446; *Allison's Opal Rooms,* 15 Park St., 267-7133; *Anina Opal and Jewellry Manufacturers,* 222 Clarence St., 267-1938. Also see the chapter "Outside Sydney" for information on the opal country of Lightning Ridge.

DINING OUT. No visit to Sydney would be complete without an adequate sampling of its over two thousand restaurants. Sydneysiders dine out quite regularly, and the climate makes gardens, terraces, courtyards, and pavements, sometimes with the added bonus of a harbor or beach view, popular selections as venues.

There are restaurants in Sydney serving fine food to suit every mood and every wallet. A diverse ethnic background among the city's population, the excellent quality and availability of fresh ingredients, the layout of the city around a magnificent harbor, as well as the talent of its chefs, combine to produce a wide enough range of restaurants to make your choice difficult.

What will it be for lunch today? A small vegetarian café serving the freshest salads and long, cool fruit juices? Or grilled John Dory fillets and a crisp white wine at a seafood restaurant by the harbor? And for dinner? Do you feel like silver service, elegant décor, fine Australian and imported wines, and the best French cuisine? Or will you take your own wine to a no-frills café serving spicy Malay sate or Thai curry expertly prepared and simply presented?

If your time in Sydney is limited, so is the number of culinary experiences you can manage. "Musts" on your sampling lists should include seafood fresh from local or nearby waters: fat Sydney rock oysters, the prehistoric-looking, crustaceous Balmain bugs, sweet king prawns, or fish such as snapper or John Dory, popular among discerning locals.

SYDNEY

You should also taste a selection of Australian wines; the Hunter and Barossa valleys are only two of the Australian areas producing world-class wines. You will notice that wine in restaurants is priced much higher than in hotels or liquor stores. This is the result of the very high price restaurants must pay for wine licenses. Before selecting a restaurant, check the type of liquor license it has. Licensed restaurants usually serve a range of beers, spirits, and wines. Unlicensed restaurants are not permitted to sell alcohol, and you will have to buy your own from a hotel or liquor store—some restaurants then charge you a corkage fee to open and serve these wines. Unlicensed restaurants are usually referred to as BYO (bring your own).

For dessert, either fresh fruits such as mango, papaw, pineapple, or strawberries or a selection of fine Australian cheeses should delight.

PRICE CLASSIFICATIONS AND ABBREVIATIONS

The price classifications (in Australian dollars) for the restaurants listed are based on the average price of a three-course dinner for one. This does not include drinks or tip. Tipping in Australian restaurants is at your discretion for good service. It is generally around 10 percent of the bill. There may be surcharges on weekends or public holidays, when penalty rates must be paid to staff.

Deluxe means over $55; *Expensive,* $35–$55; *Moderate,* $25–$35; *Inexpensive,* less than $25.

Abbreviations for credit cards are: AE, American Express; BC, Bank Card; DC, Diners Club; JCB, Japan Credit Bureau; MC, MasterCard; V, Visa. TC indicates the restaurant will accept traveler's checks, with establishments accepting only Australian or U.S. traveler's checks indicated as TC ($A) or TC ($US).

Many of Sydney's best restaurants are away from the city center; the approximate distance in kilometers and miles from the center of Sydney is indicated where relevant. Cabs can easily take you to the outlying restaurants. See also "Theater Restaurants" in the "Nightlife" section, below. ♦ = highly recommended.

AMERICAN

Moderate–Expensive

Bourbon and Beefsteak. 24 Darlinghurst Rd., Kings Cross; 357–1215 or 358–1144. American-style breakfasts, spareribs and steaks for heartier meal needs, are the fare at this establishment. Not the classiest of restaurants for women dining alone, but Bourbon and Beefsteak's food is nevertheless adequate, the service quick, and the staff friendly. Open 24 hours, its bar is a popular late-night spot. Licensed. B, L, D, daily. Reservations accepted Mon.–Thurs. only. AE, BC, DC, JCB, MC, V, TC.

Inexpensive–Moderate

Green Park Diner. 219 Oxford St., Darlinghurst (2 km/1 mi east); 357–5391. Breakfast is available here until midnight, but not early in the morning, to

DINING OUT

complement the lifestyle of the neighborhood. Mostly tasty hamburgers here, with some additions such as steak, soup, Cokes, and coffee. BYO. L, D, daily. AE, BC, MC, V.

Rockerfeller's Eastside. 227 Oxford St., Darlinghurst (2 km/1 mi east); 33–6968. A fun hamburger joint, where burgers with names like "Kick Off," "Green Bay Packer" (with avocado), and "New York Giant" complement the giant footballer models running at you out of the walls. Licensed. D, daily. AE, BC, MC, V, TC ($A).

AUSTRALIAN

Deluxe

Oasis Seros. 495 Oxford St., Paddington (4 km/2½ mi east); 33–3377. A 1980s interior within a century-old former manse is the setting for this new and fashionable restaurant. The cuisine is modern Australian, with Chinese, French, and Italian influences. Licensed. L, Fri.; D, Tues.–Sat. Reservations recommended. AE, BC, DC, MC, V. TC ($A).

Expensive

♦ **Blue Water Grill.** 168 Ramsgate Ave., Bondi (8 km/5 mi east); 30–7810. Specializes in char-grilled seafood and meat. It is brasserie style, so you can order anything from a snack to a full meal. Spectacular views back to Bondi Beach and south along the Pacific coast. There is often a wait for the outdoor tables with the best views. Licensed. L, D, daily. No reservations. BC, MC, V. T.C.

Moderate

Argyle Tavern. 12–18 Argyle St., The Rocks (2 km/1 mi east); 27–7782. The Argyle Tavern's building was erected by convict labor over 150 years ago and now houses four restaurants. The *Garrison Restaurant* here offers à la carte dining in an elegant setting, with roast lamb on the spit a specialty of the house. For an Australian experience designed for tourists, attend the *Jolly Swagman Show*. As well as some hearty Aussie tucker served by staff in colonial costume, there's a bush band, didgeridoo playing, a gumleaf player, energetic dancing, and even the shearing of a sheep. Licensed. Garrison: D, daily. Jolly Swagman: D, daily. Lowenbrau Kellar: L, D, daily. Woolshed: L, daily. AE, BC, DC, MC, V. TC ($A).

Carey Cottage. 18–20 Ferry Street, Hunter's Hill (9 km/5½ mi west); 817–3643. Dine on mouthwatering roast dinners in a charming 19th-century cottage or in the garden. Carey Cottage always does a Christmas dinner with all the trimmings midyear (winter) for Sydneysiders, who usually eat theirs in the sweltering heat of December. After Sunday lunch take a leisurely stroll through Hunter's Hill, where a village of huge stone mansions and picturesque cottages was built amid large gardens last century. BYO. Reservations recommended. L, Sun.; D, Tues.–Sat. BC, MC. TC ($A).

SYDNEY

Inexpensive

Chalkey's Family Restaurant. 22 Darley Rd., Manly (14 km/8¾ mi northeast); 977–4293. It's hard to decide whether roast dinners are more English or Australian, but in this friendly restaurant you'll find roasts of all sorts: beef, chicken, pork, and lamb, as well as delicious homemade desserts and soups. By the way, Chalkey's likes children. BYO. D, Tues.–Sat.

Convicts and Converts. 69 Willoughby Rd., Crow's Nest (5 km/3 mi north); 436–4278. If you're on the north side and want to try a good 'ol Aussie pie, here's the place: very informal, loud and cheery later in the evening, laminex table-style, and dispensing meat pies, curry pies, steak pies, and so on, with a few additional dishes. Licensed. L, Mon.–Fri. D, Mon.–Sat. AE, BC, DC, MC, V. TC ($A).

Phantom at the Opera. 21 Circular Quay West; The Rocks; 27–2755. Housed in an old bond store and on the edge of the harbor, the Phantom serves mainly French food; however, the wine list of nearly 300 choices is very Australian, as the restaurant is within the Australian Wine Centre. Licensed. L, Tues.–Sun.; D, Tues.–Sat. AE, BC, DC, MC, V. TC.

Phillip's Foote. 101 George St., Sydney; 27–2585. Basically an Aussie barbecued steak restaurant; you cook your own meat and help yourself to salad. Their steak or fish with salad and a drink is a very inexpensive fixed-price choice. Licensed. L, D, daily. Reservations recommended for Fri. lunch and dinner and Sat. dinner. AE, BC, DC, JCB, MC, V. TC ($A).

CHINESE

Expensive

Imperial Peking Harbourside. 15 Circular Quay West, The Rocks; 27–7073 or 27–6100. Innovative Chinese cuisine, specializing in Pekingese food and offering excellent service. This restaurant is a little more formal than most Chinese restaurants, yet relaxed and comfortable, and is located in the old Campbell's Bond Store in the historic Rocks area. Licensed. L, D, daily. Reservations recommended, particularly for window seats with harbor view. AE, BC, DC, MC, V. TC.

Peacock Gardens. 100 Alexander St., Crow's Nest (5 km/3 mi north); 439–8786. An excellent Chinese restaurant north of the harbor, specializing in Cantonese food. Efficient service and a most hospitable host. Licensed. L, D, daily. Reservations recommended. AE, BC, DC, MC, V. TC ($A).

Moderate

Dixon. 51 Dixon St., Sydney; 211–1619. Located in the heart of Chinatown, the Dixon is an old favorite with Sydneysiders. It is open until 1:00 A.M., Fri. and Sat.—handy if you've been to an event at the Sydney Entertainment Centre. Licensed. L, D, daily. AE, BC, DC, MC, V. TC.

Fortuna Court. 605 George St., Sydney; 267–3033. A busy and noisy restaurant, Fortuna Court can seat 300 people having fun. It is set in a huge pagoda-

DINING OUT

style building atop a drugstore and offers an inexpensive fixed-price dinner menu as well as á la carte menu. Licensed. L, D, daily. AE, BC, DC, MC, V. TC.

Ming Wah. 33–37 Dixon St., Sydney; 212–5987. Tucked inside the northern gates of Chinatown, the Ming Wah offers good service in an attractive restaurant. There's not a huge menu, but enough variety to please everyone. Licensed. L, D, daily. AE, BC, DC, MC, V. TC ($A).

Inexpensive–Moderate

Choys 1,000 A.D. Corner Harbour and Hay St., Sydney; 211–4213. Supposedly modeled on an 11th-century Chinese inn, Choys has plenty of timber and rusticity and is quite different from the flocked wallpaper and bright carpets of many Sydney Chinese restaurants. Blackboard menu with a pleasing selection of dishes. Can get extremely busy at times, particularly preperformance time at the nearby Entertainment Centre. Licensed. Reservations recommended. L, D, daily. AE, BC, DC, MC, V.

New Tai Yuen. 31–37 Dixon St., Sydney; 212–5244. The sign on the downstairs window of this restaurant promises "top quality food, happy atmosphere, friendly service, reasonable price," and also states that "this is one of the most popular restaurants in Sydney." The sign must bring people in, because it is. Licensed. Reservations advisable. L, D, daily. AE, BC, DC, MC. TC ($A, $US).

Nine Dragons. 39 Dixon St., Sydney; 211–3661. Nine Dragons is well known for its yum chas, and these are particularly busy on weekends. It offers an extensive Cantonese menu. Licensed. L, D, daily. AE, BC, DC, MC, V.

Inexpensive

China Sea. 94 Hay St., Haymarket (1½ km/1 mi); 211–1698. A Cantonese restaurant, where the clientele is mostly Chinese. Experiment with one of the dishes listed on the walls. Licensed. L, D, daily (till 2:00 A.M.). BC, DC, MC, V.

Old Tai Yuen. 110 Hay St., Sydney; 211–3782. Perched above the entrance to Chinatown, the Old Tai Yuen is an old favorite among visitors to the district. It serves all the most popular Chinese dishes in an atmosphere of laminex tables, linoleum floors, and plenty of noise. Licensed or BYO. L, D, daily. AE, BC, DC, MC, V. TC.

ENGLISH

Inexpensive

Home Cooking. 292 Bondi Rd., Bondi (7 km/4 mi east); 30–5454. A daily-changing blackboard menu includes old favorites like roast beef and Yorkshire pudding or cottage pie and puds such as trifle or fruit crumble and custard. And what English meal would be complete without bread and butter and a cup of tea? Home Cooking is small and cozy, tables have lace tablecloths, and there are old English-style pictures on the wall to add to the atmosphere. BYO. D, Mon.–Sat. BC, MC.

SYDNEY

FRENCH
Deluxe

Berowra Waters Inn. Berowra Waters (40 km/25 mi north); 456-1027. Gay Bilson has a battalion of keen patrons who return again and again to sample some of the finest cuisine in Australia. Hers is also a popular restaurant for "special occasions." For an unusual day's outing (and a really expensive experience!) take a small Aquatic Airways seaplane (919-5966) from Rose Bay to this restaurant perched right on the water's edge of Berowra Creek. Licensed. L. Sun.; D, Fri.-Sat. Reservations essential. AE, BC, DC, MC, V. TC ($A).

♦ **Claude's.** 10 Oxford St., Woollahra (4 km/2½ mi east); 331-2325. Chefs Josephine and Damien Pignolet run one of the best French restaurants in Sydney. It is small and charming, and service is excellent. Popular nights are the first Fri. of each month—bouillabaisse night—and the first Sat., when a Fine Bouche menu is offered—this is a gourmet night, with a set menu of up to six courses. BYO. D, Tues.-Sat. Reservations are essential—sometimes up to two months ahead for weekends. No cards. TC ($A).

Kables. 199 George St., Sydney; 238-0000. As elegant as the Regent of Sydney hotel it is housed within, Kables prides itself on its "cuisine de marché," using products fresh daily from the markets. Game, seafood, poultry, and meat are prepared creatively and presented by attentive staff. The fixed-price lunch menu should appeal to those who enjoy excellent cuisine but lack a deluxe wallet. Licensed. L, Mon.-Fri.; D, Mon.-Sun. Reservations preferred especially for D, Sat. AE, BC, DC, MC, V. TC can be cashed at hotel.

Expensive

Barrenjoey House. 1108 Barrenjoey Rd., Palm Beach (39 km/24 m north); 919-4001. This restaurant can be reached by seaplane (919-5966) from Rose Bay, and it nestles comfortably in one of Sydney's most attractive beach suburbs. The food is excellent: fresh and innovative. Enjoy it from a table on the large, leafy terrace on a sunny day or by the open fire in winter. Licensed. Reservations recommended. L, Sat.-Sun. and public holidays. D, daily in summer, Fri.-Sun. in winter. AE, BC, V. TC ($A).

Contented Sole. 156 Hall St., Bondi (7 km/4 mi east); 30-6261. French-style seafood is the restaurant's specialty: seafood pie is recommended. BYO. D., Tues.-Sat. Reservations advisable. AE, BC, MC, V.

Pegrum's. 36 Gurner St., Paddington (5 km/3 mi east); 357-4776. Another successful husband-and-wife team on Sydney's French restaurant scene, with Mark Armstrong as chef and Lorinda at the front of the house. Elegant but relaxing atmosphere in apricot hues with sparkling French silverware. Imaginative cuisine and interesting specials that vary according to what is available at the markets, such as pheasant or hare, or salmon, or crayfish from Tasmania. Licensed. L, Fri.; D, Tues.-Sat. Reservations a must. AE, BC, DC, MC, V. TC ($A).

Puligny's. 240 Military Rd., Neutral Bay (5 km/3 m north); 908-2552). One of the best restaurants on the North Shore: elegant and professional with food

DINING OUT

that is innovative but not fussy. Leave room for the superb dessert. This would be a good restaurant to visit on the way back to the city after a day in Manly. Licensed. Reservations necessary. L, Fri; D, Tues.–Sat. BC, MC, V. TC ($A).

Reflections. 1075 Barrenjoey Rd., Palm Beach (39 km/24 mi north); 919–5893. Palm Beach is a very attractive northern beach area of Sydney and Reflections a good spot for lunch during a Sun. drive. The cuisine is excellent and the service friendly. Licensed. Reservations necessary. L, Sun.; D, Wed.–Sat. (winter); daily (summer). BC, MC, V.

Moderate–Expensive

Bon Cafard. 379 Liverpool St., Darlinghurst (2 km/1 mi east); 357–5318. Although "cafard" means cockroach, you won't be taking any risks visiting this establishment. The food is tasty and plentiful and the environment casual. BYO. L, Fri.; D, Tues.–Sun. Reservations recommended. BC, MC. TC ($A).

Moderate

Cactus Café. 150 Victoria St., Potts Point (2 km/1 mi east); 358–3705. This is a fashionable and informal establishment: a modern look with white laminex tables, chairs in yellow (the café's main color), and two huge murals, one of the desert. The food reflects a Seychelles influence, and there is a good choice for a light or full meal. Popular are the enormous and arty cocktails, including the pina colada, cactus coola, and cactus rose. BYO. D, Wed.–Sun. Reservations recommended. AE, BC, DC, MC, V. TC.

L'Aubbergarde. 353 Cleveland St., Surry Hills (2 km/1 mi southeast); 699–5929. French-provincial-style restaurant of the red-and-white-checked-tablecloth mode. Food is unpretentious but reliable; the blackboard menu offers dishes such as coquilles St. Jacques, filet au poivre, and filet béarnaise. There is also a very reasonable fixed-price three-course menu offered for lunch and dinner, Mon.–Thurs. Licensed. L, Mon.–Fri.; D, Mon.–Sat. Reservations advised, particularly on weekends. AE, BC, MC, V. TC ($A).

The Little Snail. 96a Curlewis St., Bondi (7 km/4 mi east); 300–0042. Delicious French cuisine, attractively presented. The fixed-price menu is particularly good value for its high quality. Licensed. D., Mon.–Sat. Reservations recommended on Fri. and Sat. AE, BC, DC, MC, V.

Rush Cutter. 129 Bayswater Rd., Rushcutters Bay (3 km/2 mi east); 331–4393. The food at Rush Cutter is very good; ingredients are of excellent quality and expertly prepared. There is International food here as well as French. Casual restaurant. BYO. D, Mon.–Sat. AE, BC, DC, MC, V.

Inexpensive

La Guillotine. 9 Albion Place, Sydney; 264–1487. Informal, bistro-style restaurant with wooden tables and bench seats. It specializes in omelettes and is housed in the cinema belt of the city. Also offered are dishes such as bouillabaisse, poulet Marengo, and ratatouille. Licensed. L, Mon.–Fri.; D, Mon.–Sun. Reservations advised. BC.

GREEK

Moderate

Athens Star. 65 Alexander St., Crows Nest (5 km/3 mi north); 439–4734 or 439–8803. A selection of traditional Greek dishes are served in an informal atmosphere. Chef Dimitri recommends the "Athens Special" of lamb and stuffed vegetables. Licensed. L, Mon.–Fri.; D, Mon.–Sat. AE, BC, DC, MC, V. TC ($A, $US).

Iliad. 126 Liverpool St., Sydney; 267–7644. The Iliad is a small, informal restaurant and offers some interesting, creative Greek cuisine as well as traditional dishes. Popular with the political fraternity, so you may eavesdrop on affairs of state. Licensed. L, Mon.–Fri.; D, Mon.–Sat. Reservations advisable. AE, BC, DC, MC, V. TC ($A, $US).

Inexpensive–Moderate

Diethnes. 336 Pitt St., Sydney; 267–8956. A cheerful, friendly restaurant, Diethnes always seems busy. It offers all the Greek favorites, including taramasalata, tzatziki, eggplant and garlic sauce, moussaka, and dolmades. Licensed. L, D, Mon.–Sat. Reservations advisable. AE, BC, MC. TC ($A).

Kakavia. 458 Elizabeth St., Surry Hills (2 km/1 mi southeast); 699–3562. A simple, informal restaurant, Kakavia offers very tasty food, including kakavia, a Greek bouillabaisse. Worth a visit. Live entertainment is provided Fri. and Sat. nights. Licensed. L, Mon.–Fri.; D, Sun.–Sat. Reservations recommended. AE, BC, DC, MC, V.

INDIAN

Expensive

Mayur. MLC Centre, 19 Martin Place, Sydney; 235–2361. Sydney's most glamorous Indian restaurant, the Mayur offers spicy and delicate curries and excellent tandooris and enticingly prepares a range of chicken, lamb, prawn, fish, and beef dishes. The tandoori oven has walls that allow diners to watch the bright orange marinated meats and the naan bread being prepared and cooked. Licensed. L, Mon.–Fri.; D, Mon.–Sat. Reservations recommended. AE, BC, DC, MC, V. TC ($A).

Moderate

Shree Punjab. 121 Bondi Rd., Bondi (7 km/4-1/3 mi east); 389–2300. Offers quality food in generous proportions, delivered with pleasant service. The menu is varied and includes delicious chicken (the clientele's favorite), prawn and lamb tandoori, and a range of curries. Licensed or BYO. L, Mon.–Fri.; D, daily. AE, BC, DC, MC, V.

Tandoori House. 471 Pacific Hwy., Crows Nest (5 km/3 mi north); 439–3468. A popular and busy restaurant on Sydney's North Shore. It, too, offers the marinated, half-baked, half-smoked tandoori meat dishes prepared in an oven in public view. Curries are also served and the atmosphere is relaxed and

DINING OUT

informal. Licensed and BYO. L, Mon.–Fri.; D, daily. Reservations recommended. AE, BC, DC, MC, V.

Inexpensive–Moderate

Amar's. 39 Goulburn St., Sydney; 211–4165. Another popular Indian restaurant, on the edge of Chinatown. To sample as many dishes as possible, try Amar's "banquet," the Maharaja's Khana. It has a mixed entrée, four main courses with all the trimmings, and a dessert. Amar's has a downstairs vegetarian section and snack bar that is also a nonsmoking area. Licensed and BYO. L, Mon.–Fri.; D, daily. AE, BC, DC, MC, V.

Indian Experience. 2 Sydney Rd., Manly (14 km/8½ m northeast); 977–7086. When you're looking for somewhere to relax after a day exploring Manly, try this restaurant. There's a bar for pre-dinner drinks and a selection of very good tandoori and curries to choose from. Licensed. L, Mon.–Sat.; D, daily. Reservations recommended weekends. AE, BC, DC, MC, V. TC ($A).

Indian Experience. 2 Albert St., Circular Quay; 27–9323. Indian Experience's city restaurant is handy to the Opera House and to the Rocks area. A very reasonably priced buffet lunch available, and dinner offers an à la carte menu. Live sitar music Fri. and Sat. evenings. Licensed. L, Mon.–Fri. and Sun.; D, Mon.–Sat. AE, BC, DC, MC, V.

Param's. 222 Oxford St., Woollahra (4 km/2½ mi east); 389–3740. Some Indian and some Sri Lankan food is served here. The cooking is creative and the flavors varied and interesting. Try the traditional Thali for a variety of flavors. Param's specializes in seafood dishes (about 12 of them on the menu, depending on what's fresh at the market) and vegetarian dishes. BYO. D, daily. BC, MC, V. TC ($A).

INDONESIAN

Expensive

Bali. 80 Oxford St., Darlinghurst (2 km/1 mi east); 331–3544. A very popular restaurant that serves some unusual dishes. The Szechuan-style chicken with dry red pepper apparently has a lot of fans. BYO. L, Mon.–Fri.; D, Mon.–Sun. AE, BC, DC, MC, V.

Bali. 137 King St., Newtown (5 km/3 mi west); 51–3441. A big restaurant that serves big plates of tasty Indonesian food, including a chili prawns specialty. Licensed or BYO. L, D, Mon.–Sun. AE, BC, DC, MC, V.

Borobodur. 263 Oxford St., Darlinghurst (2 km/1 mi east); 331–3464. Very good value, with a wide choice of tasty and well-prepared food. Regulars recommend the rystaffel (for two): a generous selection of ten different Indonesian dishes. D, Mon.–Sat. BC, MC, V.

Warung Indonesia. 117 York St., Sydney; 267–1539. Favorites here are rystaffel, satay, nasi goreng, and the smorgasbord. Licensed. L, Mon.–Sat.; D, daily. Reservations necessary for more than six people. BC, DC, V.

INTERNATIONAL

Deluxe

Primo's Lafayette. 76 Elizabeth Bay Rd., Elizabeth Bay (3 km/1-8/10 mi east); 358–4516. Primo's has a fairly wealthy clientele who have felt comfortable in its heavy plush surroundings since the 1930s. The menu is extensive, with a strong Italian influence, and offers perennial favorites such as Steak Diane and spaghetti marinara, with some additional and memorable surprises. Licensed. D, Tues.–Sun. Reservations always advisable. AE, BC, DC, JCB, MC, V. TC.

Prunier's Chiswick Gardens. 65 Ocean St., Woollahra (4 km/2½ mi east); 32–1974 or 32–1619. Set in huge gardens and established over 40 years, Prunier's has a new image: decor is light, bright, and elegant, and its menu reflects a strong classic French base. Licensed. L, Mon.–Fri.; D, Mon.–Sat. Reservations daily. AE, BC, DC, MC, V. TC ($A, $US).

Expensive–Deluxe

Butlers. 123 Victoria St., Potts Point (2 km/1 mi east); 357–1988. A fashionable eating place, this is a pretty and elegant restaurant set amid sandstock brick interior walls and tables decorated with Royal Copenhagen print cloths. The food shows a nouvelle cuisine influence and alters daily according to the fresh ingredients available. Dining on the terrace gives you magnificent views across the rooftops to the landmarks of the city. Licensed. L, Fri.; D, Mon.–Sat. Reservations recommended. AE, BC, DC, MC, V. TC ($A, $US).

Expensive

Archibalds. Holiday Inn Menzies Hotel, 14 Carrington St., Sydney; 2–0232. A good small and traditional restaurant. Archibald's is a popular lunch spot and serves dishes based on the freshest of fish, meat, herbs, and fruit, using light sauces. Licensed. L, Mon.–Fri.; D, Mon.–Sat. Reservations recommended. AE, BC, DC, JCB, V, MC. TC.

Chelsea. 119 Macleay St., Potts Point (2 km/1 mi east); 358–4333. Traditional in style and cuisine, Chelsea is a spot for coffee, a drink, a snack, as well as a full meal. Charcoal grills and seafoods are popular selections from a mixed à la carte menu. Licensed. L, Mon.–Sat.; D, daily. AE, BC, JCB, MC, V. TC ($A).

Coachmen. 763 Bourke St., Redfern (3 km/2 mi south); 699–7705 or 699–5110. As well as good food and atmosphere and attentive staff, the Coachmen has a live band for dancing (except Sun. and Mon.). Reasonably formal, but relaxed atmosphere. Licensed. Reservations advisable. L, Mon.–Fri.; D, daily. AE, BC, DC, MC, V, TC ($A, $US).

Eliza's Garden Restaurant. 29 Bay St., Double Bay (4.5 km/3 mi east); 32–3656. This pleasant restaurant attracts the Eastern Suburbs social set, and no wonder: It's in the heart of their shopping area, the smorgasbord or à la carte meals are imaginatively prepared, and the environment is upscale but relaxed. A shaded garden area is perfect for summer dining, and there are open fires in

DINING OUT

winter. Licensed. L, D, daily. Reservations recommended. AE, BC, DC, MC, V. TC.

Moderate–Expensive

Different Drummer. 32 Burton St., Darlinghurst (2 km/1 mi east); 331–3290. Housed in a convict-built cottage, the restaurant has a pleasant courtyard for predinner drinks. Menu is modern in style and includes some Asian and European food and a variety of seafood. Ingredients are fresh and seasonal. Licensed. L, Tues.–Fri. in summer; D, Tues.–Sat. Reservations recommended on weekends. AE, BC, DC, MC, V. TC ($A).

Kinsela's. 383 Bourke St., Darlinghurst (2 km/1 mi east); 331–3100. Kinselas is popular and fashionable, and it really buzzes some nights. A point of interest is the section of the restaurant housed within the Art Deco chapel of the former funeral parlor that gave Kinsela's its name. There is a bar upstairs for pre- or post-dinner drinks, and the restaurant serves supper until 1:00 A.M. Kinsela's also has cabaret shows in a separate theater-style restaurant and presents some very good entertainment. (See Theater Restaurants section). Licensed. D, Mon.–Sat. Reservations recommended. AE, BC, DC, MC, V. TC ($A).

Maestro. 120 Glenmore Rd., Paddington (4 km/2½ mi east); 331–5084. Maestro has a small garden with fountain where it is pleasant to dine and be tempted by the groaning platter of today's fresh seafood. Choose your own wine from a walk-in wine cellar. Specialties include fresh pasta and suckling pig. Licensed. L, Mon.–Fri.; D, Mon.–Sat. Reservations necessary weekends. AE, BC, DC, MC, V. TC ($A).

Moderate

Miss Betty's. 242 Oxford St., Padington (4 km/2½ mi east); 331–7440. Call in here for a delicious brunch or a light meal. Salads are Miss Betty's specialty; a delicious Indian salad includes poached chicken, curry-flavored mayonnaise, celery, pecans, and papadams. Licensed for wine only. B, Sat.; L, D, daily. Reservations recommended for garden area. BC, MC, V. TC ($A).

Inexpensive

Restaurant on the Park. Art Gallery Rd., The Domain; 232–1322. As the address indicates, the Restaurant is just opposite the Art Gallery and the perfect spot for lunch after a morning's viewing of the Gallery's collection. It is set in the large grassy and tree-filled Domain and next to the Royal Botanic Gardens. Eat outdoors, and don't be distracted by the armies of joggers that pound by during the week. A very reasonably priced three-course fixed-price menu is served. Licensed. L, daily. BC, MC, V. TC ($A).

San Francisco Grill. Hilton Hotel, 259 Pitt St., Sydney; 266–0610. Expect first-class service from this formal and elegant restaurant. There are a pianist and violinist to entertain you evenings. Try the Sydney rock oysters, or a San Francisco Grill specialty: steak tartae with caviar, prepared to your liking at the table. Licensed. L, Mon.–Fri.; D, Mon.–Sat. Reservations recommended. AE, BC, DC, MC, V.

ITALIAN

Expensive

Abbey. 156 Pyrmont Bridge Rd., Glebe (3 km/2 mi. west); 660–4792, 660–1211. Set in a restored stone church over a century old, the Abbey is ornately furnished and surrounded by garden, but don't expect to see an altar when you glance up from your meal: A cocktail bar is in its place. The food is rich, with a strong traditional Italian influence. Licensed. L, Mon.–Fri.; D, Mon.–Sat. Reservations usually necessary. AE, BC, DC, MC, V. TC.

Beppi's. Corner Stanley and Yurong Sts., East Sydney (2 km/1 mi east); 357–4558 or 357–4391. Beppi has delighted Sydney palates for over 30 years. Friendly and efficient waiters in black tie tempt you with a wide menu and delicious specials. Ask for a table in the cellar area and you'll be surrounded by floor-to-ceiling wine. Licensed. L, Mon.–Fri.; D, Mon.–Sat. Reservations advised. AE, BC, DC, MC, V. TC.

Darcy's. 92 Hargrave St., Paddington (4 km/2½ mi east); 32–3706 or 32–4512. Popular with the wealthy Eastern Suburbs set and with businessmen at lunch, Darcy's has a formal atmosphere, pleasant staff, and, from the antipasto on, a satisfied clientele. Licensed. L, Mon.–Fri.; D, Mon.–Sat. Reservations recommended particularly for dinner. AE, BC, DC, JCB, MC, V. TC.

Pulcinella. 30a Bayswater Rd., Kings Cross; 358–6530. An old favorite with Sydneysiders who find dining in the vine-covered courtyard on a sunny day or balmy evening a pleasant experience. Sat. lunch here is quite an event for observing Sydney lawyers, media people, and politicians. The food is very good, and the list of daily specialties is larger than your arm; all are mouthwatering. Licensed. L, Sat.; D, Mon.–Fri. Reservations recommended. AE, BC, MC. TC ($A).

◆ **Taylor's.** 203 Albion St., Surry Hills (2 km/1 mi southeast); 33–5100. Set in a row of beautifully restored colonial cottages, Taylor's with its Georgian décor does not look very Italian. The food, however, is: northern Italian cuisine imaginatively prepared and attractively presented. Book a garden table when the weather obliges with its best. Licensed. L, Fri.; D, Tues.–Sat. Reservations essential. AE, BC, DC, V.

Moderate–Expensive.

Al Corso. 440 New South Head Rd., Double Bay (4.5 km/2-8/10 mi east); 327–7546. Al Corso offers expertly prepared cuisine in a quietly formal but friendly setting. You may dine alongside some of Sydney's top political figures here on their days off. Licensed. L, Wed.–Fr.; D, Mon.–Sat. Reservations recommended. AE, BC, DC, MC, V. TC.

Moderate

◆ **Mario's.** 73 Stanley St., Darlinghurst (2 km/1 km east); 331–4945. Noisy and cheerful, Mario's is a popular restaurant with the lunch crowd. The staff are friendly and are happy to tantalize you with descriptions of the day's

DINING OUT

specials. Licensed. Reservations recommended. L, Mon.–Fri.; D, Mon.–Sat. BC, MC, V. TC.

Sandro's. 220 William St., Kings Cross; 357-2046. Delicious seafood antipasto, veal, and liver dishes are dispensed by friendly waiters, and charm by the host, Sandro, who seems always at his post in this basement-level restaurant. Casual and relaxed environment. Licensed. L, Mon.–Fri.; D, Mon.–Sat. AE, BC, DC, MC, V. TC ($A).

The **Leichhardt area** (around 7 km/4-1/3 mi west of the city) is the center of Sydney's large Italian community. It has its own pasticcerias, fresh pasta shops, alimentari, and numerous cafés and restaurants. Every few doors, it seems, there is the opportunity to sample a delicious gelato, a bowl of creamy pasta, a veal or seafood specialty, or a custard-and-liqueur-filled pastry. A small sample of the restaurants available (bookings advisable on weekends):

La Botte d'Oro. 137 Marion St., Leichhardt; 560-1349. B.Y.O. L, Mon.–Sat.; D, daily.

La Rustica. 435 Parramatta Rd., Leichhardt; 569-5824. Licensed. L, D, Mon.–Sat. AE, BC, DC, MC, V.

La Zagara. 132 Norton St., Leichhardt; 560-7957. Licensed or B.Y.O. Mon.–Fri.; D, daily. AE, BC, DC, MC, V. TC ($A).

Pan Roma. 397 Parramatta Rd., Leichhardt. 560-5874. Licensed. L, Mon.–Fri.; D, daily. AE, BC, MC. TC ($A, $US).

Inexpensive

♦ **Atlanta.** 41 Crown St., Woolloomooloo (1 km/6/10 mi east); 33-6467. A very popular cheapie amongst Sydneysiders, the Atlanta is usually busy and noisy. Select from dishes such as pastas, quail, assorted meat casseroles. Licensed. L, Mon.–Fri.; D, Mon.–Sat. Reservations recommended. BC, MC, V.

Bill and Toni's. 74 Stanley St., East Sydney (2 km/1 mi east); 357-4702. Another cheapie that's usually noisy and packed and frequented by local Italians. There is fast service and a limited but ever-changing choice of dishes, each accompanied by a salad. Downstairs for coffee. L, D, daily. No cards.

♦ **No Name.** 81 Stanley St., East Sydney (2 km/1 mi east); 357-4711. As if further proof were needed that the locals flock to cheap Italian restaurants, No Name shows just that. There's often a line waiting on the stairs, tables are shared, and service is speedy. Included in your two-course meal is bread, milk or cordial, and a basic salad. The *Arch Coffee Lounge* downstairs serves great coffee. BYO. L, D, daily. No cards.

JAPANESE

Expensive–Deluxe

Keisan Restaurant. Holiday Inn Menzies Hotel, 14 Carrington St., Sydney; 2-0232. To enter Keisan, patrons walk past a Japanese water garden into a courtyard depicting a village street scene from 16-century Japan. Traditional Japanese cuisine is available in a number of settings; a Sushi bar, tatami rooms (private rooms where you sit on the floor), and a veranda area with tables and chairs. Licensed. L, Mon.–Fri.; D, Mon.–Sat. AE, BC, DC, JCB, V, MC. TC ($A).

Suntory. 529 Kent St., Sydney; 267-2900. A favorite with Japanese businessmen and the expense-account set, Suntory is Sydney's most exclusive Japanese restaurant. Only the best ingredients are used, and the service is excellent. The restaurant and bar overlook a pretty Japanese garden and pool. Licensed. L, Mon.–Sat.; D, Mon.–Sat. Reservations are essential. AE, BC, DC, MC, V. TC.

Moderate

Edosei. 74 Clarence St., Sydney; 29-8746. Quite an attractive restaurant, Edosei specializes in sushi but offers a range of other Japanese dishes. Licensed. L, Mon.–Fri.; D, Tues.–Sat. AE, BC, DC, JCB, MC, V. TC ($A).

Miyako. 459 New South Head Rd., Double Bay (4½ km/2-8/10 mi east); 327-2383. A fashionable Japanese restaurant, Miyako has fresh seafood as one of its specialties. Teppan meals are produced with much flourish while clients sit around the hot plates and watch the performance. Licensed. Reservations recommended. L, Mon.–Fri.; D, daily. AE, BC, DC, MC, V. TC ($A).

Inexpensive

Fuji Tempura Bar. 27 Angel Arcade, Sydney; 231-1740. A popular lunch spot, where you may have to share a table. Don't expect to linger over your meal. The tempura, as you would hope, is crisp and light. BYO. L, Mon.–Fri.; D, Wed.–Fri.

Kiyomasa. 3a Spit Rd., Mosman (7 km/5 m north); 969-1150. A high-quality, inexpensive Japanese restaurant. The menu is small, but the food is delicious. B.Y.O. D, Tues.–Sat. AE, BC, DC, MC, V. TC ($A).

Noriko Teppan Steakhouse. 10 Martin Place, Sydney; 232-5785. This is a small restaurant, closely packed with tables, and popular for lunch. To help you in your search, it is below ground level opposite the GPO. Rice, soup, and tea come as part of your meal, and there are delicious tempura and a range of teppan dishes to select from. BYO. L, Mon.–Fri.; D, Mon.–Fri. Reservations advisable at lunch. AE, BC. TC ($A).

KOREAN

Inexpensive

Golden Rabbit. 1–2 Angel Place, Sydney; 221-3087. Spicy Korean/Chinese food in a tiny restaurant. BYO. L, D, Mon.–Sat. AE, BC.

Korea House. 171 Victoria St., Potts Point; 358-6601, 358-4349. By no means a glamorous restaurant, Korea House serves some inexpensive and delicious food. A large group would enjoy the do-it-yourself beef barbecue. Licensed. L, Mon.–Sat.; D, daily. AE, BC, DC, MC, V. TC ($A, $US).

LEBANESE

Inexpensive–Moderate

Abdul's. 563 Elizabeth St., Surry Hills (2 km/1 mi southeast); 698–1275. You might suspect there's one giant underground kitchen serving the many Lebanese restaurants in this area. Abdul's is an old favorite among them and has an enormous menu to select from. BYO. L, D, daily. AE, BC, DC, MC. TC ($A, $US).

Emad's. 298 Cleveland St., Surry Hills (2 km/1 mi southeast); 698–2631. A well-established restaurant offering tasty food and a relaxed atmosphere. BYO. L, Tues.–Fri.; D, daily. Lunch is by reservation only. BC, MC.

Ya Habibi. 100 Campbell Pole, Bondi Beach (8 km/5 m east); 30–4526. Here's one situated away from the Lebanese restaurant belt, but its food is delicious and it's handy to the beach. Licensed or B.Y.O. L, D, daily. AE, BC, DC, MC, V.

Inexpensive

Omar Khayyam. 272 Cleveland St., Surry Hills (2 km/1 mi southeast); 699–3546. A pleasant and simple restaurant—although it does boast tablecloths—Omar Khayyam has an excellent-value set-price menu offering eight main dishes, with trimmings, dessert, and coffee. BYO. L, Wed.–Sun.; D, daily. AE, BC, MC, V. TC ($A).

MALAY

Moderate

Malaya. 761 George St., Sydney; 211–4659. Chinese and Malay food is served here by efficient staff. Sates are popular, and the hot prawn laskas can send some running for a fire extinguisher. Licensed. L, D, daily. AE, BC, DC, MC, V. TC ($A).

Inexpensive.

Malaysian Inn. 231 A Victoria St., Darlinghurst (2 km/1 mi east); 33–0993. Excellent service and cooking in this informal restaurant make the Inn a good place to try unusual Malaysian food. BYO. D, Mon.–Sun. AE, BC, MC, V. TC ($A).

Satay Stick. 17 Goulburn St., Sydney; 211–5556. The sates here are cooked over an open fire and are very tasty—an observer can tell from the number of empty sticks left on the plates. A variety of other dishes are also available. Licensed. L, Mon.–Fri.; D, daily. AE, BC, DC, MC, V. TC.

MEXICAN

Inexpensive

Fiesta Cantina. 306 Oxford St., Bondi Junction (7 km/4 mi east); 389–3665. Fiesta Cantina offers tasty renditions of all the favorite combinations of spicy meat, beans, cheese and corn breads, plus a few interesting specials besides. BYO. L, Mon.–Fri.; D, daily. AE, BC, MC, V.

That New Mexican Place. 681 Military Rd., Mosman (7 km/4 mi northeast); 969-7269. Quite well known, so obviously not that new anymore, this restaurant serves a comprehensive menu of Mexican goodies. BYO. D, daily. AE, BC, DC, MC, V. TC ($A).

SEAFOOD

Expensive

♦ **Doyle's on the Beach.** 11 Marine Parade, Watson's Bay (11 km/6-8/10 mi east); 337-2007. For a really comprehensive view of Sydney Harbour you might well do a seafood-restaurant crawl, and enjoy it from all sides. Here is a perfect place to start, where dining indoors (ask for a table near the front) or outdoors allows you a view up the harbor to the city skyscape across sparkling water, or of brilliant sunsets and the night lights of Sydney. The Doyle family has been catching and serving fish for many years and is an institution on the Sydney restaurant scene. Casual dress. Licensed. L, D, 7 days. BC, MC, V. TC ($A, $US).

Sails. 2 Henry Lawson Ave., McMahons Point (5 km/3 mi north); 920-5998, 920-5793. On the opposite side of the harbor, the décor of this restaurant is uninspiring but the magnificent views past the squeals and lights of Luna Park under the enormous span of the Harbour Bridge to the Opera House make that irrelevant. Fresh fish is served daily. Try the Balmain bugs—something you won't see at home. Catch a ferry across to the wharf next to the restaurant. Ask the staff for timetable details when booking. Licensed. L, D, Mon.–Sat. Reservations are advisable, particularly in summer. AE, BC, DC, MC, V. TC ($A).

Views. Lyne Park, Rose Bay (6 km/3¾ mi east); 371-6799. A little farther round the foreshores of the harbor toward the city is the first of the Sails restaurants. It is built right on the water's edge, within a park, and overlooks the comings and goings of cruisers, sailing boats, and seaplanes. Views serves modern Australian cuisine with an emphasis on seafood that is fresh daily. Meat dishes are also available. Licensed. B, Sun.; L, Tues.–Sun.; D, Tues.–Sat. Reservations advisable, particularly on weekends. AE, BC, DC, MC, V. TC ($A).

Walter's Seafoods. Corner Reservoir and Riley Sts., Surry Hills (2 km/1 mi southeast), 211-3240 or 211-2973. Walter's has a wide variety of seafood, including barramundi, a popular but not always available reef fish, and offers lobster as a specialty of the house. There is a courtesy car service available for patrons in the Sydney city area. Licenced. L, Mon.–Fri., Sun.; D, Mon.–Sun. Reservations recommended on weekends. AE, BC, DC, JCB, MC, V. TC.

Waterfront. 27 Circular Quay West, The Rocks; 27-3666. You will probably meet lots of other tourists here because of the Waterfront's magnificent views of the harbor and the Opera House and its location in the historic Rocks area. Dine inside or on the stone-flagged pavement outside beneath masts and sails of an old schooner. Delicious fresh food, including memorable hot or cold mixed

DINING OUT

seafood platters. Licensed. L, D, daily. Reservations recommended. AE, BC, DC, MC, V. TC ($A).

Moderate–Expensive

Claudine's Strand Seafood. 50 The Strand Arcade (1st floor), Sydney; 233-3473. Here's a seafood restaurant not located by the sea. Work your way through the exclusive and novel shops of the historic Strand shopping arcade and end up here for a very reasonable fixed-price lunch menu. Sit indoors or on the terrace overlooking the elegant arcade. More expensive if you select à la carte. The food is prepared from fresh ingredients and cooked with flair. Licensed. L, D, Mon.–Sat. Reservations recommended for lunch. AE, BC, DC, MC, V. TC ($A).

Mischa's Seafood Restaurant. The Esplanade, Balmoral Beach (8 km/5 mi north); 969–9827 or 969–3720. On the northern side of the harbor, Mischa's is great to reach by aquacab, which will drop you at the end of the beach. Enjoy a stroll along the Esplanade back to the wharf after your meal. Mischa, who looks as though he enjoys his fare, serves delicious seafoods, exotic cocktails, and breakfasts like the "Balmoral Schooner": hot cakes, eggs and bacon, fried potatoes, toast and coffee. Licensed. B, L, D, daily. Reservations recommended; the earlier you book, the closer you get to the window and the view. AE, BC, DC, JCB, MC, V. TC.

Moderate

♦ **Le Kiosk.** Shelly Beach, Bower St., Manly (14 km/8-6/10 mi north); 977–4185. A short stroll from Manly's main surfing beach, Le Kiosk overlooks its own very pretty beach, where you can swim after lunch. Return to the city by hydrofoil or ferry. Le Kiosk's specialty is a mixed hot and cold seafood platter. Licensed. B, Sun.; L, D, daily. Reservations are necessary. AE, BC, DC, MC, V. TC ($A, $US).

Moderate–Inexpensive

♦ **Bob and Di's.** 29 Kent St., Millers Point (3 km/2 mi north); 27–3137. Tasty and straightforward fish and chips in this simple restaurant in the wharves area. Take-out also available. Bob and Di always try to have a selection of reef fish, such as red emperor, coral trout, or parrot fish, when available. BYO. L, Mon.–Fri.; D, Tues.–Sat. (closes early). Reservations recommended. No cards.

Sorrento. 7 Elizabeth St., Sydney; 27–1419. Many old customers from its "no-frills" fish-and-chips days at Circular Quay have followed Sorrento to its classier new establishment. The meals are still good and served in generous proportions. Attracts the business crowd at lunchtime. Licensed. L, Mon.–Fri.; D, Mon.–Sat. AE, BC, DC, MC, V.

SYDNEY

SPANISH

Moderate

Captain Torres. 73 Liverpool St., Sydney; 264-5574. Generous servings of strongly flavored good Spanish fare available here, delivered by friendly Spanish waiters. Licensed. L, D, daily. AE, BC, DC, MC, V.

Don Quixote. 1 Albion Place, Sydney; 264-5903 or 264-2788. A spacious restaurant with the Spanish cowhide-and-wood look and slate or stone floors. Don Quixote has open fires in winter and a live band for dancing on Fri. and Sat. nights. If you want to try the roast suckling pig, order when making reservations. Licensed. L, Mon.–Fri.; D, Mon.–Sat. Reservations recommended. AE, BC, DC, MC, V.

Inexpensive–Moderate

Raquel's Ole Madrid. 145 Oxford St., Darlinghurst (2 km/1 mi east); 357-4618. Raquel's is another jolly, noisy Spanish restaurant, and although its menu is small, everything is tasty, spicy or garlicky. BYO. L with reservations only; D, daily. AE, BC, DC, MC, V. TC ($A).

♦ **Sir John Young Hotel.** 557 George St., Sydney; 267-3608. This may not sound like much of a possibility for Spanish food, but a small restaurant, the *Grand Taverna*, exists behind the bar area, where very tasty paella and seafood are served along with jugs of sangria. It's always packed here, and you may have to share a table. Noisy and informal and worth a visit. Closes early. Licensed. L, D, Mon.–Sat.

SRI LANKA

Inexpensive

Sri Lanka Room. Corner Harris and George sts., Broadway (2 km/1 mi south); 211-4375. Popular for both lunch and dinner, the Sri Lanka Room offers a very inexpensive fixed-price menu at lunch. The food is excellent. Licensed or B.Y.O. (but only from the pub downstairs). L, Tues.–Fri.; D, Tues.–Sat. Reservations recommended. BC, MC, V.

STEAK

Moderate

Clock Cellar. 470 Crown St., Surry Hills (2 km/1 mi southeast); 331-1832. Excellent fresh, juicy steaks of all sorts are available here with great sauces. It's a popular venue for the discriminating carnivores of Sydney, and can be packed with the business set at lunchtime. Licensed. L, Mon.–Fri.; D, Mon.–Sat. Reservations recommended. AE, BC, DC, MC, V. TC ($A, $US).

Johnny Walker's Bistro. Angel Place, Sydney; 232-6099. Also a very popular business lunch spot, Johnny Walker's offers a variety of steaks and barbecued spareribs as specialties of the house. Licensed. L, Mon.–Fri. Reservations recommended. AE, BC, DC, MC, V. TC.

Inexpensive

Century Tavern. 640 George St., Sydney; 264–3157. Watch your fresh steak being cooked and select from fresh salads to accompany it. Generous portions of tasty pavlova or cheesecake to follow. Licensed. L, Mon.–Fri.; D, Mon.–Sat. AE, BC, DC, MC, V.

Phillip's Foote. 101 George St. North, The Rocks; 241–1485 or 27–2665. Select and grill your own steak or fish. Salad and a drink included in the very reasonable price. Licensed. L, D, daily. AE, BC, DC, JCB, MC, V. TC ($A). (See also Australian restaurants.)

THAI

Inexpensive–Moderate

♦ **Bangkok.** 234 Crown St., Darlinghurst (2 km/1 mi east); 33–4804. Service and food are both very good, with delicious curries and seafood the popular choices. Licensed. L, Wed.–Fri.; D, Tues.–Sat. Reservations recommended. AE, BC, DC, MC, V.

Inexpensive

Sawaddee. 290 Bondi Rd., Bondi (7 km/4-1/3 mi east); 300–9783. Sawaddee has a long menu from which to make your difficult choice, though the chicken with ginger and honey and spiced with lemongrass is hard to beat. BYO. D, daily.

Thai Orchid. 628 Crown St., Surry Hills (2 km/1 mi southeast); 698–2097. This looks more Italian than Thai in décor, but serves delicious and inexpensive Thai food. Licensed and B.Y.O. L, Mon.–Fri.; D, Mon.–Sat. AE, BC, DC, MC, V.

VEGETARIAN

Inexpensive

Badde Manors. 37 Glebe Point Rd., Glebe (3 km/1-8/10 mi west); 660–3797. Loads of atmosphere here and always busy and noisy. There is variety in the food, and the blackboard menu changes daily. It could include spinach roulade, pasta with eggplant and tomato sauce, or spring rolls with peanut sauce. There is always a plentiful supply of rich Hungarian cakes, strong coffee, and drinks such as smoothies, whips, herbal teas, and exotic Indian and Indonesian spiced milk tea. Be prepared to share a table with one of the regulars—a student from the local university or someone in evening dress on the way home from the opera. Open till 2:00 A.M. BYO. B, L, D, daily.

Cafe Elan. 379 Crown St., Surry Hills (3 km/2 m east); 332–3858. A stylish restaurant offering a great range of rich dishes such as tofu au poivre, eggplant curry with tomato sauce, and wonderful desserts. Vegan meals are always available and exotic cocktails are a specialty. Licensed. D, Tues.–Sun. BC, MC, V.

SYDNEY

Hammonds Vegetarian. 38 Pittwater Rd., Manly (14 km/8 3/4 m north); 977-5225. After a refreshing trip by ferry you can indulge in the great fresh salads and smorgasbord offered. Guests help themselves to the selection, which is well known for variety and novelty. A friendly, relaxed restaurant. BYO. D, daily. Reservations recommended in summer. TC ($A).

Metro. 26 Burton St., Darlinghurst (2 km/1 mi east); 33-5356. Well known and constantly busy; you may have to stand in line. The food is innovative and rich, with the emphasis on homemade and fresh ingredients—pastas, pastries, salads, etc. It's worth the wait to experience Metro's delights. BYO. D, Thurs.-Sun. No reservations.

Sloane Rangers. 312 Oxford Street, Paddington (5 km/3 mi east); 331-6717. A popular café in the heart of trendy Paddington, it has a fresh, clean atmosphere and a shaded courtyard to sit in out the back. The food is interesting, filling, and cheap, and includes tasty sandwiches, pastas, quiches, and spicy tacos with chili sauce. There is a mouthwatering selection of cakes. Service is brisk, and the front seats provide an opportunity to observe the latest Sydney fashions on parade. BYO. B, L, daily.

Wei Song. 96 Bronte Road, Bondi Junction (7 km/4-1/3 mi east); 389-3108, and 125 Military Rd., Neutral Bay (5 km/3 m north); 90-6471. Sydney's only Chinese Kosher Vegetarian restaurants. The management promises no garlic, onion, eggs (unless requested) coffee, MSG or salt—only fresh juices and organic vegetables. The food is a fascinating combination of fresh fruits, nuts, vegetables, buckwheat noodles, and brown rice in light piquant sauces. Ice creams are homemade with fresh fruit. This may look like a typical Chinese restaurant, but its food is unusual—also tasty and totally satisfying. BYO. Bondi: D, Mon.-Sat.; Neutral Bay: D daily. Reservations essential Fri. and Sat. AE, BC, DC, MC.

VIETNAMESE

Inexpensive

Kim-Van. 147-149 Glebe Point Rd., Glebe (3 km/2 mi west); 660-5252. Kim-Van is a popular restaurant among the students and academics from Sydney University, up the road. It is attractive, the service is efficient, and the food is tasty. BYO. D, Mon., Wed.-Sun. AE, BC, MC.

Oriental Express. 651 George St., Haymarket (1.5 km/1 mi south); 212-3653. A simple restaurant serving authentic Vietnamese food, it has a lengthy menu to select from. BYO. L, Mon.-Sat.; D, daily. AE, BC, DC, MC, V. TC ($A, $US).

FOR THE TOURIST

Expensive–Deluxe

Sydney Harbour is spectacular from the water. The following operators give you the opportunity to enjoy a pleasant evening or lunch at a restaurant and, at the same time, to cruise on one of the most magnificent harbors in the world. The price is in the *expensive–deluxe* range because the cruising and dinner charges are combined.

DINING OUT

Captain Cook Candlelight Dinner Cruise. Circular Quay jetty no. 6; 27-4416. Captain Cook offers a table d'hôte dinner menu, candlelight, and soft music to allow you to enjoy Sydney Harbour from the water by night. There is dancing on the upper deck after dinner. Two dockings: one at 9:30 P.M. for those wanting an early night and another at 11:00 P.M. Licensed. Dinner Tues.–Sat. Reservations essential. AE, BC, DC, JCB, MC, V. TC ($A).

John Cadman Cruising Restaurant. Circular Quay jetty no. 6; Jeffrey St. Wharf, Milsons Point, 27-4416. John Cadman offers an à la carte menu for you to select from, with all meals prepared on board. Relax and watch the beautiful harbor glide by or enjoy dancing after dinner. Licensed. L, Sun.; D, daily. Reservations advisable. AE, BC, DC, JCB, MC, V. TC ($A).

M.V. Southern Cross. Commissioner's Steps, Circular Quay; 264-3510. Candlelight dining on a harbor cruise. The à la carte menu includes fresh seafoods and steaks and French and Japanese cuisine. Dance under the stars after dinner. Licensed. D, daily. Reservations essential. AE, BC, DC, MC, V. TC. ($A).

Expensive

♦ **Bennelong.** Sydney Opera House, Bennelong Point, Sydney; 250-7548. A spectacular place for the visitor to Sydney, Bennelong has extensive harbor views and an interesting à la carte menu. There is often a chamber group playing to add to the elegant atmosphere. A table d'hôte menu is available for pretheater diners, 5:30 P.M.–7:30 P.M. Licensed. L, D, Mon.–Sat. Reservations recommended. AE, BC, DC, JCB, MC, V. TC ($A).

Summit. Level 47, Australia Square Tower, Sydney; 27-9777. A fairly straightforward à la carte menu is offered at the Summit, with the food fresh and well prepared and international in style. A smorgasbord is also available. The restaurant revolves and affords diners marvelous views of Sydney. There is a dance floor, and supper is served Mon.–Sat. Licensed. L, D, daily. Reservations recommended. AE, BC, DC, MC, V. TC ($A).

Sydney Tower. Centrepoint, Market Street, Sydney; 233-3722. There are two revolving levels of restaurants atop this enormous tower. Expansive views of Sydney distract diners from their meals in the à la carte restaurant on Level 1, and in the self-service restaurant on Level 2. The self-service restaurant offers a fixed-price three course meal for a moderate sum. Licensed. Level 1: L, Mon.–Fri.; D, Mon.–Sat. Level 2: L, D, Tues.–Sun. AE, BC, DC, MC, V. TC ($A, $US).

Moderate

Captain Cook Cruises and M.V. Southern Cross. (See *Expensive–Deluxe*, above.) Both offer moderately priced lunch cruises daily, and the *Southern Cross* has a breakfast cruise on Sun. These are perfect for relaxing and scenic meals. Captain Cook provides a smorgasbord lunch and *Southern Cross* a selection of meat or fish of the day, cheese and fruit, and coffee.

Gardens Restaurant. Royal Botanic Gardens, Sydney; 27-2419. On a sunny day, lunch on the wide veranda overlooking the gardens, accompanied by twittering sparrows, is an experience to be recommended. This is a self-service restaurant offering meat dishes, pastas, and salads, and unlike in many self-service places, the menu changes regularly. Licensed. L, daily. Tea available.

COFFEE SHOPS, TEA SHOPS, BRASSERIES. Art Gallery Restaurant. Art Gallery Rd., The Domain (1 km/.6 m east); 232-5425. A nice spot for morning or afternoon tea or a light lunch while you are visiting the Art Gallery of New South Wales. Mon.–Sat., 10:30 A.M.–4:30 P.M.; Sun., midday –4:30 P.M. BC, MC, V.

Bagel Coffee House. 5 Flinders St., Darlinghurst (2 km/1 mi east); 332-1106. Freshly baked bagels with a variety of tasty fillings, as well as various salads and cakes. BYO. Tues.–Thurs., 11:00 A.M.–6:00 P.M. Fri., Sat., 9:00 A.M.–2:00 A.M.; Sun., 9:00 A.M.–10:00 P.M.

Bayswater Brasserie. 32 Bayswater Rd., Kings Cross; 357-2749. There's something for everyone here: a light or a more substantial meal, brunch, or just excellent coffee with a pastry. Fashionable spot, offers courtyard or indoor tables. Licensed. Mon.–Sat., midday–midnight; Sun., 11:00 A.M.–11:00 P.M. No reservations. BC, MC, V. TC ($A).

Cafe Roma. 189 Hay St., Sydney; 211-3909. Great coffee is dispensed in this authentic Italian café, and there's a display window bursting with delicious cakes and pastries. A wide variety of veal, poultry, pasta, and other dishes also available. Décor is no frills: laminex tables and orange vinyl chairs. BYO. Mon.–Fri., 7:30 A.M.–5:30 P.M.; Sat., 7:30 A.M.–3:00 P.M.

Coluzzi Bar. 322 Victoria St., Darlinghurst (2 km/1 mi east); 357-5420. The coffee is the great drawing card in this unpretentious café. It is often crowded with people noisily chatting or just reading their newspapers. Daily, 5:30 A.M.–7:30 P.M.

Cosmopolitan. Knox St., Double Bay (4.5 km/2-8/10 mi east); 327-1866 or 327-5520. The Cosmopolitan is both restaurant and coffee shop and has a piano bar area besides. From the sidewalk café area watch all manner of flashy and expensive cars come and go and the fashionable people around town stroll by. Licensed. Mon.–Sat., 8:30 A.M.–2:00 A.M.; Sun., 9:30 A.M.–2:00 A.M. AE, BC, DC, MC, V.

Gelato Bar. 140 Campbell Parade, Bondi Beach (9 km/5½ mi east); 30-4033 or 30-3211. The Gelato Bar serves meals throughout the day and is always busy. Gelato, ice cream, and amazing cakes bring customers from far and near; the cake display in their front window usually draws a pavement crowd! BYO. Tues.–Sun., 10:00 A.M.–midnight. BC, MC, V. TC.

Giovanni's. 550 George St., Sydney; 267-3321 or 267-3555. A chic and elegant coffee lounge opposite the Sydney Town Hall, Giovanni's serves tea, coffee, and light meals or snacks. The rich cakes are a knockout, especially the Devil's Food. Licensed. Mon.–Wed., 10:00 A.M.–midnight; Thurs., 10:00 A.M.–1:00 P.M.; Fri.–Sat., 10:00 A.M.–2:00 P.M.; Sun., 11:00 A.M.–midnight. AE, BC, DC, MC, V. TC ($A).

Harris's Coffee and Tea Shop. Ground floor, Strand Arcade, Sydney; 231-3002. Set in an attractive and historic arcade. The aroma of coffee permeates

NIGHTLIFE 119

the shop, and numerous varieties of coffees and teas line the shelves, as do a range of implements for brewing or storing same. A good spot to stop for a cuppa and a small cake or biscuit. Mon.–Fri., 7:15 A.M.–5:00 P.M.; Sat., 7:30 A.M.–2:00 P.M.

Hyde Park Barracks Café. Hyde Park Barracks, Macquarie St., Sydney; 223–1155. What a bonus! A very good café providing delicious light meals right at a major Sydney tourist attraction. Interesting selections for lunch and croissants and sandwiches for morning or afternoon tea. Licensed. Daily, 10:00 A.M.–5:00 P.M. BC, MC, V.

Le Croissant Bar. 26 Sydney Square Arcade, Sydney; 264–7296. You'll find Le Croissant Bar underground in the Town Hall Station complex. Well known mainly for its pastries, cakes, and Italian coffee, it also offers a selection of entrées and main meals such as quiches and pasta. Mon.–Wed., Fri., 7:00 A.M.–5:30 P.M.; Thurs., 7:00 A.M.–6:30 P.M.; Sat., 8:00 A.M.–2:00 P.M.

Kellett Café. 3 Kellett St., Kings Cross; 358–4209. Attracts young fashionables and is set on the ground floor of a very pretty terrace house. Light meals, coffee, and cakes are available, and there's a small garden area at the street end to sit in. BYO. Mon., 7:30 P.M.–late; Tues.–Sun., 12:15 P.M.–late. AE, BC, MC, V. TC ($A).

New Edition Tea Rooms. 328a Oxford St., Paddington (4 km/2½ mi east); 33–0744. Enter through the bookshop of the same name and enjoy excellent coffee and light meals, or morning and afternoon teas. Live music entertains both clients and passersby in the street on Sat. BYO. Mon.–Fri., 10:30 A.M.–4:00 P.M.; Sat., 9:30 A.M.–5:00 P.M. Sun., 10:30 A.M.–5:00 P.M. AE, BC, MC, V. TC ($A).

Opera Brasserie. Corner Bridge and Elizabeth St., Sydney; 27–9304. As the name implies, popular with pre- and post-Opera House patrons. It serves light French and Italian food from a small menu and is art decoish in mood. Licensed. Mon.–Fri., midday–midnight; Sat., 6:00 P.M.–midnight. AE, BC, DC, MC, V. TC ($A).

NIGHTLIFE. Sydney is *the* city in Australia for nightlife. Although some of its bars, clubs, and discotheque/nightclubs can be quiet early in the week, as the week goes on the crowds get bigger and noisier and the hours later.

Sydneysiders enjoy a variety of entertainments. Some like to dress up and go dancing until they drop at one of Sydney's fashionable discotheques. Others enjoy a quiet drink at a piano bar; some would rather jostle crowds for a beer in a friendly pub. There are cabaret evenings at the local licensed club, or bawdy entertainment and boisterous singing at a theater restaurant. Jazz buffs might choose a sophisticated supper club or a casual jazz restaurant for entertainment, while a young punk rocker finds a pub dispensing his style of music on the edge of town. Singles will find that although in Sydney there are no bars especially provided for them, most of the bars mentioned in this book, as well as discotheques and supper clubs, are even better.

SYDNEY

Whatever form of entertainment you choose, Sydney can offer it to you, whether you want to sit back and watch or jump right in and participate.

BARS

Often called hotels, due to an old licensing law that required overnight accommodations to be available, many bars close around 11:00 P.M.

The Cortile. Intercontinental Hotel, Macquarie St., Sydney; 230–0200. In the center of the historic Treasury Building that forms the heart of the hotel. A pleasant place for a drink during the day or in the evening, when a chamber group performs. A good spot to people-watch. Daily, 11:00 A.M.–midnight. No cover, no minimum.

Farthings Cocktail Bar. North Sydney Travelodge; 92–0499. A pleasant bar on the north side. A snack menu is available from the bar, or have a full meal at the adjoining restaurant. A pianist entertains Mon.–Fri. from 7:00 P.M. Open Mon.–Sun., midday–midnight. No cover, no minimum.

Forecourt Restaurant. Sydney Opera House, Bennelong Point, Sydney; 250–7557. The Forecourt is actually a cafe/restaurant, but you are welcome just for a drink as well. It is one of the best spots in Sydney from which to watch the bustling activity on the busy harbor. Daily, 10:00 A.M.–supper. No cover, no minimum.

Garden Court Cocktail Lounge. Sheraton Wentworth, 61 Phillip St., Sydney; 230–0700. A quiet, intimate, and comfortable bar, with live musical entertainment from 6:00 P.M. Mon.–Fri., 11:00 A.M.–2:00 A.M.; Sat., 6:00 P.M.–2:00 A.M. No cover, no minimum.

Hero of Waterloo. 81 Lower Fort St., The Rocks; 27–8471. Situated in Sydney's historic Rocks area, the Hero is a charming and authentic "pub" and a great spot to enjoy an Aussie beer. Open: Mon.–Sat., 10:00 A.M.–11:00 P.M. Sun., midday–10:00 P.M. No cover, no minimum.

Kinsela's. 383 Bourke Street, Darlinghurst; 331–6200. This is one of *the* Sydney nightspots and offers restaurant and cabaret besides bar facilities in a refurbished funeral parlor. Mon.–Sat., 6:00 P.M.–3:00 A.M. No cover, no minimum.

Loft. Boulevarde Hotel, 100 William St., Sydney; 357–2277. There are magnificent city and harbor views from the adjoining restaurant here, high up in the Boulevarde. Mon.–Fri., noon–midnight; Sat., 5:00 P.M.–midnight; Sun., 11:00 A.M.–3:00 P.M. No cover, no minimum.

Lord Nelson. 19 Kent St., Sydney; 251–4044. This is the oldest licensed hotel in Australia. This quaint pub attracts locals, tourists, workers from the nearby wharves, and city office workers. Mon.–Sat., 11:00 A.M.–11:00 P.M.; Sun., noon–10:00 P.M. No cover, no minimum.

Marble Bar. Sydney Hilton, 259 Pitt St., Sydney; 266–0610. This elegant and ornate bar has been re-created from the Old Adams Hotel, which was originally on this site. At times it's as tightly packed as a sardine tin. Mon.–Thurs., midday–midnight; Fri., midday–2:00 A.M.; Sat., 5:00 P.M.–2:00 A.M. Rock music after 7:00 P.M. No cover, no minimum.

NIGHTLIFE

Menzies Hotel Piano Bar. Holiday Inn Menzies Hotel, 14 Carrington St., Sydney; 2–0232. There is a pianist every night except Sun. from 7:30 P.M. at this relaxing and intimate bar. Open Mon.–Sat., noon–12:45 A.M.; Sun., noon–11:45 P.M. No cover, no minimum.

Observer Hotel. 69 George St., The Rocks; 27–4262. Often packed with regulars; the crowd is mixed, but an early-20s age group predominates. Local entertainers perform (American rock 'n' roll is popular), and almost everyone sings along. Friendly, rowdy, and unpretentious (that might be an understatement), "The Obbie" is a good place to drink beer and meet some locals. Open Mon.–Sat. 9:00 A.M.–10:45 P.M.; Sun., noon–9:45 P.M.

Orient Hotel. Corner George and Argyle sts., The Rocks; 27–2464. A bit more upscale than the Observer (see above), the Orient seems to get more of a tourist crowd. Entertainment nightly. A comfortable place for a beer break if you're exploring The Rocks. Open Mon.–Sat., 10:00 A.M.–11:00 P.M.; Sun., noon–11:00 P.M.

Phillip's Foote. 101 George St., Sydney; 27–2585. A noisy, friendly bar to drop into for a drink. You might stay for a barbecued steak, and here you cook it yourself. Open Mon.–Thur., noon–11:00 P.M.; Fri.–Sat., noon–midnight; Sun., noon–10:00 P.M. No cover, no minimum.

Piano Bar. Hyatt Kingsgate Hotel, Kings Cross Rd., Kings Cross; 357–2233. The Hyatt has a good position at the top of The Cross if you're exploring Sydney by night. Music in the evenings. Mon.–Fri., 5:00 P.M.–1:00 A.M.; Sat. 1:00 P.M.–3:00 A.M. No cover, no minimum.

Regent. 199 George Street, Sydney; 238–0000. A choice of bars here: *Club Bar* is an excellent establishment with seating on lounge chairs at low tables, looking out through a glass wall toward Circular Quay. Light snacks are available, but not on Sunday. Open Mon.–Sat., 11:30 A.M.–1:00 A.M.; Sun., 12:00 noon–1:00 A.M. *George Street Bar* is a more informal bar, with mostly standing room. There is entertainment Mon.–Fri., and Sat. nights. Lunch, and snacks after 5:00 P.M. Open Mon.–Thurs., 11:00 A.M.–11:00 P.M.; Fri., midday–midnight; Sat., 5:30 P.M.–midnight.

Sebel Townhouse Cocktail Bar. 23 Elizabeth Bay Rd., Elizabeth Bay; 358–3244. Frequented by local and visiting celebrities, but don't rush for your autograph book. Everyone plays it cool. Daily, noon–midnight. No cover, no minimum.

Sheraton Marquee. 40 Macleay St., Potts Point; 358–1955. Enjoy a drink here at the terrace harbor bar overlooking the city. Daily, 6:30 P.M.–midnight. No cover, no minimum.

CLASS ACTS

Sydney Hilton Hotel. 259 Pitt St., Sydney; 266–0610. A full meal and a show are included in the ticket to the Hilton's three-times-yearly cabaret seasons. International stars are featured in these glittering performances, held in the ballroom of the hotel. Performers have included Tina Turner, Peter Allen, and the Village People.

CLUBS

A main source of entertainment for many Sydneysiders is their local licensed club. This could be a small lawn bowling club, a golf club and accompanying facilities, one of the enormous rugby league football clubs, or perhaps an RSL Club whose membership is based on past soldiers, sailors, and airmen from Australia's armed forces.

Whatever the sporting or organizational basis of the clubs, they all share certain characteristics. They have varying numbers of bars and restaurants, sporting and other recreational facilities. As well, many provide entertainment, some of international standard, and they provide all their services at a reasonable cost. All the clubs have poker machines, or "one-armed bandits," as some people know them. These are very popular among the clientele—and particularly among visitors from other states where these machines are not legal. They provide hours of entertainment for many, small windfalls for some, and a steady source of revenue to finance the club.

Most clubs are happy to have visitors from out of town, so phone the Licensed Clubs' Association of NSW, 261-1155 for information on clubs located near you, and experience something of the recreational activities of New South Welshmen.

Three of the biggest clubs with high standards of live entertainment and excellent dining and recreational facilities are: *Revesby Workers Club.* 2b Brett St., Revesby; 772-2100. *South Junior Rugby League Club.* 558a Anzac Parade, Kingsford; 349-7555. *St. George's Leagues Club.* 124 Princes Hwy., Kogarah; 587-1022.

COMEDY

Comedy Store. Margaret Lane (off Jamieson St.); 251-1480. Some very talented new and established Australian comedians perform here, as well as some who'll never make it . . . Take your chances of having a hilarious evening's entertainment. "Talent night" on Wednesdays is when Sydney's untried comedians are given a go. Comedians perform Wed.–Sat., with dinner from 7:30 P.M. Performances from 9:00 P.M.

DISCOTHEQUES, NIGHTCLUBS, DANCING

Amy's. Hilton International Sydney Airport, 20 Levy St., Arncliffe (12 km/ 7-4/10 mi south); 597-0122. An exciting supper club/discotheque right near Sydney airport, Amy's would be a good spot for your last night in Sydney before that early-morning flight out. Licensed. Wed., Fri.–Sat., 8:00 P.M.–3:00 A.M. Cover charge, no minimum.

Cauldron. 207 Darlinghurst Road, Darlinghurst (2 km/1 mi east); 331-1523 or 331-5730. A restaurant and discotheque, the Cauldron is extremely popular and gets very crowded. Its clients include the glamorous model set. May be

NIGHTLIFE

difficult to get in unless you're dining at the restaurant. Licensed. Open Mon.–Sun. No minimum.

Hip Hop. 11 Oxford St., Paddington; 332-2568. Hip Hop boasts "the smartest show, the danciest music and the finest food." There is discotheque music, a dinner show at 7:00 P.M., and then a live show at 11:00 P.M. Hip Hop is very popular, but don't don your silk dress or shirt; good casual clothes are OK. Licensed. Tues.–Sat., 7:00 P.M.–3:00 A.M.; Sun., 7:00 P.M.–4:00 A.M. Small cover charge, no minimum.

Jamison Street. 11 Jamison St., Sydney; 251-1480. A supper club and discotheque, Jamison Street has great music, lights, and effects, as well as a quieter bar area upstairs for conversation, from which you can see the dancing below. Licensed. Tues.–Sun., 9:00 P.M.–3:00 A.M. Cover charge, no minimum.

Juliana's. Sydney Hilton, Reception floor, 29 Pitt St., Sydney; 266-0610. Dress up for this elegant disco. There is a modern jazz combo Fri., 5:30 P.M.–8:30 P.M., and a floor show, then discotheque Tues.–Sat. until 3:00 A.M. Licensed. Cover charge, no minimum.

Old Sydney Bar. Sheraton Wentworth Hotel, Phillip St., Sydney; 230-0700. Brolly's is on the Bligh St. level of the hotel and operates as a discotheque every Fri. and Sat. night, 8:00 P.M.–1:00 A.M. It draws a fairly dressy crowd. Licensed. No cover, no minimum.

Red Rock Cafe. 666 New South Head Rd., Rose Bay (6 km/4 mi east); 371-5566. A rock and roll venue, popular among the 18–21-year-old Eastern Suburbs social set. Licensed. Thurs.–Sun., 10:00 P.M.–3:00 A.M. No minimum. Cover charge.

Rogue's. Laneway, next to 165 Riley St., Darlinghurst (2 km/1 mi east); 33-6924. Preference is given to members at this glamorous restaurant-cum-bar/disco—unless you have a reservation at the restaurant. There's also a piano bar with live music. Tues.–Sat. 7:30 P.M.–3:00 A.M., with disco from 10:30 P.M.; Sun. disco from 9:00 A.M.–3:00 A.M. Licensed. No minimum.

Steps Nightspot. Metropole Hotel, 305 Military Rd., Cremorne; 909-8888. Dance to music from the 1940s on Wed., to upbeat music on Thurs.; see a floorshow Fri., and party the night away on Sat. Open Wed.–Sat., 8:00 P.M.–3:00 A.M. Cover charge, no minimum.

Tivoli. 656 George St., Sydney; 267-5499. Sydney's biggest rock venue and video dance club, for visitors who like to "rage." Mon.–Sat., 7:30 P.M.–3:00 A.M.; Sun., 5:00 P.M.–10:00 P.M., but phone first because times alter when no live band is appearing. Cover, no minimum.

William's. 100 Williams St., Sydney; 356-2222. One of Sydney's newest classy nightspots, William's has two very comfortable lounge bars, an elegant restaurant, and a dance floor. Licensed. Wed., Fri., Sun., 5:30 P.M.–3:00 A.M.; Thurs., Sat., 7:00 P.M.–3:00 A.M. Entry is by membership, dinner reservation, or payment of cover charge. No minimum.

SYDNEY

GAY BARS

Men

Albury Hotel. 6 Oxford St., Paddington (1½ km/1 mi east); 33-6555. Cleverly decorated art-deco-style hotel with elegant cocktail bar, piano bar, and large, extremely popular public bar with regular events, including drag shows, fashion parades, male strippers, and live music. Dress from cutoffs to Armani leather suits. No cover, no minimum. Nearby dining room serves Cajun food. Accommodations available. Licensed. Mon.–Sat., midday–midnight; Sun., 1:00 –11:00 P.M.

Exchange Hotel. 34 Oxford St., East Sydney (1 km/½ mi east); 331-1936. Leading new-wave spot featuring clientele in bizarre clothes and spiked hairdos, dancing and drinking in three bars—one with a DJ, one cavernous and noisy, and one relaxed and called the Twilight Zone. No cover, no minimum. Dress the more outrageous the better. Licensed. Mon.–Fri., noon–2:00 A.M.; Sat., 6:00 P.M.–midnight; Sun., 6:00 P.M.–2:00 A.M.

Midnight Shift. 85 Oxford St., Darlinghurst (2 km/1 mi east); 357-4319. Sydney's premier gay dance bar. High-energy environment with a large, power-packed dance floor. Two quieter bars for conversation. Informal dress, mainly jeans and T-shirts. Restaurant on first floor. Licensed. No drink minimum. Mon.–Sat., 10:30 P.M.–3:00 A.M.; Sun., noon–10:00 P.M. No cover charge Sun.

Patches. 33 Oxford St., Darlinghurst (2 km/1 mi east); 267-7380. Big, brash, and noisy, featuring a large dance floor, large conversation bar, and 2 floor shows each night. A younger crowd here, varying from new-wavers to the surf crowd. Dress any way you want. Licensed. No minimum. Mon.–Sat., 6:00 P.M.–11:00 P.M. as restaurant; 11:00 P.M.–3:00 A.M. as cabaret. Fri., Sat., cover.

Unicorn Hotel. 106 Oxford St., Paddington (4 km/2½ mi east); 357-6371. Labeled "Home of Entertainment," this friendly pub offers different drag shows Thurs.–Sun. Atmosphere might best be described as "down home with diamente." Restaurant and accommodations available. Licensed. No cover, no minimum. Mon.–Sat., midday–midnight; Sun., midday–10:00 P.M.

Women

Ruby Fruit Jungle Bar. 504 Elizabeth St., Surry Hills (2 km/1 mi southeast); 699-5917. Playground has a restaurant upstairs and bar and disco/cabaret downstairs. It is a fairly spacious nightclub, and there are tables close to the music and the action and others away from it for conversation purposes. Dress is casual. It draws the 25–40s crowd. Licensed. Thurs.–Sat., 6:00 P.M.–3:00 A.M. Cover charge after 11:00 P.M. Fri. and Sat., no minimum.

FOR JAZZ

From the number of places where you can listen to excellent jazz in Sydney, it would appear that this is one of the city's most popular music forms. Most of the jazz performers appear in restaurants or bars, and although there may

NIGHTLIFE

be no cover charge or drink minimum, the management expects you to dine or buy drinks on the premises.

A very helpful organization to contact if you are seeking out what's going on in jazz during your visit to Sydney is the Jazz Action Society, 24 Pitt St. North, The Rocks; 232–1419. See also "Music," above.

Some of the more well-known jazz clubs are:

Aircrew Club. Texas Tavern Building. Fifth Floor, 44 Macleay St., Potts Point (3 km/2 m east); 358–1211. There are jazz performances here daily at 9:00 P.M., and the Tavern is open 24 hours for when hunger sets in. No cover, no minimum.

Basement. 29 Reiby Place, Circular Quay; 27–9727. All jazz fans gravitate to the Basement. It offers one of the most interesting and varied jazz programs in Sydney—the house band, Galapagos Duck, is one of the best jazz groups in Australia. Dinner is also available here, Mon.–Sat., as is supper on Fri. and Sat. Licensed. Mon.–Wed., 6:30 P.M.–1:00 A.M.; Thurs., 6:30 P.M.–2:00 A.M.; Fri.–Sat., 6:30 P.M.–3:00 A.M. Cover charge, no minimum.

Don Burrows Supper Club. The Regent of Sydney, 199 George St., Sydney; 238–0000. This is a sophisticated nightspot where some of the best Australian and overseas jazz musicians and vocalists perform. A snack menu is available. Licensed. Mon.–Thurs., 9:00 P.M.–2:00 A.M.; Fri., 5:00 P.M.–3:00 A.M., Sat., 9:00 P.M.–3:00 A.M. Jazz from 9:00 P.M. Cover charge; no minimum.

Musician's Club. 36 Chalmers St., Sydney; 212–3817. Although this is a club for musicians, visitors are welcome on jazz nights, every first Wed. of the month, 8:00 P.M.–midnight. Licensed. Cover charge.

Orient Hotel. 89 George St., The Rocks; 27–2464. A very popular drinking spot in The Rocks. The Orient's trad jazz has everyone swinging on weekend afternoons. Licensed. Music Sat.–Sun., 3:00–6:00 P.M. No cover, no minimum.

Red Ned's Bar & Bistro. 11 Spring St., Chatswood (12 km/7½ mi east); 412–1559. Enjoy a meal and listen to jazz on the north side. Good bands, and variety too: Dixieland, mainstream, and jazz rock bands perform on different nights. Licensed. L, Mon.–Fri.; D, Mon.–Sat., with music 8:00–11:00 P.M. from Tues.–Sat. No cover, no minimum.

Richmond River Boat. Pier One Pontoon, Walsh Bay; 27–2979. Enjoy a harbor cruise and some of Sydney's finest jazz bands at the same time. (Some nights are comedy, so check before booking.) Food available. Licensed. Usual times: Fri., 7:30 P.M.–11:30 A.M.; Sat., Sun., noon–4:00 P.M.

The Rocks Push. 109 George St., The Rocks; 27–2588. The Rocks Push includes a restaurant, cocktail bar, and small dance floor. It is the scene for some very good jazz bands and some very good fun. Licensed. L, Mon.–Fri.; D, daily. Jazz dinner music Wed.–Thurs., 7:30 P.M.–11:00 P.M.; Fri.–Sat., 8:00 P.M.–11:30 P.M. No cover, but they prefer that you eat dinner; no minimum.

Soup Plus Restaurant. 383 George St., Sydney; 29–7728. One of Sydney's most popular jazz venues with a good mix of modern and traditional. L, D Mon.–Sat., with music from 7:30 P.M.–10:30 P.M. No cover, but minimum for dinner.

Strawberry Hill Hotel. 453 Elizabeth St., Surry Hills (2 km/1 mi southeast); 698-2997. A popular jazz venue late in the week. No cover, no minimum.

FOR ROCK, POP, AND BUSH MUSIC

Bevey's Wine Bar Bistro. 789 Military Rd., Mosman; 969-1807. A small and comfortable place for soft rock music, jazz, and country and western. Licensed. Small cover charge, no minimum.

Didi's. Roger St., Brookvale (18 km/11 mi north); 93-2334. There's a dance floor and some seating from which to enjoy local rock bands. Licensed. No cover charge, no minimum.

Hotel Manly. 1 Belgrave St., Manly; 977-5599 (or 977-0393 for information on what's playing). This hotel is just opposite the Manly ferry wharf and rocks with music most evenings and weekend afternoons. As the hotel is earmarked for redevelopment sometime during 1988, phone before making a special trip to hear bands there. Open til 3:00 A.M. Cover charge for some bands. No minimum.

Marble Bar. Hilton Hotel. 259 Pitt St., Sydney; 266-0610. Rock music in the fabulous atmosphere of this Victorian-era bar draws quite a crowd. Licensed. Bar is open Mon.-Thurs., midday-midnight; Fri., midday-2:00 A.M.; Sat., 5:00 P.M.-2:00 A.M. Rock music from 7:00 P.M.

Rose, Shamrock, and Thistle Hotel. 193 Evans Street, Rozelle (5 km/3 mi west); 810-3424. Affectionately known as the "Three Weeds," this is a popular place for live rock music later in the week. Licensed. Small cover charge, no minimum.

Selina's. Coogee Bay Hotel, 253 Coogee Bay Rd., Coogee (8 km/5 mi southeast); 665-0000. This is a large, stand-up club for rock bands, attracting a young "down market" trendy audience. Before the show there is disco music and dancing. For a woman alone this might be a bit rough, though a number of female Sydneysiders count this among their favorite nightspots. Licensed. Cover charge, no minimum.

Sheila's Tavern. 77 Berry St., North Sydney (3 km/2 mi north); 922-7489, 922-7682, or 922-7902. Sheila's has a restaurant and live rock music, also two bars and big-screen video music. There is a large dance floor and it is often quite crowded, even during the week. Licensed. Cover charge after band commences playing, no minimum.

There are numerous city and suburban taverns and hotels where rock groups perform regularly. Consult Metro guide in Friday's *Sydney Morning Herald* for what's on at venues such as *Lucy's Tavern,* City, 231-4738; *The St. James,* City, 221-2468; *The Rest Hotel,* Milson's Point, 929-6387.

THEATER RESTAURANTS

Kinsela's. 383-387 Bourke St., Darlinghurst (2 km/1 mi east); restaurant reservations 331-3100, box office and theater reservations 331-6200, 331-6399, or 331-3299. Kinsela's is a fashionable Sydney nightspot, a combination of restaurant, bars, and cabaret. The food is OK, and the shows are usually bright and satirical. Licensed. Nightly performances at 8:00 P.M.

Les Girls. 2C Roslyn Street, Kings Cross; 358–2333. An all-male revue, Les Girls presents spectacularly costumed drag shows, often to quite staid audiences. At dinner and supper shows, glamorous performers dance and mime to recorded music. Disco afterward. Licensed. Wed.–Sat.

Sydney has a number of other theater restaurants that offer dinner and an evening's entertainment (usually fairly bawdy) on a particular theme. These are fun for group outings, and generally it's a good time rather than a gourmet meal that the patrons look forward to. Prices are moderate for dinner and a show. A selection of these establishments is:

Argyle Tavern. 18 Argyle St., The Rocks; 27–7728. The Jolly Swagman Show (see "Dining Out," above). Show nightly.

Beachcomber. 233 Victoria Rd., Drummoyne (7 km/4 mi northwest); 819–6333 for bookings. Tropical luau feast and island show with live band. There's even an indoor blue lagoon to complement the activities. Licensed. Shows Fri.–Sat. evenings.

Dirty Dick's. 313 Pacific Hwy., Crow's Nest (5 km/3 mi north); 819–6333 for bookings. Bawdy Elizabethan banquet theme, with a king leading the entertainment and much participation from you, his subjects, at the tables. A filling meal of soup, hot crusty bread, roast beef, and plum pudding is served. Shows Fri. and Sat. and sometimes Wed. and Thurs. evenings.

Northside Theatre-Restaurant. 2 Marian St., Killara (14 km/8½ m); 498–3166. For a theater restaurant of a different variety. Here the productions are serious drama and you dine before the performance, not during it. The cast is from the Northside Theatre Company.

Roman Scandals. 159 Kent St., Sydney; 819–6333 for bookings. A Roman musical romp and feast, with dancing after the show. Licensed. Shows Fri. and Sat. and sometimes Wed. and Thurs. evenings.

Outside Sydney

by
DAVID SWINDELL

Actually, many of the attractions included in the Sydney chapter are literally outside the city limits. Almost any visitor who spends time in Sydney will move beyond the city proper. Dinner may take you to a suburb, as noted in the "Dining Out" section, above. A drive north along the coast will bring you to the beautiful beaches mentioned in the Sydney chapter. Head south and there is Royal National Park, with woodsy areas, lakes, spectacular views, hang-gliding, and more beaches.

In this chapter we focus on areas that are popular day tours for Sydney visitors. The majestic Blue Mountains, the wine country in the Hunter Valley, the opal country of Lightning Ridge, and the Outback town of Dubbo can all be visited by organized tour. We list accommo-

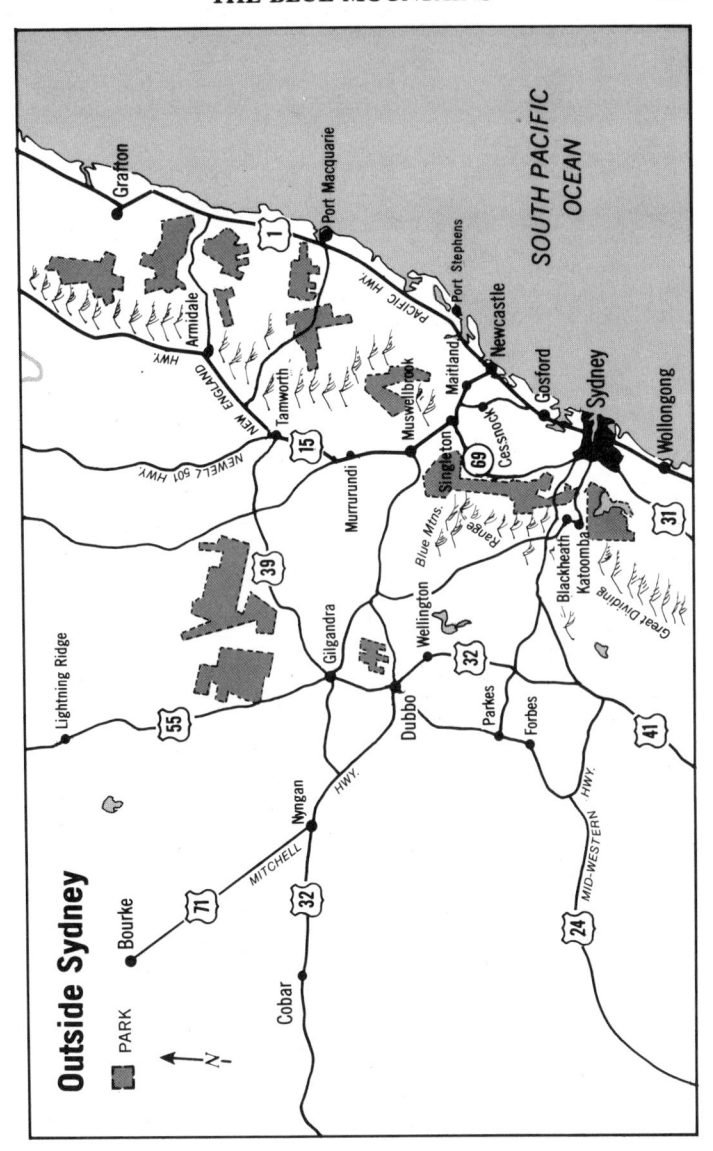

THE BLUE MOUNTAINS 129

OUTSIDE SYDNEY

dations in these areas, but there is actually no need to check out of your city hotel: Book a day tour through the Travel Centre of New South Wales (see "Tourist Information" in *Practical Information for Sydney*) and get a taste of what the rest of Australia is like.

EXPLORING THE BLUE MOUNTAINS

One of Australia's most majestic mountain ranges is one of Sydney's most popular year-round playgrounds. The Blue Mountains to the west of the city have beckoned Sydneysiders to its resorts since the last century, but only after World War I have the pleasures of the Blue Mountains been developed to attract foreign visitors as well. The main town in the mountains is Katoomba, 104 km (62 mi) west of Sydney.

Spring and fall are the most beautiful times of year here. In springtime, millions of wildflowers and trees bud, and the many planned gardens in the region start to flourish. In fall, the North American species of trees introduced long ago to the region—oak, elm, chestnut, beech, and birch—do the same in the Blue Mountains as they would in the Catskills: turn brilliant reds, oranges, and yellows. Summer finds campers and hikers descending on the mountains in throngs, and winter is the time the mountains are at their quietest and most peaceful, offering perfect solitude for city escapees.

If you're looking for a swinging resort, the Blue Mountains may not be for you. There is little nightlife; what there is centers around local restaurants and hotels. In many secluded yet accessible places in the Blue Mountains, about the only sounds you're likely to hear are birdcalls, the wind blowing through trees, and waterfalls.

One of the main attractions in the Blue Mountains is the Jenolan Caves, a massive underground system of limestone caverns that has been lighted for tourists. The caves are eons old and quite fascinating. Guides will take you through the caves from 9:00 A.M. to 5:30 P.M. daily. Each tour lasts about 1½ hours, and there are several payment scales, starting at $5.00, depending on how many are in your party and how many of the caves in the system you care to visit. The Jenolan Caves are a 1½-hour drive from Katoomba.

PRACTICAL INFORMATION FOR THE BLUE MOUNTAINS

HOW TO GET THERE. The *New South Wales State Rail Authority* runs frequent trains from Central Station in Sydney to Katoomba and other mountain towns. If you drive, the Great Western Hwy. (Hwy. 32) runs from Sydney via Parramatta to Katoomba and includes the F4 Freeway.

ACCOMMODATIONS. Accommodations can usually be booked on the spot, but space may be tight during weekends and holidays. A *deluxe* hotel or motel will run around $135 and up for a double room; *expensive,* $70–$135; *moderate,* $45–$70; *inexpensive,* under $45.

KATOOMBA-LEURA-BLACKHEATH AREA

Alpine Motor Inn. *Moderate.* Corner Great Western Hwy. and Orient St., Katoomba; (047) 82-2011. Television, telephone, radio in all rooms; air-conditioning; sauna; pool; laundry facilities.

Avonleigh Guest House. *Expensive.* 174 Luvline St., Katoomba; (047) 82-1534. Nine rooms with bathrooms. Central heating and unlicensed restaurant. Rates include dinner, bed, and breakfast.

Clarendon. *Moderate.* Corner Lurline and Waratah Streets, Katoomba; (047) 82-1322. Television radio, in all rooms; heated pool; sauna.

Cleopatra. *Deluxe.* Cleopatra St., Blackheath; (047) 87-8456. A charming guest house of five rooms (three bathrooms). $160 per person includes dinner, bed, and breakfast.

Echo Point Motor Inn. *Moderate.* Echo Point Road, Katoomba; (047) 82-2088 or 008-02-4879. Television and radio in all rooms, fans and heating in all rooms.

Everglades (part of Leura Resort). *Moderate.* 70 Gladstone Rd., Leura; (047) 84-1317. Television, radio, telephone in all rooms; pool; sauna; squash court; tennis court; laundry facilities; fans and heating in rooms.

Fairmont Resort. *Deluxe.* Sublime Point Rd., Leura; (02) 327-6677. Television, video, radio and air-conditioning in all rooms. Room service; pool; spa; sauna; squash and tennis courts; barbecue and laundry facilities.

Felton Woods Guesthouse. *Moderate.* Corner Lurline and Merriwa sts., Katoomba; (047) 82-3933. Television and telephone in all rooms; pool; recreation room; spa; laundry facilities.

Leura Resort. *Moderate.* Fitzroy St., Leura; (047) 84–1331. Television, telephone, and radio in all rooms; air-conditioning; pool; sauna; squash court; tennis court; laundry facilities.

Hoylake Lodge. *Inexpensive.* 16 Fitzroy St., Leura; (047) 84–1311. Television, radio, telephone in all rooms; room service; sauna; pool; laundry facilities.

Katoomba. *Inexpensive.* 15 Parke St., Katoomba; (047) 82–1106. Television lounge room, laundry facilities.

3 Sisters. *Inexpensive–Moderate.* Katoomba St., Katoomba; (047) 82–2911. Television, radio, telephone in all rooms.

TOURIST INFORMATION. The *Travel Centre of New South Wales* at the corner of Pitt and Spring sts. in Sydney has complete information about the Blue Mountains and can book day and extended tours to the region (see *Practical Information for Sydney*). Once you're in the area, the *Blue Mountains Tourist Association,* Echo Point, Katoomba, (047) 82–1833, can answer visitor's questions.

TOURS. From Sydney, a legion of day tours to the Blue Mountains are available. The most active tour operators are *AAT King's, Ansett Pioneer, Australian Pacific, Clipper Tours,* and the *New South Wales State Rail Authority.* Each company varies its itinerary a bit, but there are tours that combine a trip to historic Parramatta with the mountains, for example, and tours that will take you to the Jenolan Caves or Featherdale Wildlife Park, where you can see the koalas used by Qantas in all its advertisements. Many tours call in at Katoomba as well. Day tours are priced around $30 per adult. Overnight tours are also available. All tours can be booked at the Travel Centre of New South Wales in Sydney (see "Tourist Information" under *Practical Information for Sydney*).

BUSH WALKING. The best way to get to know the Blue Mountains is by hiking the well-planned trails that have been designed by the New South Wales Forestry Commission. There are numerous walks available in lengths from an hour to a full day. Itineraries are available at information offices in the mountains or from the Blue Mountains Tourist Association in Katoomba (see "Tourist Information," above).

CAMPING. Facilities for camper vans and tents are located at campsites and trailer parks throughout the Blue Mountains. The Travel Centre of New South Wales in Sydney and the Blue Mountains Tourist Association in Katoomba have information about campsite locations, facilities, and fees.

THE BLUE MOUNTAINS

POINTS OF INTEREST. While it's true that Mother Nature is the big draw in the Blue Mountains, there are other things to do if you're not the outdoors type. They include:

Historic Hartley Courthouse and Village. The village of Hartley had 16 streets in 1838; today it still has 16. So little has changed that the town is a history buff's delight, with many buildings restored to their 19th-century elegance. Convicts built the courthouse in 1837.

Nepean Belle. This historic paddlewheeler still steams the Nepean River and is ideal for a cruise through the mountains. There's a restaurant on board the two-deck riverboat. Board at the jetty off Nepean Avenue in Penrith.

Norman Lindsay Gallery and Museum. The Blue Mountains have always drawn many artists to their tranquility, and one of the most famous was Norman Lindsay, one of Australia's geniuses of the canvas. Many of his works are displayed at the gallery and museum bearing his name, located at 128 Chapman Parade, Springwood. Fri., Sat., Sun., public holidays, 11:00 A.M.–5:00 P.M.

Scenic Railway and Skyway. Reputed to be the steepest rail line in the world, this train climbs from Katoomba into the heart of the Blue Mountains. Next to it is the Scenic Skyway, where some of the most dramatic scenery in the mountains can be viewed from a gondola in the air. Located off Cliff Drive in Katoomba. Open daily, 9:00 A.M.–5:00 P.M.

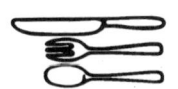

DINING OUT. Most motels and hotels in the Blue Mountains have restaurants that serve basic home-style Australian meals. Freshwater fish from mountain lakes, streams, and rivers pops up on many menus. One restaurant is of particular note (but not for the food): the *Skyway Revolving Restaurant* in Katoomba, which provides patrons with spectacular mountain views while they dine. Tearooms, once popular with honeymooners, are reemerging in the Blue Mountains after years in decline. In towns throughout the mountains there are tearooms that serve Devonshire tea and a plate of hot scones and jams. A *deluxe* dinner will run around $45 and up for one person without drinks; *expensive*, $30–$45; *moderate*, $25–$30; *inexpensive*, under $25.

KATOOMBA

Clarendon Restaurant. *Moderate.* Clarendon Hotel, Lurline St.; (047) 82-1322. Australian cuisine is the fare, and there is a cozy log fire in winter. Operates some nights as a theater restaurant presenting musicals, comedies, and reviews.

Fork and View. *Expensive.* Cliff Drive; (047) 82-1164. Has a bush view for the eyes and French nouvelle cuisine for the tastebuds.

Paragon. *Moderate.* Kotoomba St.; (047) 82-2928. A well-preserved Art Deco restaurant that includes a confectionary shop and a bar well worth viewing.

Skyway Revolving Restaurant. *Inexpensive.* Violet St.; (047) 82-2577. This restaurant revolves 360 degrees once every 11 minutes, offering diners spectacular panoramic views of the Blue Mountains. Open for basic self-serve lunches and morning and afternoon teas.

BLACKHEATH

Some of the finest meals in the mountains can be tasted in Blackheath, and often in restaurants that service their own guesthouse as well. Examples of these are:

Cleopatra. *Deluxe.* Cleopatra St.; (047) 87-8456. Lunch is served on Sunday and dinner Fri. to Sun. Cuisine is French, with a set menu, and you may bring your own wine.

Glenella. *Expensive–deluxe.* 56 Govetts Leap Rd; (047) 87-8352. French. Lunch and dinner served Fri.–Sun.

Kubba Runga. *Expensive.* 9 Brentwood Ave; (047) 87-8330. French, with a Vietnamese influence. B.Y.O. for dinner Thurs.–Sun.

EXPLORING THE HUNTER VALLEY

The Hunter Region, 100 km (60 mi) north-northwest of Sydney, is one of Australia's two major wine-producing areas. But in addition to vineyards and wineries, the Hunter Valley is also an area of ocean beaches and secluded seaside resorts, lakes, rivers, and lush forests that perfectly lend themselves to escapes from the bustle of city life in Sydney.

Many of the large wine estates in the Hunter Region are open to the public for tours, tastings, and sales. Two major wine trails have been mapped out so that tourists can visit several estates in a single day. The Pokolbin Wine Trail encompasses almost 30 estates, from large international wineries such as Lindemans, McWilliams, and Wyndham Estate to small makers of exclusive wines like Terrace Vale and Saxonvale. The small towns of Branxton and Cessnock are the usual jumping-off points for drives along the Pokolbin Wine Trail. The other major trail in the region is the Upper Hunter Wine Trail, where you will find the Rosemount Estate, Arrowfield Wines, Mt. Dangar Vineyards, and Horderns Wybong Estate, all respected names in Australian wines. Tours of this area are best begun in the town of Warkworth or Singleton.

One of the most popular attractions in the area is Old Sydney Town, a theme park, created expressly for the entire family, that is a faithful reproduction of Sydney in 18th-century colonial times. Soldiers, minstrels, townspeople, craft workers, and shopkeepers are on hand in authentic costumes to tell you about the early days and times of Australia's first European colony. Old Sydney Town is located just south of the city of Gosford, about an hour's drive from Sydney.

PRACTICAL INFORMATION FOR THE HUNTER VALLEY

HOW TO GET THERE. A modern highway links Sydney with Newcastle, the largest city in the Hunter Region, and from there highways and country roads fan out to every corner of the Hunter Valley. The *New South Wales State Rail Authority* operates regularly scheduled trains to Newcastle and many of the smaller towns in the region, and Newcastle is served by domestic and commuter airlines from Sydney's Mascot Airport. *Batterham's Coaches* provide express bus service to Cessnock, and many other towns in the Hunter Region are connected by local bus services.

ACCOMMODATIONS. Motels and hotels are located throughout the Hunter Region. An *expensive* lodging will run around $65 and up for a double room; *moderate*, $40–$65, *Inexpensive*, under $40.

NEWCASTLE

Newcastle Parkroyal. *Expensive.* Corner King and Steel sts.; (049) 26–3777. Television, radio, telephone in all rooms; air conditioning; pool; lounge; laundry facilities; room service.

Novocastrian Motor Inn. *Expensive.* 21 Parnell Pl.; (049) 26–3688. Television, radio, telephone in all rooms; air conditioning; room service; pool; laundry facilities.

Settlers Newcastle Motel. *Expensive.* Corner Shortland Esplanade and Zaara St.; (049) 25–181. Television, radio, telephone in all rooms; air conditioning; room service.

The Casbah. *Inexpensive–Moderate.* 465 Hunter St.; (049) 2–2274. Television and telephone in all rooms; laundry facilities.

GOSFORD

Bermuda Motor Inn. *Moderate.* Corner Henry Parry Dr. and Pacific Hwy.; (043) 24–4366. Television, telephone, radio in all rooms; pool; air conditioning; laundry facilities.

136 OUTSIDE SYDNEY

Gosford Motor Inn. *Moderate.* 23 Pacific Hwy.; (043) 23–1333. Television, radio, telephone in all rooms; barbecue; pool; laundry facilities.

Rambler Motor Inn. *Moderate.* 73 Pacific Hwy.; (043) 24–6577. Television, telephone, radio in all rooms; pool; spa; barbecue facilities; air conditioning.

Willows. *Moderate.* 512 Pacific Hwy.; (043) (28–4666.) Television, telephone, radio in all rooms; heated pool; air conditioning; spa; recreation room; cooking facilities available.

MAITLAND

Monte Pio Court Motel. *Expensive.* Dwyer St.; (049) 32–5288. A modern motel built within the shell of an old orphanage. Telephone, television, radio; room service; air conditioning; pool, spa, sauna, gym, and tennis.

East Maitland Motel. *Moderate.* New England Hwy.; (049) 33–5488. Television, telephone, radio in all rooms; spa; pool; air conditioning.

Molly Morgan Motor Inn. *Moderate.* New England Hwy.; (049) 33–5422. Television, telephone, radio in all rooms; pool; laundry facilities; air conditioning.

Maitland Siesta. *Inexpensive.* New England Hwy.; (049) 32–8322. Television in all rooms; air conditioning; laundry facilities.

TOURIST INFORMATION. The *Travel Centre of New South Wales* has complete travel information about the Hunter Valley (see *Practical Information for Sydney*), as does the *Hunter Tourist Association,* City Hall, Newcastle 2300; (049) 26–2323. The *Hunter Valley Wine Association,* 4 Wollombi Rd., Cessnock, phone (049) 90–6699, prints a free map of the region, which contains information about estates that are open to the public for tours and tasting.

TOURS. If you want to visit the Hunter Region on a day trip from Sydney, the most efficient way is probably on an organized tour packaged by several Sydney-based operators. *Australian Pacific Tours* and *AAT King's* package identical day tours that leave every Thurs., Sat., and Sun. from Circular Quay for a day in the Hunter Region, including visits to several wine estates. The tours leave at 8:45 A.M. and return at 7:30 P.M. and cost $44, including lunch and wine tastings. These tours and tours packaged by *Ansett Pioneer* can be booked at the Travel Centre of New South Wales. (See "Tourist Information" under *Practical Information for Sydney*.) *Royal Newcastle Aero Club* will fly you over the Hunter Region on flights of 20 minutes or more from $33 per person (call 049-32-8888. You can also fly over the area in a hot-air balloon. *Balloon Aloft,* (02) 818–1212, will fly you over the Hunter Region for $150 for about an hour's flight over the vineyards. Finally, the *New South Wales State Rail Authority* sells a six-day, five-night package called "Hunter Valley Discovery," which is $322 per adult, all inclusive. Any rail office has details. There are also farm, ranch, and adventure vacations that can be planned in the Hunter Region,

THE HUNTER VALLEY

and several companies charter houseboats for cruises on the lakes and rivers in the area. Both the Travel Centre of New South Wales in Sydney and the Hunter Tourist Association in Newcastle (see "Tourist Information," above) have details on these and on the weekend "Hunter Explorer" bus. *Australian Pacific Tours* also has full-day tours to Old Sydney Town on Wednesdays to Sundays.

THEME PARKS. *Old Sydney Town,* in Somersby, 70 km (43 mi) north of Sydney, is a re-creation of 18th-century Sydney featuring authentic-looking period buildings and costumed people. Regular bus service from Sydney is available. Wed.–Sun., 10:00 A.M.–5:00 P.M. Closed Christmas. Phone (043) 40–1104.

HIKING TRAILS AND CAMPING. Few areas of Australia lend themselves to camping or trekking in the great outdoors more than does the Hunter Region. Caravan parks that have electric and water hookups for camper trailers and facilities for tents are located in the towns of Newcastle, Lake Macquarie, Port Stephens, Cessnock, and along the Pacific Hwy. and the New England Hwy. Many excellent drives and walks through the Hunter Region have been carefully mapped out by the New South Wales Forestry Commission, and detailed brochures about each trail, with map, are available from most tourist information centers in the area or from the Hunter Tourist Association.

SPORTS. The Hunter is an active region, and the Hunter Tourist Association or the Travel Centre of New South Wales can tell you where you will find facilities for golf, boating, sailing, fishing, swimming, and other sports.

MUSEUMS AND ART GALLERIES. There are about 20 museums and numerous art galleries in the Hunter Region. In addition, craft and antique galleries are located in many parts of Hunter Valley; the Hunter Tourist Association can tell you where they are. Of particular note: *Newcastle Maritime Museum and Newcastle Military Museum.* Fort Scratchley, Newcastle; (049) 2–2588. The maritime museum charts Newcastle's early importance as a seaport, while the military museum exhibits collections of weapons, uniforms, and other wartime memorabilia. Maritime museum open Tues.–Sun., noon to 4:00 P.M.; military museum open Sat. and Sun., noon–4:00 P.M.

Regional Art Gallery, Newcastle; (049) 26–3644. Contains works by William Dobell, a famous Australian artist who lived in the region. Open Mon.–Sat., 10:00 A.M.–5:00 P.M. Sun. and public holidays, 2:00 P.M.–5:00 P.M.

OUTSIDE SYDNEY

Royal Australian Infantry Corps Museum. Singelton Army Camp; (065) 78-8257. One of the finest collections of small arms in the Southern Hemisphere. Open Wed.–Sun., 9:00 A.M.–4:00 P.M. (Closed in October.)

Von Bertouch Galleries. 61 Laman St., Newcastle; (049) 2-3584. Paintings and sculpture by Australian artists are displayed and sold. Open Fri.–Mon., 11:00 A.M.–6:00 P.M. or by arrangement.

Windermere Homestead. Lochinvar near Maitland; (049) 30-7204. Historic home in the heart of the Hunter Valley, which contains a family museum depicting life on a rural homestead in Australia in the last century. Open by appointment. Refreshments available on request.

HISTORICAL SITES. History buffs may want to stop in the township of *Murrurundi* in the northern reaches of the Hunter Valley, as it contains a collection of 19th-century buildings that have been classified as landmarks by Australia's National Trust. However, the pasts of most towns and villages in the Hunter Region are reflected in their architecture. Also of interest historically and architecturally are the towns of Maitland, Merriwa, Booral, and Cessnock. The Hunter Tourist Association is the best source of information about the region's past and its architecture.

DINING OUT. A *deluxe* dinner will run around $45 and up for one person without beverages; *expensive*, $30–$45; *moderate*, $25–$30; *inexpensive*, under $25.

NEWCASTLE

The Billabong Restaurant. *Moderate–Expensive.* Corner Hunter and Crown sts.; (049) 2-1997. A pleasant restaurant serving Australian meals.

Istana Malaysia. *Moderate.* 32 Market Town Shopping Centre, King St.; (049) 2-3522. Exotic Malay dishes are the specialty here.

Kelly's Villa Franca. *Moderate.* 2 Scott St.; (049) 2-2344. Seafood and shellfish, caught daily in the waters off Newcastle, have made this restaurant a success.

Lock's. *Moderate.* 146 Darby St.; (049) 2-1565. Australian cuisine is the fare.

Maharaja Indian Restaurant. *Moderate.* 653 A Hunter St.; (049) 26-1665. Indian and Tandoori dishes are served.

MAITLAND

Old George & Dragon. *Expensive–Deluxe.* 48 Melbourne St., East Maitland; (049) 33-7272. French cuisine is served in an old-style pub setting.

The Pines. *Expensive–Deluxe.* Monte Pio Court Motel, Dwyer St., Maitland; (049) 32-5288. International cuisine in a restaurant that was once part of an orphanage. Accommodations available.

EXPLORING OPAL COUNTRY AND THE OUTBACK

Australia is the world's largest producer of opals, and many of the nation's most productive mines are located in western New South Wales, in the vicinity of Lightning Ridge, 763 km (458 mi) northwest of Sydney. Lightning Ridge is a frontier town reminiscent of the Old West in the United States. It sits atop the world's only known supply of black opals. It is not exactly a tourist mecca, but you'll probably find the best prices on earth for opals in Lightning Ridge.

Almost as soon as Sydney's city limits end, the great Australian bush country, the legendary Outback, begins. The Outback is a part of every Australian's life whether he or she has ever been there or not, because, like the Old West, it is part of the nation's folklore. It is stark country, unaccustomed to frequent rains, but beautiful in its austere way. Kangaroos, emus, wombats, koalas, and many other creatures unique to the Australian Outback call this area home.

Many of Australia's largest sheep and cattle stations (ranches) are located in western New South Wales, and some of them open their doors to visitors who'd like to get a close-up view of a working station. Hazleton Air Services operate day and extended tours of the area from Sydney. Ask at the Travel Centre of N.S.W. about Hazleton's "Meet a Cocky" tour, where you can meet a cocky (Australian farmer) at home, from $200 per person. One of the most popular tour series to the area is packaged by Air New South Wales and called "Jolly Swagman Tours." There is a one-day tour to the country town of Dubbo that features a visit to a working sheep station and a bush barby (barbecue), priced from about $279 per adult, all inclusive, and several three-day tours of the opal mining centers that are priced from $330 per adult, all inclusive. Opal tours take visitors right into the mines to demonstrate how opals are carefully removed from way beneath the earth. Plenty of time is allowed for opal shopping under the guidance of experts who can tell you what you're buying and how much you're saving compared to world market prices.

PRACTICAL INFORMATION FOR OPAL COUNTRY AND THE OUTBACK

HOW TO GET THERE. *Air New South Wales* flies to the outback or you can take a *New South Wales State Rail Authority* train. *Greyhound* and *Ansett* run express coaches from Brisbane and Melbourne through N.S.W. These stop at Dubbo and other outback towns.

ACCOMMODATIONS. An *expensive* room will run around $55–$65 for a double; *moderate* $45–$55; *inexpensive*, under $45.

DUBBO

Ashwood Country Club Motel. *Expensive.* Whylandra St; (068) 81-8700. Telephone, television, radio and air-conditioning in all rooms; room service; pool; spa; tennis; barbecue and laundry facilities.

Atlas. *Moderate.* 140 Bourke St.; (068) 82-7244. Television, radio, telephone in all rooms; pool; air-conditioning.

Blue Lagoon Motor Inn. *Moderate.* 81 Cobra St.; (068) 82-4444. Television, telephone, radio in all rooms; room service; pool; air-conditioning; spa; laundry facilities.

Cascades Motor Inn. *Expensive.* 141 Cobra St; (068) 82-3888. Telephone, television, radio and air-conditioning in all rooms. Room service; pool and laundry facilities.

Country Comfort. *Moderate.* Peak Hill Rd.; (068) 82-4777. Television, telephone, radio in all rooms; air-conditioning; pool; room service; sauna; tennis court; laundry facilities.

Golden West. *Moderate.* 87 Cobra St.; (068) 82-2822. Television, telephone, radio in all rooms; pool; sauna; air-conditioning; room service.

Dubbo Centre Point. *Inexpensive.* 146 Bourke St.; (068) 82-7644. Television, radio, telephone in all rooms; air-conditioning; pool.

Forest Lodge Motor Inn. *Inexpensive.* 248 Mayall St.; (068) 82-6500. Television, telephone, radio in all rooms; air-conditioning; room service; laundry facilities and pool.

LIGHTNING RIDGE

Lightning Ridge. *Moderate.* Onyx St.; (068) 29-0304. Radio and television in all rooms, air-conditioning, laundry facilities.

OPAL COUNTRY AND THE OUTBACK

Wallangulla. *Moderate.* Corner Morella and Agate Sts.; (068) 29–0142. Air-conditioning.

Black Opal. *Inexpensive–moderate.* Opal St.; (068) 29–0518. Air-conditioning.

TOURIST INFORMATION. For helpful information, as well as tour bookings, contact the *Travel Centre of New South Wales* in Sydney. (See *Practical Information for Sydney.*)

DINING OUT. An *expensive* meal will run around $30 and up for one person without drinks; *moderate*, $20–$30; *inexpensive*, under $20.

DUBBO

Dubbo Eating House. *Inexpensive.* Macquarie St. For under $10 all you can eat Chinese smorgasbord.

The Eidelweiss. *Moderate.* 215 Macquarie St. Surf 'n' turf Australian style, as well as fondue.

Fu Lee Wah. *Moderate.* 127 Macquarie St. Chinese. Mee Lee's competition.

Jules Crepes. *Moderate.* 195 Macquarie St. Crepes and pancakes.

Mee Lee Wah. *Moderate.* 236 Macquarie St. Chinese.

Philippes. *Moderate.* 208 Brisbane St. French cuisine has made it to the Outback via this establishment.

LIGHTNING RIDGE

Lightning Ridge is a small and unsophisticated outback town memorable for its lifestyle and local characters rather than its restaurant experiences. However, you will be able to get nourishing meals at:

Lightning Ridge Motor Village's Restaurant. *Moderate–Expensive.* Onyx St. (see *Accommodations* section).

Lightning Ridge Bowling Club. *Inexpensive.* Agate St. Hearty meals for around $10 per person.

INDEX

General Information

Accommodations, 6
Alcoholic beverages. *See* Dining out; Drinking laws
Auto rentals, 6

Banks, 3
Beaches, 25
Bed & breakfast. *See* Accommodations

Climate, 2–3
Clothing. *See* Packing
Costs, 4–5
Credit cards, 3
Cruises, 5
Cultural life, 23–24
Currency & exchange, 3
Customs
  entering Australia, 2

Departure tax, 12
Dining out, 6–7
Drinking laws, 7
Drinking water. *See* Dining out

Electricity, 10

Facts & figures, 1, 15–16
Food & drink, 23

Gambling, 9

Handicapped travelers, 10

History, 16–18
Holidays, 8
Hotels & motels. *See* Accommodations
Hours of business, 3, 8

Information sources, 1
Introduction to Sydney, 13–26

Local time, 8

Metric conversion tables, 10–11
Motoring hints, 5–6

Nightlife, 25

Packing, 3
Passports & visas, 2
Postage, 10

Restaurants. *See* Dining out

Seasonal events, 2, 8–9
Security precautions, 11
Shopping, 20–21
Sports, 9, 25

Taxis. *See* Motoring hints
Telephones, 11
Tipping, 7
Traveler's checks, 3

Women visitors' information, 9

Geographical and Practical Information

Admiralty House, 73
Airport transportation, 57–58
Air tours (in Sydney), 62
Air travel to Sydney
  from abroad, 51
  from elsewhere in
    Australia, 52

Anzac War Memorial, 37
Archibald Fountain (The), 37
Architectural sites, 73–80
Argyle Arts Centre, 78
Argyle Cut, 41, 78
Argyle Steps, 41
Argyle Terrace, 41, 78

INDEX

Art galleries, 92–94
Art Gallery of New South Wales (The), 37–38, 80
Austinmer Beach, 69
Australia Square, 73
Australian Ballet (The), 34, 90
Australian Centre for Photography, 80
Australian Fishing Museum, 80
Australian Museum (The), 37, 80–81
Australian Opera (The), 34, 78
Australian Steam Navigation Co. (bldg.), 40
Australian Wine Centre, 33
Auto rentals, 58
Avalon Beach, 68

Ballet. *See* Dance
Balmoral Beach, 70
Bare Island Historical Site, 73–74
Beaches, 67–70. *See also alphabetical listings*
Bellambi Beach, 70
Bennelong Point, 33
Bilgola Beach, 68
Blackheath
  restaurants, 134
Blue Mountains (The), 130–134
  camping, 132
  hotels, 131–132
  information sources, 132
  restaurants, 133–134
  sightseeing & points of interest, 132–133
  tours, 132
  transportation to, 131
Boating, 71
Bondi Beach, 69
Bronte Beach, 68
Bulli Beach, 70
Bus tours, 28, 61
Bus travel
  in Sydney, 58–59
  to Sydney from elsewhere in Australia, 52

Cadman's Cottage (maritime museum), 40, 77

Camp Cove Beach, 33, 50, 70
Captain Cook's Landing Place Historic Site (Kurnell), 85
Carss Cottage Museum (Blakehurst), 85
Cenotaph (The), 38
Centennial Park, 63–64
Centrepoint Tower. *See* Sydney Tower
Chauffeur-driven tours, 61
Chinatown, 42–43
Church Hill, 74
Circular Quay, 28, 29, 33, 74
Circular Quay West, 78
Clark Island, 65
Coalcliff Beach, 69
Coledale Beach, 69
Collaroy Beach, 68
Collingwood House (Liverpool), 85
Colonial House Museum, 81
Colonial Secretary's Building, 74
Concord Historical Society, 85
Conservatorium of Music, 35, 74, 87, 89
Coogee Beach, 69
Corrimal Beach, 70
Counting House (bldg.), 41
Cricket, 72
Cronulla Beaches, 69
Cruises to Sydney. *See* Ship travel
Cruise tours (in Sydney), 62–63
Curl Curl Beach, 68
Customs House, 74

Dance, 90
Darling Harbour, 43, 74
Darlinghurst Jail & Courthouse, 46, 74
Dawes Point Park, 41, 64
Dee Why Beach, 68
Dixon Street, 42–43
Domain (The). *See* Sydney Domain (park)
Don Bank Museum, 81
Double Bay, 49–50
Dubbo, 139
  hotels, 140
  restaurants, 141

INDEX

Eastern Suburbs, 49–50
Elizabeth Bay House, 46, 81
Elizabeth Farm (Parramatta), 50, 75
Entertainment Centre. *See under* Sydney
Ervin (S.H.) Museum & Art Gallery, 81
Exploring Sydney, 27–50

Fairy Meadow Beach, 70
Farm Cove, 29
Featherdale Wildlife Park, 66
Ferries, 29, 59–60, 62–63
Film, 86–87
Fishing, 71
Football, 72
Fort Denison, 29, 75
Free music, 90

Garden Island, 29
Garie Beach, 69
Garrison Church, 78
Geological & Mining Museum (The), 41, 81–82
George Street, 40–42
Golf, 71
Gosford, 134
  hotels, 135–136
Government House, 29, 35, 75
Great Synagogue, 75
Greyhound Racing, 72

Hall of Champions, 82
Harbord Beach, 67–68
Harbour Bridge. *See under* Sydney
Harbour Natl. Park. *See under* Sydney
Harness Racing, 72
Harrisford House (Parramatta), 50
Hartley (historic courthouse & village), 133
Hickson Road, 40
Hills District Historical Society Museum (Castle Hill), 85–86
Historic interest sites, 73–80. *See also alphabetical listings*
Horse racing, 72

Hotels & motels, 52–57. *See also other localities & areas*
  airport area, 52
  deluxe, 53
  expensive, 53–55
  inexpensive, 56–57
  inexpensive–moderate, 56
  moderate, 55–56
Hunters Hill Historical Society Museum, 82
Hunter Valley (The), 134–138
  camping & hiking, 137
  historical sites, 138
  hotels, 135–136
  information sources, 136
  museums & art galleries, 137–138
  restaurants, 138
  sports, 137
  theme parks, 137
  tours, 136–137
  transportation to, 135
Hyde Park, 37, 64
Hyde Park Barracks, 35, 37
Hydrofoil transportation, 29, 59–60

Information sources, 60. *See also other localities and areas*
Intercontinental Hotel, 75
Ivan Dougherty Gallery, 82

Jazz, 88–89, 124–126
Jenolan Caves, 130

Katoomba, 130
  hotels, 131–132
  information sources, 132
  restaurants, 133–134
Kendall Lane, 41
Kings Cross, 43–45
  map, 44
  nightclubs & entertainment, 45
  restaurants, 45
  shopping, 45
Kirribilli House, 75
Knox Street (Double Bay), 50
Koala Park, 66
Ku-Ring-gai Chase Natl. Park, 64

INDEX

Lady Jane Beach, 33, 50, 70
Lancer Barracks, 75
Leura
  hotels, 131
Lewers Bequest & Penrith Regional Art Gallery (Emu Plains), 86
Lightning Ridge, 139
  hotels, 140–141
  restaurants, 141
Long Reef Beach, 68
Lower Fort Street, 78
Luna Park, 29, 66
Lydham Hall (Rockdale), 86

Macleay Museum, 82
Macquarie Place, 75–76
Macquarie Street, 35, 37, 50, 76
Maitland
  hotels, 136
  restaurants, 138
Malabar Beach, 69
Manly, 33
Manly Art Gallery, 82–83
Manly Beach, 67
Manly Ferry, 29, 60
Manly Museum, 83
Maps
  Australia, viii–ix
  Domain-Macquarie-Hyde Park, 36
  harbor & beaches, 32
  Kings Cross, 44
  Outside Sydney area, 129
  Paddington, 47
  Rocks (The), 39
  Sydney, 30–31
Maroubra Beach, 69
Martin Place/Plaza, 15–16, 38, 76
Mint Museum (The), 35, 37
Mona Vale Beach, 68
Monarch Historical Society (Dee Why), 86
Motor racing, 72
"Mounting of the Ceremonial Guard" (exhibition), 38
Movies. *See* Film
Murrurundi Township, 138
Museum of Fire, 83

Museums, 80–86. *See also alphabetical listings*
Music, 87–90

Nagoya Park, 37
Narrabeen Beach, 68
National Folkloric Festival, 34
National Maritime Museum, 83
National Trust of Australia, 78
Nepean Belle (riverboat), 133
Newcastle
  hotels, 135
  information sources, 136
  restaurants, 138
Newport Beach, 68
New South Wales Fire Service Museum, 83
New South Wales Parliament House, 35, 37
Nicholson Museum of Antiquities, 83
Nielson Park Beach, 70
Nightlife, 119–127
  bars, 120–121
  class acts, 121
  clubs, 122
  comedy, 122
  dancing, 122–123
  discotheques, 122–123
  gay bars, 124
  jazz, 124–126
  nightclubs, 122–123
  rock & pop music, 126
  theater restaurants, 126–127
Norman Lindsay Gallery & Museum (Springwood), 133
North Wollongong Beach, 70

Observatory Hill, 78
Observatory Park, 64
Old Government House (Parramatta), 50, 76
Old Mariner's Church, 40
Old Police Station, 77
Old Sydney Town (theme park) (Somersby), 134–135, 137
Opal Country & The Outback, 139–141
  hotels, 140–141

INDEX

Opal Country & The Outback (*continued*)
  information sources, 141
  restaurants, 141
  tours, 139
  transportation to, 140
Opal Skymine (The), 38
Opera, 89
Opera House. *See under* Sydney
Oxford Street, 46–49
  coffee & tea shops, 49
  pubs, 48
  shopping, 46, 48–49

Paddington, 46–49, 76
  coffee & tea shops, 49
  map, 47
  pubs, 48
  shopping, 46, 48–49
Paddy's Market, 43
Palm Beach, 68
Parks & gardens, 63–66. *See also alphabetical listings*
  general information, 63
Parliament House, 77
Parramatta, 50
Parramatta Experiment Farm Cottage, 50, 86
Pokolbin Wine Trail (Hunter Valley), 134
Port Jackson, 14
Port Kembla Beach, 70
Power Gallery of Contemporary Art, 83
Power House Museum, 83

Queens Square, 37
Queen Victoria Building, 28, 77

Randwick & District Historical Society, 84
Reef Beach, 33
Restaurants & other eating facilities, 97–119. *See also other localities and areas*
  American, 98–99
  Australian, 99–100
  brasseries, 118–119
  cafes, 118–119
  Chinese, 100–101
  coffee shops, 118–119
  English, 101
  French, 102–103
  Greek, 104
  Indian, 104–105
  Indonesian, 105
  international, 106–107
  Italian, 108–109
  Japanese, 109–110
  Korean, 110
  Lebanese, 111
  Malay, 111
  Mexican, 111–112
  seafood, 112–113
  Spanish, 114
  Sri Lanka, 114
  steak houses, 114–115
  tea shops, 118–119
  Thai, 115
  tourist & cruise restaurants, 116–118
  vegetarian, 115–116
  Vietnamese, 116
Rock/pop music, 89, 125–126
Rocks (The), 28, 38–42
  map, 39
  pubs, 42
  restaurants, 42
  shopping, 40–42
  visitor centre, 40
Rose Bay, 29
Rosenblum (A.M.) Jewish Museum, 84
Royal Botanic Gardens, 29, 33, 34, 35, 64
  sightseeing tours, 63
Royal Mint, 84
Royal Natl. Park, 64–65
Rushcutter's Bay Park, 29, 65

Sailing
  participant, 71
  spectator, 73
St. Andrew's Cathedral, 78
St. James Church, 37
St. John's Church (Parramatta), 50
St. Patrick's Church, 41
Sandon Point, 69
Scarborough Beach, 69
Scenic Railway & Skyway (Blue Mountains), 133

INDEX

Sergeant Majors Row, 41
Shark Island, 65
Ship travel to Sydney from abroad, 52
Shopping, 94–97
Sightseeing (special-interest), 63
Sports (participant), 71–72. *See also alphabetical listings*
Sports (spectator), 72–73. *See also alphabetical listings*
Stage. *See* Theater
Stanwell Beach, 69
State Archives (The), 41
State Library of New South Wales, 35, 84
State Theatre, 78
Steam Train & Railway Museum (Parramatta Park), 86
Strand Arcade (The), 38, 79
Surfing, 71–72
Surfing Carnivals, 73
Sydney Centre for Educational & Social History, 84
Sydney Cove, 38
Sydney Dance Company, 34, 90
Sydney Domain (park), 37–38, 65
Sydney Entertainment Centre, 43
Sydney environs, 128–141
Sydney Harbour, 28–29, 33
  map, 32
Sydney Harbour Bridge, 14, 29, 33, 41
Sydney Harbour Natl. Park, 33, 65–66
Sydney Hospital, 35, 79
Sydney Maritime Museum, 84
Sydney Observatory, 84
Sydney Opera House, 14, 28–29, 33–35, 76, 89
  sightseeing tours, 63
Sydney Symphony Orchestra, 34, 87
Sydney Tower, 28, 79
Sydney University, 79
Sydney University Music Department, 88

Tamarama Beach, 69
Taronga Zoo, 66–67
Taxis, 58
Taylor Square, 46
Tennis
  participant, 72
  spectator, 73
Theater, 91–92, 126–127
Theaters, 92
Theme parks, 66, 137
Thirroul Beach, 69
Tours, 61–63
Town Hall, 79
Towradgi Beach, 70
Train travel
  in Sydney, 59
  to Sydney, 52
Transportation in Sydney, 57–60. *See also specific modes of transportation*
  economy fares, 60
Transportation to Sydney
  from abroad, 51–52
  from elsewhere in Australia, 52

Union Bond (bldg.), 41
Upper Hunter Wine Trail, 134

Vaucluse House, 79
Victoria Barracks, 79–80

Walking tours, 62
Waratah Park, 67
Warriewood Beach, 68
Watson's Bay, 29, 50
Whale Beach, 68
William Street, 45
Windsurfing, 72
Wollongong Beach, 70
Woonona Beach, 70
Wynyard Park, 66

Yarranabbe Park, 66

Zoos, 66–67. *See also alphabetical listings*

FODOR'S TRAVEL GUIDES

Here is a complete list of Fodor's Travel Guides, available in current editions; most are also available in a British edition published by Hodder & Stoughton.

U.S. GUIDES

Alaska
American Cities (Great Travel Values)
Arizona including the Grand Canyon
Atlantic City & the New Jersey Shore
Boston
California
Cape Cod & the Islands of Martha's Vineyard & Nantucket
Carolinas & the Georgia Coast
Chesapeake
Chicago
Colorado
Dallas/Fort Worth
Disney World & the Orlando Area (Fun in)
Far West
Florida
Fort Worth (see Dallas)
Galveston (see Houston)
Georgia (see Carolinas)
Grand Canyon (see Arizona)
Greater Miami & the Gold Coast
Hawaii
Hawaii (Great Travel Values)
Houston & Galveston
I-10: California to Florida
I-55: Chicago to New Orleans
I-75: Michigan to Florida
I-80: San Francisco to New York
I-95: Maine to Miami
Jamestown (see Williamsburg)
Las Vegas including Reno & Lake Tahoe (Fun in)
Los Angeles & Nearby Attractions
Martha's Vineyard (see Cape Cod)
Maui (Fun in)
Nantucket (see Cape Cod)
New England
New Jersey (see Atlantic City)
New Mexico
New Orleans
New Orleans (Fun in)
New York City
New York City (Fun in)
New York State
Orlando (see Disney World)
Pacific North Coast
Philadelphia
Reno (see Las Vegas)
Rockies
San Diego & Nearby Attractions
San Francisco (Fun in)
San Francisco plus Marin County & the Wine Country
The South
Texas
U.S.A.
Virgin Islands (U.S. & British)
Virginia
Waikiki (Fun in)
Washington, D.C.
Williamsburg, Jamestown & Yorktown

FOREIGN GUIDES

Acapulco (see Mexico City)
Acapulco (Fun in)
Amsterdam
Australia, New Zealand & the South Pacific
Austria
The Bahamas
The Bahamas (Fun in)
Barbados (Fun in)
Beijing, Guangzhou & Shanghai
Belgium & Luxembourg
Bermuda
Brazil
Britain (Great Travel Values)
Canada
Canada (Great Travel Values)
Canada's Maritime Provinces plus Newfoundland & Labrador
Cancún, Cozumel, Mérida & the Yucatán
Caribbean
Caribbean (Great Travel Values)
Central America
Copenhagen (see Stockholm)
Cozumel (see Cancún)
Eastern Europe
Egypt
Europe
Europe (Budget)
France
France (Great Travel Values)
Germany: East & West
Germany (Great Travel Values)
Great Britain
Greece
Guangzhou (see Beijing)
Helsinki (see Stockholm)
Holland
Hong Kong & Macau
Hungary
India, Nepal & Sri Lanka
Ireland
Israel
Italy
Italy (Great Travel Values)
Jamaica (Fun in)
Japan
Japan (Great Travel Values)
Jordan & the Holy Land
Kenya
Korea
Labrador (see Canada's Maritime Provinces)
Lisbon
Loire Valley
London
London (Fun in)
London (Great Travel Values)
Luxembourg (see Belgium)
Macau (see Hong Kong)
Madrid
Mazatlan (see Mexico's Baja)
Mexico
Mexico (Great Travel Values)
Mexico City & Acapulco
Mexico's Baja & Puerto Vallarta, Mazatlan, Manzanillo, Copper Canyon
Montreal (Fun in)
Munich
Nepal (see India)
New Zealand
Newfoundland (see Canada's Maritime Provinces)
1936 . . . on the Continent
North Africa
Oslo (see Stockholm)
Paris
Paris (Fun in)
People's Republic of China
Portugal
Province of Quebec
Puerto Vallarta (see Mexico's Baja)
Reykjavik (see Stockholm)
Rio (Fun in)
The Riviera (Fun on)
Rome
St. Martin/St. Maarten (Fun in)
Scandinavia
Scotland
Shanghai (see Beijing)
Singapore
South America
South Pacific
Southeast Asia
Soviet Union
Spain
Spain (Great Travel Values)
Sri Lanka (see India)
Stockholm, Copenhagen, Oslo, Helsinki & Reykjavik
Sweden
Switzerland
Sydney
Tokyo
Toronto
Turkey
Vienna
Yucatán (see Cancún)
Yugoslavia

SPECIAL-INTEREST GUIDES

Bed & Breakfast Guide: North America
Royalty Watching
Selected Hotels of Europe
Selected Resorts and Hotels of the U.S.
Ski Resorts of North America
Views to Dine by around the World

AVAILABLE AT YOUR LOCAL BOOKSTORE OR WRITE TO
FODOR'S TRAVEL PUBLICATIONS, INC., 201 EAST 50th STREET, NEW YORK, NY 10022.